Work
Backwards

Also by Tim Duggan

Cult Status: How to Build a Business People Adore
Killer Thinking: How to Turn Good Ideas Into Brilliant Ones

"This is a rare book: both profound and useful." —Seth Godin

Tim Duggan

Work Backwards

The revolutionary method to work smarter and live better

WILEY

This edition was published 2025.

© 2025 Tim Duggan

Edition History
This edition was first published 2024 by Pantera Press Pty Limited.

Registered Offices

John Wiley & Sons, Inc., 111 River Street, Hoboken, NJ 07030, USA
John Wiley & Sons Ltd, The Atrium, Southern Gate, Chichester, West Sussex, PO19 8SQ, UK

Editorial Office

The Atrium, Southern Gate, Chichester, West Sussex, PO19 8SQ, UK

For details of our global editorial offices, customer services, and more information about Wiley products visit us at www.wiley.com.

Library of Congress Cataloging-in-Publication Data is Available:

ISBN 9781394298174 (Cloth)
ISBN 9781394299997 (ePub)
ISBN 9781394300006 (ePDF)

Cover Design: Wiley
Author Photo: Courtesy of Cybele Malinowski

SKY10085588_092024

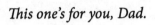

This one's for you, Dad.

Contents

Work Backwards Step 2: Know your 'enough'

WORK

Work Backwards Step 3: Use the right tools

Work sucks
So don't listen to anyone who says that
It can be fulfilling and enjoyable
As despite what you might think
The only reason we work is for money
It's wrong to say that
We have to prioritise life over work
Because it is the most important thing

(Now read it backwards)

Introduction: The end

The way we are working is broken, and it's up to us to fix it.

We are crowded into cubicles, worn out on worksites and exhausted in executive roles as office towers stretch high into the heavens, dominating our horizons and psyches. Over the last few decades, almost every industry has been squeezed by longer hours, higher expectations and increased stress, and the end result is literally killing us.

Too many of us are overworked, disengaged and increasingly apprehensive about the future, and much of this malaise can be traced directly back to the role and importance we've placed on our jobs, giving it top priority in our lives – to the detriment of everything around us. We have let work dictate how we should live, and now something is about to break. If we don't make changes soon, that something will be us.

This was the heavy realisation that hit me as my father lay on his deathbed. In those final, delicate moments where time stands still before it's up, life's unimportant trivialities, unfinished jobs and never-ending to-do lists finally melt away, leaving only a wide metallic hospital bed, clammy white hands and an unquenchable thirst. At least, that's what it felt like during the last few hours of my dad's life.

I'd driven him to hospital a few weeks earlier, the pain of years of compounding cancers growing inside his body breaking his usually stoic facade. My dad had battled through various illnesses over decades, from lung cancer in his forties to bowel cancer in his fifties. But the one that got him in the end was multiple myeloma, a type of blood cancer that grows inside bone marrow. This incurable disease, sometimes morbidly nicknamed 'liquid cancer', can be temporarily dampened by a smorgasbord of drugs, radiation and chemotherapy that zaps any remaining energy, until you're the patient in Room 628 counting down your hours.

In his final weeks, my father experienced the piercing clarity that comes from knowing your days are numbered. When a visiting priest delivered his final rites, alone in a darkened room, he emerged with tears in his eyes. 'In all of my years,' the priest said, 'I've never seen someone so at peace with their life. He told me that he has not one single regret, and is ready to die a contented man.'

Work was an important part of my dad's life and identity, but never his primary personality. He started a business with a friend, then spent four decades building a successful company with his name on the front door. Outwardly, it was his biggest achievement, but on his deathbed, almost none of that mattered. In the remaining few days, as his breathing slowed and became guttural, all that dominated his thoughts were the people who'd been part of his life: my mum, me and my siblings, his family and friends. As we flitted around his bedside like moths, taking turns to stroke the back of his hand or moisten the inside of his mouth with a tiny wet sponge, he revisited stories of adventures on holidays, family birthdays around the dining table, personal and sporting achievements and time spent on the ride-on lawnmower at his beloved farm. Work hardly rated a mention. All those promotions, late-night emails, corner offices and pay rises won't mean a damn thing when you're on your deathbed, holding the hands of your loved ones as you wheeze your final breath.

The loss of a parent feels like being violently knocked off a bike that you've spent your whole life learning to ride. When you finally pick yourself back up, you realise one of the handlebars, something you assumed would always be there, is missing. It takes some practice, and many more falls, to learn how to ride properly again, but eventually you get back up and balance, moving forward on a bike that will never be the same.

The years leading up to my dad's inevitable death ignited something deep inside me as I sorted through fresh memories, earmarking those to keep. He lived an extremely full life, balancing work while fostering deep relationships, pushing his own body and mental capacity right up until the end. Any death is a sobering moment for those lucky enough to still live; a time to stop and reassess, spending quiet moments in reflection to confirm that your values and priorities are aligned with the direction you want to go in.

For years I'd had a gnawing sensation that something wasn't quite right with the way we are living and working. I'd begun working full-time in the mailroom of an advertising agency straight out of school, before co-founding my first digital media title with friends in my mid-twenties. Over the next 15 years I gave everything I had to work, helping to build a business with 60 full-time staff – a company we sold in 2016 and I left in 2020.

Inspired by the sense we were in the middle of a momentous shift in the way we work, supercharged by the global pandemic, I began experimenting with different ways of living and working. First, I experimented with location, spending six months working out of a motorhome as my husband and I drove to the sunburnt edges of Australia. We mixed up the usual Monday to Friday schedule, packing as much work as we could into the first few days of each week, leaving the rest of the time free to do what gave us joy, like travelling, exploring, hiking, cooking, reading and snorkelling.

Luckily, my husband's job, like mine, could be done from anywhere with a power point and an internet connection, and we soon swapped our campervan for six months living in Australia's Top End, basing ourselves in Darwin. Each working day, we'd dial into video calls from our sun-soaked apartment, then close our computers and spend the afternoon in the pool or at the local swimming hole to cool down.

But the biggest experiment of all came in 2021, when we moved to Europe to combine travelling and working into one occasionally messy but always glorious journey. We crawled through Greece, Israel, Mexico and Finland before making a home on the Spanish island of Mallorca. Here, we wake up early a few mornings to communicate with Australia during the time zone crossover, and then have several precious hours of deep, productive thinking before knocking off for a late lunch, a siesta or an afternoon swim in the Mediterranean. I acknowledge the enormous privilege I have in terms of financial and travel freedom; I've sold several businesses and I don't have any children, but my own journey is just a starting point for the ideas explored in this book through the perspectives of scores of people you're about to meet. It took me a long time, and many different experiments, to learn my ideal way of living and working, and that discovery has redefined the role work plays in my life.

The happier I felt experimenting, the more obsessed I became with understanding why it took over two decades to find a way through the noise and make work finally work. I started seeking out others who were also experimenting with different ways of working and living, emboldened by an unprecedented opportunity to bend the rules to achieve the lives they wanted. Many were motivated by the depressing reality of the path they saw laid out ahead of them, a conveyor belt that they didn't want to blindly travel on.

I read and spoke about the future of work with dozens of the world's leading experts to try to understand where we are heading. In doing so, I became dismayed. I discovered that hundreds of independent research studies are all flashing amber, their combined alarms warning us that our current approach is broken, making us overworked, disengaged and apprehensive about our trajectory.

Harsh truths

The research on work is overwhelming and depressing. A global Gallup study found that average stress levels at work increased by 42% between 2009 and 2022.[1] Burnout is at an all-time high across most professions,[2] and that's not confined by borders – McKinsey Health Institute[3] showed that almost a third of all employees worldwide reported experiencing burnout symptoms sometimes, often or always. In the highest-ranked country, India, almost 40% of workers reported feeling this way. In China, there's a common expression, '996', which means pride in working 9 a.m. to 9 p.m., six days a week, something Alibaba billionaire Jack Ma called a 'blessing'.[4] Japan even has a term, *karoshi*, that translates as 'death by overwork' – which the Ministry of Health legally recognised as a severe problem in 1987, and which continues culturally to this day.[5]

The way we are working is literally killing us. The World Health Organisation concluded that long working hours led to 745,000 deaths from stroke and ischemic heart disease in 2016 alone, a 29% increase since 2000.[6] The study, in partnership with the International Labour Organisation, showed that working 55 hours or more per week – the equivalent of the relatively common white-collar timetable of 8 a.m. to 7 p.m. Monday to Friday – is associated with an estimated 35% greater risk of a stroke and a 17% higher risk of dying from heart disease, compared to working the standard 35 to 40 hours a week.

But, I can already hear you whisper in defence, what about all of the positive changes that emerged thanks to the global pandemic and the shift to working from home and working remotely? We'll get to those in detail later, but for now it's important to point out that some of those changes have actually exacerbated our overwork culture. Microsoft, which collects data every time you interact with one of their products, tracked the amount of hours that people around the world spend using their Teams software. They found that when many office workers shifted to logging in from home instead of the office, the length of the average workday increased by 13%, or 46 minutes, in the two years after the pandemic began in March 2020.[7] And where traditionally most professional workers had two productivity peaks in their day, before and after lunch, the same researchers observed the emergence of an additional peak since the pandemic, with a third bump of work taking place in the late evening. They call this phenomenon a 'triple peak day'.[8]

No matter which way you look at it, we are caring less about work. Data from workers in 155 countries shows that almost two-thirds of us are emotionally detached at work,[9] and only half of US workers said they were really satisfied with their jobs.[10] In the aftermath of the pandemic, almost 40% of people said the importance of work had diminished for them during the Covid years.[11]

Lastly, we're becoming increasingly nervous about the uncertain future we're heading into. Alongside growing climate and general anxiety, an increasing number of people are apprehensive about the effect of artificial intelligence (AI) on the labour market. A PwC report found around 60% of Australians are worried about the future of their work and their job prospects,[12] and around a third of workers are already worried that their roles could be replaced by AI technology in the next three years.[13]

Combined, that's a lot of research screaming that something has to change, and fortuitously, it's all happening at the most extraordinary moment for us to rethink our relationship with work. During the years that the pandemic ravaged the globe, we collectively lived through the largest global workforce experiment in a century, exposing us to what a tantalising new future could look like. And now we have a once-in-a-generations chance to rethink it all – but exactly how do we go about it?

That's the thorny question I've spent years getting to the bottom of. I've spoken to workers in a wide variety of professions. I met a couple of bakers in Glasgow who only open their bakery two days a week in order to reclaim some of their lives from their work. I met a start-up CEO who lives in Thailand to be closer to his family, while the rest of his employees work from another country. I met a photographer and his wife who've built a successful business out of him going surfing with a camera every morning. I met a tradesman in Southern Virginia who balances his week so he can spend more time doing what he loves. I met an office worker in Sydney who now works three days a week so she can spend more time with her kids, and ironically earns more than when she worked five full days. I found each of them inspiring in their own way – and you're about to meet them too, plus dozens more.

The reasons why our approach to work has broken can be roughly lumped into two categories, structural and individual. Many of the structural causes are interlinked with growing inequality. There is structural inequality in the way our economy operates, and income inequality where salary levels can determine life outcomes. There are also gender, race, class and other inequalities that have been hardwired into the way our society operates. Trying to shift these root causes will take radical, long-term political pressure to achieve ideas such as a universal basic income and fair legislation that takes into account all members of an economy.

Unfortunately, it's going to take more than a book to solve these structural problems. What we can control is the way we as individuals think about how and why we work, which can have an enormous impact on our own lives. How change happens is something I've been studying for over a decade. When I was running the media company I co-founded, Junkee Media, we ran one of the largest longitudinal studies on Australian youth, and there was one particular question I found extremely illuminating. We asked our audience, 'Where do you think change for the better in society will come from?' to find out if there was a specific area, age group or institution who would drive the societal change we so desperately need.

We originally forced respondents to choose only one option, and when we did that, most people deflected the responsibility of change onto someone else. The highest-ranked answer regarding where this change would come from, at 16%, was the federal government and media. This was followed by scientists (14%), friends and family (14%) and lobby groups (12%). One of the lowest-ranking options, at just 6%, was 'me'. In other words, when given only one option, most people overwhelmingly thought change for the better would come from someone other than themselves.

However, when we gave respondents the ability to choose multiple options in response to this same question, something truly fascinating happened. Personal responsibility, or the number of people who said change was going to come from 'me', alongside any of the other options, jumped dramatically, from 6% to 46% – the same level of responsibility as the federal government. This shows that people do want to play a role in bringing about change, but they can't do it alone. The desire for change is strong, as long as it's effected in tandem with other institutions. When we examined the data further, we found that an even larger proportion of women (50%) than men (43%) said that change would come from them in partnership with others. There are many examples of businesses, government, scientists and the media that are agitating for a change to the way we work, and you'll meet them throughout this book. We need to seize this moment, and use that momentum to push, provoke, challenge and change how we think about work forever.

All of these years of experiments, research, interviews and thinking have led me to a simple conclusion about the problem and solution on an individual level: the way we are working is broken because we are living our lives in the wrong direction. We're beginning at the incorrect starting line and aiming for the wrong destination.

Wrong direction

Most of our lives play out in a fairly typical way, without us giving it much active thought. The default path for many people is that you leave school or university, and start looking for a job in an area that matches your skills and experience. You land a job with a company, starting in the most junior position. In exchange for your labour, your employer decides how much they will pay you per hour, week or month. That payment drops into your bank account, and gets divvied up to cover bills, credit cards, rent, petrol, food, necessities and Netflix, until it all seems to dissipate just as quickly as it appeared.

The next month, another salary is deposited and the cycle repeats again. This continues over and over, until work becomes primarily a means of getting enough money to pay for the lifestyle you've developed. There's even a term for this: lifestyle inflation. It helps to explain why the more your salary increases, the more you spend, until you realise you're caught in a common, dangerous rip that's hard to get out of. Most of us repeat this cycle over and over, with very few chances to draw breath, until we retire. No wonder we feel overworked, disengaged and apprehensive.

The bad news is that the way we are currently working – and, by extension, living – is broken. The good news is that it doesn't have to be this way. Instead of the default mode we have become accustomed to, where we think about work, money and life in that order, we need to reverse it and see it in a fresh light.

This is what it means to Work Backwards, and this book is structured in the order that we need to approach these elements: life first, then money and, lastly, work. Alongside these stages are three simple steps to show you how to do this. You'll get inspiration, ideas and new tools that anyone – full-time employees, contract workers, students, business owners and freelancers – can use to make work actually work for you. The lessons in this book will serve you at different times of your life, and can be referred back to as you progress. For simplicity, everyone will fall somewhere on the scale of three primary categories of readers: early, mid and late career. Note that I have intentionally not divided these by age, as there's nothing worse than someone telling you where you 'should' be at based on how many birthdays you've had. We all have unique lives with winding career journeys and can forge our own paths at our own pace.

Early career means you're at the beginning stages of your working life, where you have enormous opportunity to consider the direction you want your life to head in *before* you've really got started. While this might seem like the easiest time to resist the default mode of living, it's also one of the times when you're the most vulnerable.

Without as much real-world experience, you can easily be led astray by well-meaning people who apply their own biases and personal experience. This book aims to question your expectations and show you alternative ways of working and living; it is a hopeful roadmap that you can apply right from the beginning, to set you up in the best possible way to live a fulfilling, happy and productive life.

If you're mid career, you've spent a decade or two in the workforce and you understand how the game works. You've likely begun to question if the way you are working and living is right for you, but it can be hard to know what steps you can take to regain some balance. Also, you might theorise, you're in the stage of your life where work is meant to be hard, right? But the longer that goes on, the more you realise it's up to you – and only you – to reclaim your life. The mid-career stage is also the time when many people start young families, injecting a larger priority into your life that screams, quite literally, for your attention. In the midst of all this, it can be difficult to think about making any seismic changes, but even small tweaks to the way you work can have a big impact at this stage.

People who are late in their career are the most experienced of all. You've seen your workplace, and life, evolve in unexpected ways. You've lived through ups and downs of relationships, family changes, wars and economic booms and busts. By this stage, there is little that fazes you, and that's a superpower of its own. Paradoxically, the later in your career you are, the more options you have regarding how to live your life. Your family might be grown up, you might have some resources saved up or inherited, and at this stage you have less to lose by using this framework to change the way you work and live.

It doesn't matter which stage you're in, this is a radical invitation to take your life back and wring every last drop out of it. At times, applying these principles might feel like trying to rebuild a plane while you're flying it, but the reward is worth all the effort. You will spend up to one-third of your life at work, so changing your approach will have cascading benefits on how you live.

Let's also be brutally honest here. There are always going to be periods of your life when that idealised vision that you know you *should* be heading towards feels further away than ever. Take the first few years after becoming a parent, when everything gets turned upside down, the starting chapter of a new business, or a particularly intense patch of your career, when you decide you're going to give work every ounce of energy for a set time period with a clear end goal in mind. That is perfectly normal, and the path to a healthy way of working is not always linear. The important thing is that you know what you're aiming for.

As individuals, we each play an important role in deciding how and why we work, and there's never been a better time to rethink it than this moment right now. If enough of us redefine what it looks like together, we have the real ability to pick up some of the broken pieces and reassemble them in a much better way.

A better way

I t's easy to get lost in the narrow, winding streets of Jerusalem. The ancient city is carved up into four distinct quarters, each inhabited by Jews, Muslims, Christians and Armenians respectively, who have each fiercely and passionately protected their corner of the historic town for centuries.

But despite its significance as the centre of multiple religions, the old city is crammed into a tiny parcel of land that totals less than one square kilometre, walled in on all four sides by stony, sunburnt walls. Internally, each quarter is separated by differences in archaeology and ideology. The Jewish Quarter is dominated by the Western Wall and dozens of crumbling synagogues. The Muslim Quarter is packed tight with sellers hawking spices, incense and brassware on every corner. The Armenian Quarter is mostly walled off, allowing its residents to live quietly away from the crowds. And if you wander through each of the quarters and follow the natural slope of the streets downwards, you'll eventually end up in a small, unassuming courtyard in the Christian Quarter that faces directly towards two large wooden doors. These doors guard the most contested church in the world.

It's estimated there are between 8 and 16 million churches[1] on Earth. No one is quite sure of the exact number, but there is consensus at least on which of those is the holiest for the two billion followers of Christianity. The Church of the Holy Sepulchre is built on the supposed sites of two of the most important locations in Christian history: the rock that Jesus was said to be crucified on, and the empty cave where it's believed he was buried and resurrected.

Unsurprisingly, this church is *always* teeming with people. At every hour of the day, thousands of tourists queue ten-deep to enter the altar built over the land where the tomb once stood, lining up to shuffle underneath a small table and place their hand into a dark crevice to rub the surface of the rock formation that Jesus may have been crucified on. The combination of emotional pilgrims, hazy processional smoke, noisy tourists and a haphazard layout make it an overwhelming experience.

Part of the reason for this chaotic feeling inside the church is that no one actually takes full responsibility for the maintenance of the holiest building on Earth. There are six denominations that all share the burden: the Greek Orthodox, Armenian Apostolic, Roman Catholic, Coptic Orthodox, Syriac Orthodox and Ethiopian Orthodox, and none of them can agree on who controls the church. After centuries of fighting over who had the right to use the building, in the 1700s all six denominations reluctantly came to the agreement that they would not do anything to change the building in any way without the consent of all the other owners. This agreement means that nothing *ever* changes. The most important church in the world remains frozen in time due to fear of action.

If you stand in front of the Church of the Holy Sepulchre today, watching dazed tourists spill out into the sunlight, and raise your eyes a few metres above the main entrance towards a small ledge, you'll notice something unusual: a single ladder – five rungs, wooden – leaning casually up against the wall. It looks like a tradesman may have left it there and will return any minute now to pick it up.

But nobody will be moving it. This rogue ladder has been leaning against the facade of the church since at least 1728, when a black and white engraving of the building first captured it there.[2] For three centuries it's remained stuck in place, because none of the six groups can agree on who should be the one to move it. This solitary ladder is a stubborn tribute to doing nothing, purely because that's the way things have always been done.

The immovable ladder of Jerusalem is an extreme example of what happens when you get so blinded by the mirage of stability that you give up on trying to make any sort of change. It's a perfect symbol of the price of inaction, and once you become aware of these symbols you start seeing them everywhere.

Humans are hardwired to take the path of least resistance. We lean towards what our ancestors and peers have always done, often unconsciously modelling our behaviour on what is most familiar to us without questioning if it's the right or best course of action. Neuroscientists call this our Default Mode Network, an interconnected series of brain areas that are most active when you're not focused on what is happening around you. While you might not know the scientific name for this, you're certain to have felt it in action. Have you ever commuted to work without consciously thinking about where you are going? There's a part of your mind that can switch into autopilot, telling you which bus stop to get off at, what direction to turn and when you should cross the street. When you arrive at work, your mind has been so busy thinking through other things – daydreaming, solving problems, going over old conversations or planning for the future – that you hardly remember the journey you took to get there. That is your brain's Default Mode Network in action, and it's what happens when we perform tasks without thinking much about what we're doing.

This is what many of us are doing with our lives. We are living on autopilot, giving little thought to where are we heading. This is a behaviour that pops up in all aspects of life, from relationships to financial habits and everything in between. It is especially pertinent to the ways that we traditionally work, such as a typical Monday to Friday, nine-to-five work week and other workplace norms. The 40-hour work week has been the status quo for roughly a century, since workers around the world began revolting against the longer weeks that the industrial revolution had ushered in. There has been little change to this system since the late 1800s, despite almost everything else we do evolving significantly since then.

This sleepwalking way of living is driven by fear of the unknown. We are so used to it that it's easier to just shrug and put up with it – just like the immovable ladder of Jerusalem. The direction of our lives hasn't changed in a century. Don't you think it's about time it did?

Default mode

Our standard approach to work tends to follow a cycle that begins around our early twenties and continues on a loop until we retire. It goes like this: when you finish school, some people head to university to study, others move overseas to travel, and many head straight into the workforce, trying to learn new skills you can use to build a career over the coming decades. Most of us have no idea what we want to do, so the area you begin working in might be influenced by factors such as proximity to your house, a suggestion from a careers counsellor, someone you saw in popular culture, a connection through friends or family, or an available job that requires little experience. We tend to go with what's most convenient at the time, without really considering that this could set us on a path that we might follow for the next four decades.

Eventually, after graduating, returning from travel, or fuelled by a need to earn money, you start looking for full-time work. This is usually Monday to Friday, but it can also be shift work or after-hours work, depending on the industry. You scour job boards, sign up to endless daily career-website emails and suggestions from LinkedIn. If you're connected enough, you might try to network with people you know in the field, leaning heavily on contacts for introductions, leg-ups and anything that might give you an advantage over other candidates.

With enough luck, and patience, you eventually find a job ad that looks interesting. You apply, often along with hundreds of other applicants, crossing your fingers that your experience and neatly typed CV are good enough to land you an interview. Then, finally, yes! You get an email inviting you to attend an interview.

You get excited, research the company, practise the interview, and then nervously turn up on the day. It's all a bit of a blur. Afterwards, you can't recall many of the questions they asked, except that one time you floundered a bit, desperately trying to give them the answer they wanted. You're certain that was the moment you lost the job. You constantly check your emails and phone for the fortnight they said the interview process would take, convincing yourself that you messed it up and the job will go to someone else.

After an agonising wait, you get an unexpected phone call. They offer you the job, and you're over the moon to finally have some paid work. They email you a contract, and you get to properly read the details of the offer – the title, the salary, the start date. Of course, you'd like a higher salary (who wouldn't?), but it sounds pretty reasonable, and you're just happy to have secured a steady job and a regular income. You return the signed contract enthusiastically. Congratulations, you've got a job.

The value exchange of labour for resources is as old as time. The primary reason most people work is to earn money to feed, clothe and advance ourselves and our family. When you start any new job, your employer will inform you how much you will earn to compensate you for your time and effort. Occasionally there's some room for negotiation, but this figure is generally set by the employer with little input from the employee.

From then, your salary is paid every week, fortnight or month. For a hot minute, you check your bank account and feel rich, but that temporary relief is quickly replaced by reality once your bills have all been paid: food, rent or mortgage, credit cards, transport and on and on and on. But here's the thing about this part of the cycle: you don't have much control over what your salary is. Sure, you can affect this by working hard and getting promoted, or through deft negotiation, but it's broadly determined by your employer. They give you a fixed salary, and you have to make your life work around how much you get.

Once you've got your salary in your bank account, it's quickly dispersed to pay for your life. What this means is the most personal part of this process. Life might mean that a fifth of your pay goes on your car repayment so you can drive your dream car. Or maybe half goes towards the mortgage you took out to buy your first apartment. Or to paying off the credit card you took out to pay for your last European holiday. Whatever your salary is spent on, it's being used to fund your lifestyle. The problem here is that most of us haven't consciously decided what this lifestyle is. It's just something that creeps up, with bills, costs and commitments that seem to appear out of nowhere. And the more you are paid, the higher these bills are. Sometimes your pay is barely enough to pay for basic needs like food and accommodation, and not much more.

In this scenario, life is what's left over once you've paid your bills. It can all be a bit depressing, sad and unfulfilling. It's also not uncommon. In 2022, almost two-thirds of Americans lived from pay cheque to pay cheque, an increase from 57% in 2021. It's not just low-income earners either. Almost half of those earning over US$100K a year reported that they were doing the same, up from 38% in 2021.[3]

If we were to visualise the default mode of living, it would look like this:

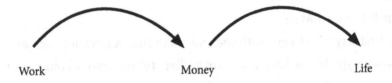

Work   Money   Life

It's a familiar flow that underpins our modern capitalist society; the same order our parents followed, as well as their parents, and theirs before them. The cycle begins with our first job, all novel and exciting when we're early in our career and everything is new to us. As we enter our mid careers and ingrained work habits begin to form over a decade or two of the same pattern, the cycle begins to grate. 'Is this it?' you might think. By the time we're in our late career, the cycle has truly worn thin, and many are left holding on by a single thread as they eye off their retirement.

Surely there has to be a better way? As it turns out, there is.

Work Backwards

Instead of just sleepwalking along the regular path, we have to start with the end point first. Instead of work–money–life, we need to reverse our thinking, starting with life, then money, and then work to design the life you want. This book is divided into those three sections, and at the end of each section is a step on how to put it into practice. This is what it means to Work Backwards, and this is what it looks like:

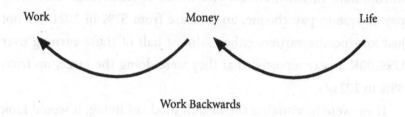

Work Money Life

Work Backwards

Life

Step 1: Create a MAP

The first step is to begin with the end result that you want to achieve. Consciously decide how you want to live, taking into account your passions, skills, happiness and the impact you want to have. You wouldn't set off in a new direction, to chart an unknown course, without having some idea of where the heck you want to go, right? To put life first, you need to create a MAP, which stands for knowing your Meaning, Anchors and Priorities.

Money

Step 2: Know your 'enough'

Once you've defined where you want to go, you need to work out how much money it will cost to get there. In this second step, you have to know what 'enough' means for you, then plan out in detail exactly what that looks like. You need to take back control and consciously plan what it costs to live a life that aligns with what you want, including how much money, success and 'things' you require to be happy.

Work

Step 3: Use the right tools

In the final section, you'll better understand all the extraordinary tools you now have access to, and how to best use them. You have to cut through the noise around where work is heading, and instead see things like hybrid workplaces and four-day work weeks as tools to be experimented with, evaluated, used and adapted to meet your needs. The tools you use will change depending on your situation, life and career stage.

This is what the Work Backwards framework looks like in a single image:

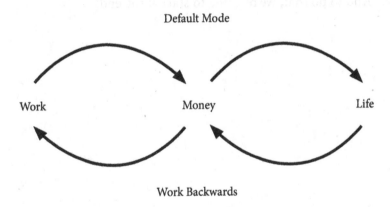

Default Mode

Work   Money   Life

Work Backwards

To help you apply the Work Backwards framework to your life, at the end of each of the three steps is a section called IRL. In case you don't live on the internet, IRL stands for 'in real life' and it's a series of ten exercises where you can apply the theory you learn in this book into real-world action today.

This book is yours to use it in whatever order you like. You might want to stop at each IRL exercise and complete it right then, or you might prefer to read the entire book first and then return to the exercises you want to complete. It doesn't matter how you use it, just that you do, and even applying some small changes to how you work can have a revolutionary impact on your life. You can also download a free detailed workbook to help you complete each of the ten IRL exercises from WorkBackwards.com/IRL that will make it even easier.

The future of work is personal, messy and here right now, but my future of work is very different from yours, which will be different again from your neighbour's. The life that you want is unique to you, and in this book you'll learn a simple three-step process to rethink how and why we work, helping you design a better way to live. And to do that, we're going to start at the end.

Life

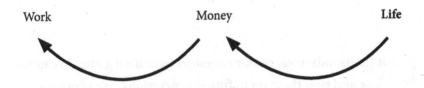

Work Money Life

'To live is the rarest thing in the world.
Most people exist, that is all.'

– Oscar Wilde

The games we play

For thousands of years, our ancestors have used games to capture ideas and pass them on to future generations. We play games to teach spiritual and ethical lessons, for fun, to pass time, to learn how to deal with complex emotions and how to interact with others. Canadian philosopher Marshall McLuhan wrote that 'the games of a people reveal a great deal about them'.[1] They are one of the more primitive ways that we've passed down morals, world views and principles, and there's no more successful teacher than the most popular board game in history.

Since the Parker Brothers released Monopoly in 1936, it's sold over 275 million sets, and been played by an estimated one billion people. Monopoly's aim is a capitalist's dream: to buy and sell properties, collect rent from other players and ultimately try to accumulate as much wealth and property as possible to the detriment of others, who we're actively trying to bankrupt in order to win.

According to Monopoly's official lore, its origin story begins in the 1930s, when Charles Darrow, long credited as the game's inventor, was invited to a friend's house in Philadelphia for an evening of drinking and fun. His friends pulled out a tattered, homemade board game that involved buying and selling properties. The game had been passed around between local households. The rules had never been properly written down, and were verbally dictated. Charles loved the excitement he felt while playing, and asked his friend to write down the rules.

In 1933, Charles took his version of the game, which he had named Monopoly, to executives at the Parker Brothers game distributors. They rejected him, citing a long list of reasons why it would never work. Undeterred, Charles printed 5000 cardboard sets, which he promptly managed to sell through a department store. When he returned to Parker Brothers a few months later with evidence of his sales success, they were impressed and bought the rights, agreeing to pay him a royalty for every game sold. Monopoly was an instant hit. Within a year, 20,000 games were being sold every single week, making it the best-selling board game in America that year, and Charles a millionaire many times over.

This scrappy entrepreneurial story has been repeated endless times over the last 80 years. Until recently, Hasbro's official website[2] included a timeline of the game's creation that began in 1935. Countless media stories have celebrated Charles's ingenuity in conjuring up Monopoly almost from thin air. The only problem with this inspiring story is that it's not true.

Charles Darrow was not the original creator of Monopoly, and it was never intended to be the ode to capitalism that it is today. In fact, the game that spreads the principle of winning at all costs was originally devised as a dire warning about the dangers of capitalism. The true inventor of the most popular board game in history was a progressive woman in her forties named Elizabeth Magie, who once took out a newspaper advertisement offering herself as a 'young woman American slave' to highlight gender politics in the late 1800s. 'Girls have minds, desires, hopes and ambition,' she wrote, somewhat controversially, at the time.[3]

In addition to fighting for gender equality, Elizabeth was a vocal anti-capitalist, believing that growing wealth and greed was leading to increased poverty and an uneven society that was leaving people behind. Inspired by her father and a book written by Henry George in 1879, *Progress and Poverty*, which favoured taxing successful people to reinvest back into the community, Elizabeth created a game in 1904 to help spread this important message.

The Landlord's Game was laid out in a square circuit, populated with landmarks and streets that players could purchase when they landed on them. In each of the four corners of the board was a starting point, a jail, a public park and a sign telling players to 'go to jail'. Players moved around the board buying and selling property with each roll of the dice.[4]

In Elizabeth's original game, however, there were two sets of rules, each designed to teach a different lesson. The first set of rules was called 'Prosperity'. Under these rules, each time someone bought a new property, every player earned money. This reflected the idea of taxing wealthy people whenever they bought land and redistributing the spoils equally to everyone. In this version, the game was won when the player who began with the least amount of money had doubled their earnings. It was an idealistic representation of a fair society where everyone had the chance to win collectively.

The second set of rules was called 'Monopolist'. Unlike the equitable way of playing, these rules rewarded players who owned properties by requiring other people who landed on them to pay rent. The game was won by the player who collected the most money from all the other players, until they had nothing left.

Elizabeth's original idea evolved over time into the game we know today, with the core elements being tweaked and refined by successive iterations until Charles Darrow walked into Parker

Brothers with his version under his arm.[5] The Parker Brothers, acknowledging the similarities between the two games, eventually bought the rights to The Landlord's Game for the grand sum of $500, with no royalties paid to Elizabeth on subsequent sales.

Elizabeth died in relative obscurity in 1948 as a widow with no children. Neither her headstone nor her obituary mentioned her role in creating the world's most successful board game.[6] And for much of the last century, her story went untold,[7] until author Mary Pilon rediscovered her pivotal role in the game's development in 2015,[8] based on a 1970s lawsuit and research by Ralph Anspach.

Monopoly has promoted its winner-take-all mentality around the globe for close to a century, but it was never meant to be that way. Elizabeth's original intention was to highlight the two possible versions of living, and didactically demonstrate how joint prosperity is a better model than sheer capitalism. But sadly, Charles's opportunistic vision of Monopoly seeped into the way society judges success in work and life. The unspoken rules for life, silently taught to children for generations, state that you need to keep playing until you win. Keep going around the board, working and spending, until you earn as much money as you can, so you can buy as much as you can. It is the polar opposite to the message Elizabeth was trying to deliver.

But Elizabeth Magie was right. There is a better way, and we should constantly be fighting to reclaim it. We don't have to live in a zero-sum world where only one party wins, and everyone else has to lose. As more people are questioning work, they're also looking at the entire system that underpins it: capitalism.

There are some positive effects of capitalism, of course, such as the way it encourages efficiency and innovation, but as the prevailing system that rules over our lives and dictates the way society behaves, it's beginning to fall apart. There is only so much tension that capitalism's dark sides, like inequality, short-termism and irreversible environmental costs, can take before the system no longer works.

We're getting dangerously close to that moment. A 2019 survey by Edelman found that over half of respondents thought that capitalism, as it exists today, does more harm than good, and a Pew Research study in 2022 showed that just 40% of 18–29-year-old Americans had a positive view of it.[9]

The default mode of living places us on a one-way conveyor belt from birth to death. But when you decide to put your life first, instead of automatically placing work at the centre, you're raging against a system that's been designed to entrap us in a never-ending cycle of wanting more than we have. And that's something worth fighting for.

A life worth living

How much is your life worth? This is one of those big, messy, existential questions that most of us don't really have an answer for, but British comedian and presenter Jimmy Carr reckons he does. In his early twenties, Jimmy was working in advertising and marketing and was pretty miserable. He quit his job to chase his dream of becoming a comedian, something that took him a decade of hard work, low pay and searching inside himself to properly achieve.

Now, when someone asks him about how he discovered happiness in his own life, he asks a provocative question in response. 'How much would you sell your life for?' he proposed on a podcast.[1] He followed this up with more questions: 'How much to not live your life? How much to not follow your dreams? How much do I have to give you across a table?' Without missing a beat, Jimmy gave his answer: 'Thirty thousand pounds is what people are doing,' he says. 'For most people, in their mid-twenties they've just left college … and they [employers] give you 35 grand to compromise on everything and always be tired and work to my time. And people go, "OK!"'

Jimmy believes that the pressure to enter full-time work before you've even had a chance to consider what kind of work is meaningful to you is a recipe for a lifetime of unhappiness. His solution, unique to his abilities and desires, was to leave his job and become a comedian. Although that's not the path for everyone, it was the right path for him, combining everything he loved into one profession. To do this, he connected with himself, and started with the kind of life that he wanted to live first.

I want to be absolutely clear on something here: prioritising life over work does not mean being lazy or not working at all. It is perfectly natural to work extremely hard during different stages of your career. The tension of work – where at times your relationship with it is frayed and at others it's perfectly balanced – is all part of its design. There are times in your career when you need to buckle down and work hard, knowing that a break is around the corner. Tradespeople and others who work for themselves refer to this as a 'feast or famine' situation, where there are heavy periods of back-to-back work that feels non-stop, but they know there will be less busy periods to balance that out. The same principle can be applied to professional workers.

Sometimes the period of intensity lasts for years, however, with no end in sight, and that's when it becomes a problem. When I was in my mid-twenties I co-founded an LGBT community website with some friends that morphed over the next decade into Junkee Media. With the ups and downs of a primarily advertising-based revenue model, at its peak we needed to bring in around AU$700,000 every single month just to keep the office lights switched on. It was exhausting, never-ending, and drained every bit of energy I had. It was also one of the most fulfilling and rewarding times I've ever experienced at work.

But after a decade of a baseline stress level that constantly buzzed away in the background, it had become too much. By the time I neared my forties I was completely wiped out. My identity *was* work. I sometimes joked that my surname was 'From Junkee' after being introduced multiple times a week – in meetings, at conferences, in a bar, to new friends – as 'Tim From Junkee'. My identity was so bound up in my job that I couldn't properly separate the two.

It was fun and exhilarating and interesting, until one day it wasn't. I don't remember the exact date, but I do remember something I'd promised myself in my early career days. 'I'd keep doing this job,' I told anyone who asked, 'until it was no longer fun.' It was just a throwaway line that didn't mean much, until the day I was walking to work and was overcome by a sudden overwhelming feeling of sickness, the type that clenches your stomach muscles into a feisty ball and refuses to budge.

My regular walk to and from the office, from leafy Paddington to trendy Surry Hills, was one of my daily highlights. I'd intentionally bought a house within a 15-minute radius of our office, believing that the ability to walk to work was one of the true simple pleasures of life. I remember reading a study once that said being able to walk to work made you happier and more focused.[2]

But this wasn't the first time I'd felt this way, and what I'd done previously nudged me out of my default mode and into the next stream of my life. The first time I'd experienced that feeling, I was 21 years old. I had started working straight out of school, aged 18, in the mailroom of an advertising agency in North Sydney. Work was a shiny, new, wondrous machine, and I was impatient to figure out how all the levers functioned. I delivered mail and packages to every floor of the agency, getting to know what different people did, making lifelong friends and valuable connections as the magical world of work was slowly demystified.

Without knowing what my limits were, this was also my first taste of overwork, especially in the stressful days leading up to important client pitches. In a culture that had normalised intense bursts of working, there were countless midnight taxis home after long nights in the office, and my first experience of an 'all-nighter', where production, creative and I – as the junior helper on everything – would refine artworks, print out concepts and glue them onto thick cardboard all through the night, until the sun rose the next morning and colleagues wandered in and spotted us still in yesterday's clothes. Occasionally that next day would continue right up to presentation time, sometimes late afternoon, clocking over 30 hours of non-stop working inside an office with no time in lieu to make up for it. This wasn't every day, of course, but it happened often enough that we'd joke about which team had pulled an all-nighter to get their work completed.

After a few years in advertising, I simply wore out. I'd expend all my energy, and sometimes rivers of tears, adjudicating fights between creatives and clients, trying hard to find common ground on campaigns. I'd put everything into it, during hours, after hours, on shoots, balancing spreadsheets, only to come to the sad revelation that the average person quickly turned the page of a newspaper, or switched off the television, whenever they encountered an advertisement I'd spent every ounce of my energy on.

It was very demoralising to realise that what I was doing had little value to others, and that sucked any remaining meaning I derived from my job. It all came to a head one day on the way to work. I was on a Sydney ferry, soaking up the early morning sunshine on the front deck as I cruised through one of the most beautiful harbours in the world. I felt something funny, deep down inside the pit of my stomach, and the closer I got to work the tighter the ball of muscles became. By the time I got off the ferry beneath the wide grin of Sydney's Luna Park and began the trudge up the streets to the office, my stomach was violently telling me I didn't want to be here. *Listen to me*, it urged. *Do not ignore me.* I walked straight into my manager's office and quit my job on the spot. I didn't have anything else lined up, but I knew, in that moment, that something had to break, or I would.

Almost two decades later, as I wound through the backstreets of Surry Hills trying not to inhale the pollen from the constantly shedding plane trees, I was on my way to a bigger office. This time, the responsibility I felt was to my own staff and colleagues, some of whom I'd spent 15 years in the trenches of workfare with. There were parts of my job that I still enjoyed, but I was no longer as engaged by what I was doing. I was tired, sometimes so exhausted that I'd fall onto the couch on a Friday night and not want to move much for the entire weekend. I was so focused on one part of my life – work – that everything else was suffering. I didn't feel like a great husband, son, friend or colleague.

The worst part was that it wasn't just me. I looked around my friendship group and recognised similar themes: stressed workers who had to see psychologists to get them through the week. Tired employees who were so anxious they needed sleeping tablets to knock them out every night. People so overworked they dragged themselves through the year just to get to their few weeks off work, which they'd spend inside their hotel rooms thawing out from their busy lives and trying to recover in time to go back to work.

I widened my gaze, looking to younger generations like Gen Z, who had recently entered the workforce and were struggling to balance the demands of older bosses with their own expectations of why and how they wanted to work. I was determined not to be yet another statistic of an overworked, disengaged workforce. I knew something had to change, but it would take me a few more years of research to figure out exactly what, and how.

There is no age limit to looking internally and asking if you're happy with the way you are living and working. When Gabrielle

Foreman tells someone about the twists in her life, they always tell her she should write a book. Gab joined the New South Wales police force in 1998, following in the footsteps of her grandfather. Gab never wanted to work on the front lines, however; she had her heart set on being a police prosecutor, a sworn officer who examines a criminal brief of evidence to determine whether there's a 'reasonable prospect of guilt' and if so, appears in court on behalf of the arresting police officer and the victim to prosecute the case. In the state of New South Wales, these legal advocates prosecute about 95% of police cases, with a success rate of over 90%.[3] Within 12 months of graduating, Gab was transferred to the legal unit and spent the next 13 years as a police prosecutor.

The work was draining, leaving little room for joy in her life. 'You're dealing with people on the worst day of their lives, whether it's the victim or the offender,' she says. 'And it's depressing.' Her final few years in the police force also coincided with some big changes in her own life, including a relationship breakdown and the death of her father. All of this led her to feeling burnt out and tired.

Around this time, Gab was offered a role with the Royal Commission into Institutional Responses to Child Sexual Abuse, which was formally established in 2013 by the Australian Government. The Royal Commission would go on to hear from 1200 witnesses and hold 57 public hearings that went on for over 400 days. It was a watershed moment in how the country treated victims of child sexual abuse, but it needed experienced people to help research and compile the mountains of evidence.

Gab initially jumped at the unique opportunity, fuelled by a desire to do important, helpful work that would have a lasting positive impact for victims and their families. In her first week, based in the Department of Public Prosecution, she was led into an office piled up with hundreds of briefs that she had to pick out, read and write reports on. The work, as you might expect, was harrowing. 'It was just brief after brief after brief of misery and despair and just the most horrific crimes against children that you could ever imagine,' she says. What was meant to be a 3-month contract turned into 13 months that left her feeling distressed. 'I was often in tears, it was just horrible,' she recalls.

When the contract finally wrapped up, she began applying for other work in the legal field. For each job application, Gab had to write lengthy answers about why she wanted the job and was passionate about it. It didn't take her many attempts to realise that she just couldn't do it anymore. Any last drops of passion had been drained out of her, she had nothing left to give. She resolved to reconnect with herself and try to understand who she was when she wasn't working. She got out a piece of paper and listed all the things she loved doing that gave her life meaning. They were simple categories, like music, fashion and dogs. Alongside this, she thought about her core values, such as joyfulness, pride and equality, which were missing from her life.

Around this time, a friend asked Gab if she could mind their dog, Buddy, while they were on holidays. Excited to have something to do, Gab moved into their house, and noticed how happy she felt when looking after the dog. She started looking into walking local dogs, and was googling local dog walkers in her area. This led her to a jobs-listing website, where she discovered that an older couple were selling their small dog-walking business. They had around 15 dogs in the business, and would walk all dogs at once every day.

Gab crunched numbers with her accountant and saw it had potential. She had never even considered swapping her stressful day job as a police prosecutor for something as diametrically opposed as a professional dog walker, but she closed the traumatic legal briefing books for the last time and bought the small business instead.

Straightaway, she became excited by the possibilities. She changed the name to Rumble & Bark and had fun developing the branding, marketing and social media. Thanks to the social nature of pet owners, who often chat while their dogs are running around parks, she soon had more business than she knew what to do with. Within a few years, Gab's business expanded to six staff, four dog vans and hundreds of clients all over Sydney's eastern suburbs and inner west. 'It's the best thing I have ever done in my life,' says Gab, her face lighting up. 'I bound out of bed every morning now. I'm happy to go to work, and even if I'm not having a great day I get to the first doggy's place, I open the door and all my troubles just melt away.'

Gab has finally connected her job with who she wants to be. She no longer dreads waking up, and feels pride in the business she's built, the accomplishments of her team around her and the lifestyle that comes with it. 'I feel grateful, and also proud of myself for making such a massive life change that has given me balance, and I just know I've done the right thing.'

After working through the distress she felt from those years of wading through heavy content, she now has a philosophical take on life. 'You have to weigh up how much more of this can you take. Can you take it for another year? Can you take it for another two years? Can you take it for another ten? ... For me I couldn't bring myself to open another brief because I knew what was going to be inside and it was the same thing that ruins lives, and I just didn't want to be part of it anymore. And I realised that there *is* life outside that.'

Gab's story shows what happens when a job loses meaning, and how you can claw your way back to finding some. Thankfully, most of us don't have to completely quit our jobs and find an alternative career path to get there, but we do have to know one important thing: what kind of meaning do we want to get from our work, and outside of it?

We can't unsee

One hot summer's day my husband and I took our two-year-old godson to the zoo in Sydney. It was one of those days when you can't sit in direct sunlight for more than a few minutes before sweat beads start forming on every square centimetre of your skin. We moved methodically around, collecting memories with each animal: little Hugo clapped with the seals, roared at the lions and laughed at the monkeys. Finally, several long sweaty hours later, he'd expended enough energy to steer him towards the exit.

But, as with any good public institution, you had to leave through the gift shop. We had agreed in advance to buy him a stuffed animal as a keepsake, and entered the gift shop to see an army of floppy, soft toys in front of us. Through his tired, foggy eyes, which were struggling to even stay open, little Hugo spied a shelf of huge animals. His eyes locked on a tiger that was basically life-sized, about double the size of Hugo. 'That!' he slurred out. 'That!' He was definitely awake now, his round eyes bulging as he ran towards the stuffed tiger and embraced it with both arms. It was so large he couldn't even wrap his chubby arms the whole way around. 'That!' he proclaimed.

Out of respect for (and, well, fear of) his parents, we obviously couldn't buy him a life-sized tiger to bring home, no matter how much he wanted it so, and we tried to prise it from his arms. 'That!' he repeated, louder, on the verge of tears as we wrestled it away. But Hugo wasn't letting go. Each time we tried to put it back, he'd pick it up again and try to run away. I tried to reason with him, but I may as well have been trying to negotiate with a tree stump.

My husband ran around the store, collecting an army of alternative toys in a vain attempt to distract him. 'Look, Hugo, a whale! A monkey! A long green snake!' But it didn't matter what we showed him, he had seen the life-sized tiger, and now he couldn't unsee it. His screaming and wails escalated until we eventually had to drag him out of the gift shop, along with an adorable average-sized stuffed sloth that he would eventually grow to adore.

I learnt a valuable lesson that day: when you show someone something, you can't take it back. In a strange way, there are parallels between that and what happened to all of us during the pandemic years. For the first time, we were given a taste of what it felt like to control our working lives ourselves. We could determine the hours we worked, where we worked and the best ways of doing it. Our work lives were uprooted overnight, forcing all of us to catch up quickly. The global pandemic shut down factories and offices, curtailed travel, sent office workers home to set up desks inside their bedrooms and disrupted the usual way of working all around the world. And, just like my two-year-old godson, we saw some of the benefits of flexible and remote work, and now we can't unsee them. We can't just revert back to the way it was before.

As the pandemic spread around the globe in the early months of 2020, a filmmaker in Los Angeles, Julio Vincent Gambuto, wrote about what we were experiencing. Covid was 'the greatest gift ever unwrapped,' he wrote in a post that went viral with over 21 million reads.[1] 'What the crisis has given us is a once-in-a-lifetime chance to see ourselves and our country in the plainest of views ... This is our chance to define a new version of normal, a rare and truly sacred (yes, sacred) opportunity to get rid of the bullshit and to only bring back what works for us, what makes our lives richer, what makes our kids happier, what makes us truly proud.'

New ways of working burst into mainstream consciousness from the chaos: remote working, video meetings, digital everything, home offices, no commuting, group messaging, virtual networking. Some experiments worked well, while others failed, but – for the first time in history – we were all forced into a clamour to figure it out collectively. The lessons from this period are still crystallising as employers and employees continue to tussle over who will control the future, but one thing is certain: the way we work will never be the same again.

This peek at newer ways of working jolted many of us into a new reality. Nearly two-thirds of employees in the US surveyed by McKinsey in 2021 said that the global pandemic caused them to reflect on their purpose in life, with half of those going even further and saying this has caused them to reassess the type of work that they do.[2] It's a monumental life shift that will continue to reverberate for decades.

While many of the changes we glimpsed during those years promptly snapped back to where they'd been before, some trends have shifted irrevocably. In America, the national average office occupancy level dropped to less than 20% in the first few months of Covid, and after three full years still hadn't rebounded back. In fact, it has inched back to around just 50% of the occupancy levels pre-Covid,[3] a sign that changes from this period are here to stay. Interestingly, it's the opposite in Asia, where some countries are seeing office occupancy rates ranging from 80 to 110%, which means that in a few places there are now more people in the office than there were before the pandemic.[4] The push and pull between workers and employers was one of the biggest shifts resulting from those years, a power shift that is still playing out in workplaces everywhere.

Shervin Talieh argues that the relationship between workers and employers is woefully outdated. Born to Iranian parents while stationed in Turkey, Shervin lives in California where he's the founder of PartnerHero, an operations company that hires talented people around the world and connects them with growing new-economy businesses.

For two decades Shervin worked in management consulting, travelling often and using alcohol to try to ease the disconnect he felt with how he was living. 'This happens in every industry,' he says. 'Dentists, the clerk working at the food store, it doesn't matter ... the more I looked around, the more I saw that everyone was hurting. This was a universal condition. That's why for me, any conversation around the future of work is really about the future of humanity.'

Shervin firmly believes that the way we are working is broken, and it's taken him time and introspection to discover it for himself – the hard way. 'I recognised in my mid-forties that the theatre of work had forced me to adopt a persona that was different from my natural identity,' he says. 'That chasm just kept growing and growing, the more senior I became, the more experienced I was, the more power I had. I observed around me this very interesting ritual where people in all walks of life, in all professions, they had a professional identity and then they had a personal identity and there was a gap. In some industries, the gap is massive, in others it's smaller, but there's still a gap.'

We need to radically rethink how businesses operate, and Shervin has a two-part solution. The first part is to increase awareness by having more conversations. 'It's the flashlight,' he says. 'You'll find there are some of us who are not subscribing to the older playbook' – the playbook of prioritising constant growth and optimising a business for the bottom line. The second part to his solution is a bit more blunt. 'Frankly, the other pillar for this transformation is just a generation of old men have to die and leave. We must see a complete transformation of who are leading these companies.'

The bad news is that our current approach is broken. The good news is that it doesn't have to be this way, and we can reframe each of the collective emotions that we're feeling.

Overworked? As well as trying to successfully address any systemic issues in our workplaces, we need to rebalance the role of work in our lives. Work should not be the most important aspect of our lives. It does not love us back, and we will not fondly recall the nights we worked late when we're on our deathbeds. There are so many more important aspects to life, such as family, health, relationships and ourselves. These things are far more meaningful than just clocking on and off until we retire.

Disengaged? We need to consciously name and refine the meaning we want to take from our work, as well as the meaning in our lives outside of work. Workplaces were never designed to fulfil our every emotional need, and expecting them to do so will only lead to disappointment. There are simple ways to learn how to derive incrementally more meaning in your lives, and we'll explore some of them throughout this book.

Apprehensive? A lot of fear and trepidation is caused by what we don't know. When there are too many unknowns, we tend to fill the gaps with catastrophising, hyperbole and long lists of all the things that might go wrong. To overcome this, we need to arm ourselves with knowledge about the future of work so we understand all the tools we now have available, and how we can best use them.

By addressing and reframing each of the main emotions we're experiencing, we can begin to live a life that's tailored towards our priorities, making us happier, more energised and fulfilled. Once you realise that you can reverse the usual way of thinking, a whole new world of possibilities opens up, regardless of your career stage, employment status or finances.

Make life work

Reorienting your life to Work Backwards isn't always easy, and it might take a few tries until you get it right. Anna and Sam Luntley run a small bakery on the south side of Glasgow. Set on a quiet street corner surrounded by three-storey tenement houses with blond sandstone facades and generous windows, the bakery opened its doors in 2021. Out the front of the shop are half a dozen garden beds that burst with in-season herbs or vegetables, their edges doubling as sturdy seats for customers to gobble up a range of freshly made tarts, pastries, cookies, pies and bread that changes each week depending on produce and productivity.

Anna and Sam are art-school graduates who realised they could express themselves better through food than art, using creativity in the kitchen as their primary medium. It only takes one bite of their delicious baked goods, such as macaroni hand-pies or smoked dunlop and garlicky kale croissants, to see why their small shop was named 'the best little bakery in Glasgow' by *Observer Food Monthly* in 2022.[1]

As well as serving their local community, Anna and Sam's bakery, two.eight.seven., acts as an experiment to help them figure out how best to balance the seesawing priorities of work and life.

This is their third attempt to perfect their relationship with work, and it's only just starting to finally feel right for them.

The first iteration of Anna and Sam's business grew out of an artistic residency in the Scottish Highlands, where they baked obsessively in a bothy in the woods for a week, then distributed their loaves around the local community. When they returned to Glasgow they continued to bake from their small apartment, using baking as a way to forge connections.

Their customers grew over a few months, until people began pre-ordering loaves for friends and family, creating enough demand that they could quit their full-time jobs to bake. Each week they'd send out an email talking about their adventures, meals and ideas, and would spend the rest of the time baking in their home kitchen, sometimes sleeping only two hours a night in order to keep up with the demand. 'It was all-consuming,' says Anna. 'We did this for almost three years and there was no divide between work and life ... We couldn't maintain this crazy and intense way of living and working. We were exhausted.' In their first experiment with the tug-of-war between working and living, work won decisively.

For their second attempt, they knew something needed to change. So they moved their business out of their home and into a shopfront about 15 minutes from their apartment. They opened to the public from Thursday to Sunday, but continued to honour their wholesale clients by baking seven days a week, starting at 4 a.m. most days and often not leaving until midnight. But as good as their intentions were, work once again took over. 'We were all consumed again,' recalls Anna as the store quickly grew into a busy bakery and brunch spot, with eight staff and constantly exhausted owners. 'We had gone too far down the business road and felt the need to step out, get out of the city, see the world, and refresh our inspiration and creativity,' says Anna. After three years of running their shop, one day they just ended the lease, closed it all up and left town.

Anna and Sam travelled, worked sporadically and enjoyed life for a few years, eventually finding themselves back in Glasgow with a reignited passion for baking. This time, however, they were determined to correct the errors they'd made in their first two attempts and run the business completely their own way, putting their own fulfilment and values at the forefront to ensure it was sustainable.

They took into account the mistakes they'd made in the past, their life goals, and how and why they wanted to work. The first thing they agreed on was how many days they wanted to work each week, and how many rest days they needed – at least two full days off. 'We had burnt out before,' says Anna, 'so we knew we needed time to rest and recuperate. It made our business better and our product more careful and considered.'

They discussed how to remain creatively fulfilled, and how to maintain space in their lives to see friends and family who live further away. To do this, they decided to completely close the shop down for one week roughly every eight weeks, take a break at Christmas and Easter (two of the busiest periods for bakeries), and take a month off in summer. When they plotted it all out on a calendar, they saw that it basically looked like the academic timetable a university or school runs by, with sprints of hard work followed by regular intervals of rest.

Once they had their ideal work vision, they set about bringing it to life. Their aim was to work just as much as the two of them could, without hiring any additional staff, so they could do it on their terms without the added responsibility that comes with having employees. In other words, they had a finite capacity, and they wanted to build a business around that, instead of growing their output – and staff numbers – with each new order. They knew what 'enough' looked like for them.

Anna and Sam have now set up their bakery as a kind of artist studio, where they can develop their creativity through baking, and use it as way to connect and contribute to the community around them. Their bakery only opens to the public on Saturday and Sunday. In a typical week they take Monday and Tuesday off, spend Wednesday doing admin tasks, and cook on Thursday and Friday ahead of the weekend opening hours. Of course, clear lines of delineation are never as simple in reality, but it's the closest they've ever come to balancing work and life. 'We now run a bakery which, at least some of the time, feels like we control it rather than it controls us,' says Anna. 'There is a space between life and work when we want there to be.'

Their approach is an example of intentionally choosing to live their lives in a way that brings them closer to how they want. It's not perfect, and is an ongoing process, but they know clearly what direction they're facing in and where they want to get to.

The future of work will be uneven. Some workers will be able to take advantage of every new tool and opportunity to tweak their jobs, while others will be left behind as everything changes around them. Too often, the conversation about what work will look like in the future rotates solely around professional workers. In America, it's estimated that around 60% of the workforce are classified as 'white-collar',[2] but that's according to an admittedly loose definition of exactly what 'white-collar' means. One researcher, who broadly defined the alternative 'blue-collar' worker in the US as someone who doesn't manage others but is subject to the control of management, and where the work is manual without the associated autonomy found in professional offices, concluded that 62% of the economically active population could be classified as such.[3] Given the murky border between the two, it's not inconceivable to conclude that around half of the population can be classified as 'white-collar' and the other half as 'blue-collar'. Despite this, the discourse still heavily favours the former.

That's something that Rusty Carter is trying to change. When Rusty graduated from high school, he felt an invisible string pulling him in a certain direction. 'Here in the States,' he explains from south-east Virginia, 'the proverbial message is that you have to go to college to get a good job. That's the mantra they beat into your head for at least the last few decades.'

And so, without thinking, that's what Rusty did. He signed up for a community college because most of the adults in his life, including his teachers, guidance counsellors at school and his parents, gave him the impression that was his only option. But he quickly realised that it wasn't for him.

Around this time he met new friends who were all skilled tradespeople, opening his eyes to an alternative career path that he'd never considered. Rusty left college, completed an apprenticeship in ironwork and has been a proud tradesman ever since. Rusty calls the path from school to university to a white-collar job a 'self-feeding machine'. He argues that because many of our parents and other people we look up to went to college or university and their lives generally turned out pretty well, this creates a singular model that future generations feel pressured to follow. 'I can tell you from experience that they're wrong. There are other avenues out there ... it's a bit nauseating.'

Rusty is a fierce advocate for the trades, and spends most of his free time helping people discover which career path best suits them, based on starting with themselves. 'Who are you as a person? What do you like? What are your interests? ... How about we look where the opportunity is and pursue that? That's what my advice is to everybody: "where is the opportunity?"'

As well as working as a foreman on job sites and a construction safety manager, Rusty publishes podcasts and blogs under the moniker 'The Wealthy Ironworker', and this work is designed to educate people like him. The name is intended to get people thinking about how they define wealth. 'What is real wealth?' he asks. 'The conventional definition of wealth is the acquisition of something for money, but I also think that health, time and good advice are all forms of wealth ... I have a wife who I've been with for 12 years, I have three wonderful kids, I have a pretty good work and life balance – all of these things make me wealthy. I can make all the money in the world but I can't get my time back.'

Understanding what you value in life, what meaning you derive from work and outside it, and what your priorities are is the first step on your path to Work Backwards.

Work Backwards Step 1:

Create a MAP

Start with the end result you want by defining
what meaning you get from work and outside it,
your anchors and your priorities.

Meaning

Just after midnight on a cool Sunday in 1666, Thomas Farriner finished work after a long day of baking on Pudding Lane in the centre of London. A strong breeze blew through the city as he closed up the ovens and retired one level above the shop, where he lived with his young family. However, in his rush to pack up, he forgot to properly close the oven doors. As he drifted to sleep, residual heat inside the ovens created sparks that leapt out of the doors and up the walls of his wooden home. Fierce winds fanned the flames in minutes, and the building next door soon caught fire. The heat and noise woke Thomas, and he rushed his family out of a window and onto the other neighbour's roof to escape.

In a matter of hours the fire jumped from shop to shop, wooden structure to wooden structure, engulfing everything in its path. Over the next four days, almost all of the city – some 13,000 homes and 87 churches – was burnt to the ground, in what became known as the Great Fire of London. The fire didn't discriminate, burning every building it came in contact with, from cramped dormitories to the imposing St Paul's Cathedral, located at the highest point of the city of London. While many buildings were rebuilt over the next few years of manic construction, St Paul's took over three decades to restore to its former glory. From the rubble of this fire, a simple parable emerged that can help us understand the different ways of looking at work.

The story goes that one day, a young man walked past three workers who were toiling away laying bricks for what would eventually become one of the Cathedral's internal walls. He asked the first bricklayer what he was doing. 'I am laying bricks,' he said, 'working hard to feed my family.' The young man walked further along, and asked the second bricklayer what he was doing. 'I'm constructing a wall,' he responded. 'I'm a builder and I'm helping to rebuild this cathedral.' The young man walked along to the third bricklayer, and repeated the same question: 'What are you doing?' The third man puffed his chest out and responded with pride. 'I am building the house of God.'

Each man was doing the exact same work, laying bricks next to each other to form a structure, but the way they each viewed their job was starkly different. Although the parable is made up, the science behind it is real. Researchers have identified three main ways that we tend to view work: as a job, a career or a calling. It's important to understand this when talking about what meaning we get from our workplace. The three categories can be summed up like this:

Job: A lot of us simply have a job that we do. When you think of work as a job, you tend to focus on the financial rewards that you receive for doing the work, without gaining much additional satisfaction or fulfilment from it. People who consider work as a job typically angle their life outside the workplace, thinking of work primarily through the lens of what they can do with the money they earn from it. You know you have a job when the purpose of work is just to make money.

Career: This is where you work for a pay cheque, but also something more. You might have an interest in being promoted, in getting more training to help you perform the job better, or you might enjoy being part of an environment where you feel you are learning and progressing. Those with a career focus on advancement and moving up the 'ladder'. You know you have a career when the purpose of work is to build skills and to grow professionally.

Calling: Some people are able to find a deep alignment between their own personal values and the work that they do. They might feel an emotional connection to their work, and that often means they work harder, longer and with a deep sense of enthusiasm. You know you have a calling when the purpose of work is to make a positive difference.

In the case of the bricklayers, the first man had a job, which he used as a means of gaining income to provide for his family. The second man had a career, where he worked with a team that focused on the key aim of rebuilding the cathedral. Part of his identity was entwined with his job. The third man had a calling. For him, work contributed to something bigger than himself.

Often these three ways of looking at work are seen as a hierarchy, as though finding a calling is the ultimate destination that we should all be aiming towards. In most textbooks, it's positioned as a pyramid, with 'calling' at its apex. However, viewing work in this way is an ingrained, outdated perspective that centres work as the main driver of meaning in our lives, and that way of thinking is fast changing. In recent years, the pandemic forced many people to re-evaluate the primary role of work. Different generations, particularly Gen Z and Millennials, are just not as motivated to spend their whole lives striving to reach the top of the pyramid.

Instead of thinking of the 'job–career–calling' framing as a one-way journey to fulfilment that we have to move through, we need to angle our work lives to provide different types of meaning at distinct times. A job is not a single destination; it evolves as we do, morphing and changing with our moods, bosses and workload.

Lorna McDougall is a senior social care officer in a Scotland school for children with complex and enduring additional support needs, but it's not her first career. For over a decade Lorna was a hairdresser, something that just she fell into. 'I didn't know what I wanted to do,' she says. 'I did hairdressing because I had funky hair, but hairdressing for me was a way of making money.'

For Lorna, being a hairdresser was, by definition, a job. She enjoyed parts of it, such as the social aspect, but it didn't fire her up emotionally. What did was working with kids – she just didn't know how to turn that into a career without any formal qualifications. One day a friend told her about a job opening at the school where she worked. Lorna's friend knew she loved kids, and encouraged her to apply for the role, despite not having any experience. To Lorna's surprise, she got the job. On the first day, her boss told her she was either going to love it or hate it. 'I remember walking into a classroom and there were some girls in there,' she recalls. 'One of them was drooling, one of them was biting her hand, one of them was just staring at me, one was in a wheelchair. By the time I left at the end of that day they were all just young girls with their own personal stories.'

Lorna adored it from the start, and now considers her work as her calling. 'Carry me out in a box because I love my job and working with young people,' she says. For the past 18 years, Lorna has learned everything on the go (or 'on the hoof', as she describes it in Scottish slang), and when you ask what meaning she gets from her work, you almost can't get her to stop talking. 'I get so much joy out of it,' she says. 'I have watched young people coming in at nursery. They can't walk, they can't talk … And I've watched people who can't do those things accomplish that. And that's the greatest joy in the world, to help and support them to be the best they can be in their world.'

Not everyone needs to find a transition from a job to a career to a calling. Lorna was perfectly happy as a hairdresser, and still uses those skills today, but didn't realise how much she needed to work with kids until she was doing so. 'I think you should take your time,' she now tells anyone who asks. 'You need to live life a little bit. You need to enjoy, and find out what the things are that give you that nugget of joy.'

Sometimes work is just a pay cheque, at other times it's a way to learn new things and advance, and occasionally it feels like we're part of something bigger. In this new world, work can be a job *and* a career *and* a calling at different times. And there is nothing wrong with just having a job, if that is what we want. To live a fulfilled life, you need to understand what meaning you want to get from work and outside of it.

Meaning at work

It can be easy to tune out when someone begins talking about finding meaning at work. It's straightforward to say that some jobs have meaning, like a doctor who saves people's lives, or a primary school teacher who passes on to young children the building blocks of education. Sometimes meaning is a straight line from vocation to outcome, but if I asked most people to define what meaning they got from their job, they'd stare blankly back at me.

Once you demystify what meaning is, and understand that you can look at it in many different ways, you soon realise that deriving meaning from work is one of the key factors to feeling fulfilled and content in your life. Your meaning doesn't need to be some worthy aim that will solve all of the world's problems – it's a lot more personal than that. In order to Work Backwards, you need to be clear on the meaning you get from your work, as well as what meaning you get outside of work. If you only get satisfaction during work hours, then you're likely to spend too much time, energy and focus on one aspect of your life, to the detriment of the others. On the flipside, if you're only fulfilled from the minute you clock off and head into the weekend, work will become an endless chore that will never become enjoyable.

One of the biggest fallacies of modern management theory is that every job you have has to be meaningful. It doesn't – you just have to have *some* meaning in it, not zero. It also doesn't matter what industry you work in or what you do. We can all find small amounts of meaning at work that can have a big impact on how we feel about our job. In fact, most us are looking for ways to increase meaning in our jobs. Research published in *Harvard Business Review* found that more than nine out of ten people were willing to trade a percentage of their lifetime earnings to do more meaningful work.[1]

Researchers have identified four main, and equally valuable, sources of meaning in work[2]: service to others, realising your full potential, unity with others and self-integrity (which refers to behaving authentically, self-discovery and character development). These sources of meaning are industry-agnostic, and apply equally to a mechanic or a mathematician. You need to find meaning in any of those areas, and then keep refining it until you find more.

Take Brooke Hill, who lives in a tiny village with a population of 431 people tucked into the folding hills of Australia's Southern

Highlands, a two-hour drive from Sydney. There, from her home office surrounded by lush green countryside, she runs a content agency where she and her team write copy for clients like Virgin Money and fitness group F45 Training. Sounds idyllic, right? But it didn't used to be this way. Brooke was a self-described 'chronic overworker'. Starting her career in magazines, she soon found herself working in public relations and communications in London, devoting long hours to working extremely hard each day. She ran events and hosted media in Paris, Milan and New York, and lived out fantasies of her 'dream job' in Europe. 'But it means that I was working to the absolute bone with lots of late nights, backed up with really fast-paced, busy days,' she recalls.

Brooke completed timesheets detailing how long she spent working for each of her clients, and was shocked to see she was sometimes racking up to 70 hours of work a week. Her overwork had a serious effect on her mental and physical health, with her stress resulting in extreme outbreaks of psoriasis. 'My face was literally peeling off,' she says.

After a few years of intense hours, Brooke returned to a senior role in Sydney, where she was sent on a leadership course to learn how to work better. One of the exercises involved uncovering the meaning she derived from her work, and how disconnected she was from it. Brooke realised that she felt most alive in her job when she was using her imagination, instead of the time spent micromanaging events and schedules for other people. 'That was a lightbulb moment,' she says, 'where I realised how much of my day was caught up in doing things which didn't work towards what I loved doing.'

Brooke leaned into her writing skills, refining her craft through a short course and starting a graduate diploma in creative writing literature. She began prioritising the areas of her job that she wanted to spend more time on, focusing intently on them and setting boundaries around anything that took her too far away from them. The result was that her work, and that of her team, who she also encouraged to connect with their meaning, got better. 'By saying no to some things, and saying yes to the right things, we were infinitely more productive, and achieved incredible things in our time together.'

After Brooke gave birth to her first daughter, she applied the same principles to building her own business, a content agency, around her life. 'I wanted to work, and work hard – I love what I do – but I also didn't want to miss a minute of her growing up,' she says. As a new mother, Brooke worked in roughly 40-minute bursts throughout the day, whenever her daughter slept. 'I became militant about it,' she says. Brooke created clear boundaries around when to work and when to be a parent. 'There is nothing like the cry of a baby to force you to stop working!' Within a year, she estimates she was working around 10 hours a week, and was soon able to raise her fees in line with her increased confidence and experience, until she was making more than she'd earnt as a full-time senior executive.

Today, Brooke works on her company, The Contented Copywriter, for three to four days a week, working from 9 a.m. to 3 p.m. This leaves her afternoons free to pick up her kids from school and do activities with them, and the other weekdays to spend time with her youngest son, as well as weekends. Brooke worked backwards to build her life around her vision. She consciously planned what she wanted, which was to spend as much time with her family as possible, and then let work fill in the rest of the time. 'Three days a week works really well for me and our family right now,' she says. 'That may change, but it will be led by my desire of enjoyment of life rather than business demands.'

Brooke's story shows what happens when you lean into the parts of your job that give you meaning, and lean away from the parts that don't, and there's now a growing field of scientific research that's backing it all up.

If you want to know more about your own approach to work, **IRL exercise 1** on page 102 at the end of this section will help you put pen to paper to better understand what level of meaning you currently get from your job.

Job crafting

In 2001, Amy Wrzesniewski and Jane Dutton wrote a research paper together that proposed a novel theory.[3] They are now professors at the University of Pennsylvania and the University of Michigan respectively, and two of the leading experts in how we experience work. But two decades ago they defined a simple way that anyone could use to increase their ability to find meaning at work.

Their theory was born when they noticed that most employees didn't follow the job descriptions that were handed to them when they started a new position. Job descriptions are one of these things most people have at the commencement of a job, which are then promptly filed away and seldom seen again. They are usually drafted by managers and HR teams based on an idealised view of what a worker should theoretically do in a job, and rarely match up with the work someone actually does. It was this sleight-of-hand that inspired Amy and Jane, when they observed that many employees took their job descriptions as a starting point from which they actively shaped their jobs to fit their own needs, values and preferences.

They named their theory *job crafting*, and it's emerged as one of the most interesting areas studied by researchers who investigate meaning at work. Amy defines it as 'the physical and cognitive changes individuals make in the task or relational boundaries of their work', which basically means having a clear awareness of which tasks you personally find meaningful at work, and altering parts of our job to emphasise those areas. Most of us have more leeway than we realise in how we do our jobs, and scores of researchers have now proven that making small changes to the way you work can increase how engaged you feel, your performance and your psychological well-being.[4]

Job crafting is an approach anyone can use to consciously increase the amount of meaning they get from their job. You don't need to have a career or calling for this to function, and even a slight increase in the meaning that you get from your work will have a positive effect on your life. It is also a tool that can be applied across industries, regardless of the field you work in. In fact, the first empirical study of job crafting in 2006 looked at manufacturing engineers and special education teachers, and concluded that the approach enhanced individual job satisfaction, performance and commitment levels.[5] Similar findings have since been repeated on a range of workers including salespeople and midwives, who were able to craft their jobs to better cope with adversity at work.[6]

There are three main areas that can be improved through this method:

Tasks: You can actively decide to take on more or fewer tasks to improve the way you feel about your job. For example, if you have an interest in design, you can try to spend more time using programs like Canva or Photoshop to create your own designs for work projects. The more of this you do, the more likely you are to foster feelings of deeper meaning at work. On the flipside, if you detest certain tasks, trying to spend less time on them will make you feel better about work. To shape your job, you can add tasks, emphasise areas you like or redesign them to make them more meaningful.

Relationships: You can alter which interpersonal relationships to lean into and which to decrease in order to improve your work environment. To create more meaning at work, build relationships with people you want to spend time with, reframe existing relationships in a more positive light, or adapt how you interact with others through initiatives such as mentoring, which benefits both parties.

Cognitive: Lastly, you can change the way you think about your job on a wider scale. This one requires some mental gymnastics in order to reframe your motivations. Take the example of an administrative assistant whose job is to keep the office tidy, organise calendars and perform other odd jobs. They can think about their role in terms of the tasks they have to do, or they can reframe it cognitively, seeing their job as helping make other people's lives easier. This simple flip can allow you to find more meaning, just by thinking about it differently.

Laurie Santos is a Yale professor who specialises in the science of happiness. Her course on how to live a life that's happier and more fulfilling has become Yale's most popular course in over 300 years, with almost one out of every four students enrolled. She's a big fan of using job crafting to find more meaning in your job. 'There's a lot of work showing that when we act in ways that are consistent with our values or the strengths that we bring to any activity, we wind up feeling happier,' she says. 'There's evidence ... that the act of job crafting can really make a not-so-great job feel a lot better. Job crafting can be a powerful way to improve your overall wellbeing, and also how much you love your job. It's also something that any of us can do, no matter what our profession.'

It should be pointed out that a form of job crafting happens all the time, often without our awareness. We tend to spend more time with the people at work who we can learn from and enjoy being around, and minimise time spent with those we don't. Job crafting takes habits that happen beneath the surface and elevates them to a formal, manager-sanctioned activity that employees and employers can perform together to improve everyone's experience at work. It's not a process that happens once only; it's an active, ongoing conversation about your job, and should occur regularly.

To create the first part of your MAP, you need to know what meaning you get from work. It doesn't matter if you consider yourself as having a job, a career or a calling, you don't need to find every aspect of your work life meaningful. In fact, research has shown that you only need to find around one-fifth of your work activities meaningful to experience the maximum positive effect. A 2009 study[7] found that doctors who spent 20% of their time doing tasks that were meaningful to them were less at risk of burning out than those who didn't. Each doctor had the ability to define which areas gave them the most meaning, such as caring for patients, research, education or administration, and then ensured that at least one-fifth of their time was spent doing that. The doctors who devoted less of their time to activities they personally found meaningful were more likely to be burnt out. The researchers also found a 'ceiling effect', which showed that even if doctors spent more than 20% of their time on meaningful tasks, the effect on their levels of burnout was the same.

All of this goes some way towards dispelling the notion that every aspect of your job has to be meaningful. You just need to find *some* level of meaning in it. This brings us to the first big question you need to answer in order to Work Backwards: what meaning do you get from work? As soon as you know that, you can begin designing the rest of your life around it. If the answer to this question is that you simply do not get any meaning whatsoever from your workplace, then you need to seriously consider how you can find some, however minimal. One way of answering this question is to think in terms of the three areas that job crafting can help with: tasks, relationships and cognitive.

Tasks: What work activities do you most like doing?

Relationships: Who in your workplace do you enjoy spending time with?

Cognitive: Which parts of your job can you view through a positive, impactful lens?

If you want to do some job crafting of your own, you can complete **IRL exercise 2** on page 106 at the end of this section. It will help you identify what meaning you get from work, and how you can craft your job in order to increase that meaning.

Meaning outside work

Kathryn Dekas is the Director of People Operations – Future of Work at Google, but before starting at the tech company over a decade ago she was an academic who spent years researching and writing papers on how to find meaning at work. One of the seminal research papers Kathryn published in 2010 with Amy Wrzesniewski and Brent Rosso included several studies showing that people who find meaning outside work were able to buffer themselves from any shock and reduced meaning that might occur if they lost their job or retired.[8]

However, it wasn't until around a decade after publishing that paper that Kathryn really understood what that meant. In 2018 Kathryn had her first child, followed by her second two years later. She always found meaning in her life outside work, but having a young family took that to another level. 'I will say that that's been a real eye-opener for me,' she says. 'I think having such a robust commitment outside of work has made me appreciate the value of that and I think a lot of working parents would say this. I haven't reduced my commitment to my paid employment, I've just figured out how to do the job differently, and I don't think that I would probably go back to the way that I did it before.'

Kathryn half-jokingly says that she now has two jobs. 'I have my paid employment and I have my work at home. I've been doing my paid employment for decades but I've been doing this new job at home for only a few years, and it feels like that's my new job. It's harder, and there is a tension between the two … I am somebody who likes to try to keep firm boundaries so that I can be "all in" on whatever I'm doing when I'm doing it so at least I feel like I am present and able to derive the meaning and the joy from each one, which are very different.' But there are still daily struggles trying to reconcile the two, and Kathryn has noticed that the way she works has changed with the addition of her 'home job'. As well as learning how to be more efficient in completing tasks and with her time, Kathryn has noticed that she has grown better at prioritising. 'I am better at identifying if something needs my full attention … as opposed to just getting through everything because that's what's on my to-do list.'

Having a young family is one of the most common ways of deriving meaning outside work, but it's just one of the paths. Leaning into hobbies you enjoy, enjoying sports you obsess over or throwing yourself into communities you're a part of are other ways.

Finding meaning in your life outside of work is an active pursuit, and not something that passively happens.

Purpose vs meaning

What is your life's purpose? I don't actually expect you to know the answer to that – there's no quicker way to make you feel like a failure than to ask you what your life's purpose is. Some enlightened individuals who have spent a lot of time interrogating themselves might have an answer, but for most of us, figuring out our purpose will take our entire lifetime. And even then, when they're on their deathbed, many people still won't have any idea.

A purpose is an ambitious, audacious goal to aim towards – but the reality is that not everyone has a clearly defined purpose, and sometimes trying to find it can be an existential graveyard that's littered with the best of intentions. A personal purpose often makes sense in retrospect, but ironically is harder to nail down when you're right in the middle of it. This doesn't mean you don't have one, just that it's hard to figure out.

There are literally mountains of books written about how businesses need to have a clear vision of where they are going or else their employees will feel lost and disconnected. I covered this in depth in my first book, *Cult Status*, exploring the importance of a business having an impact statement. And it's true: purpose in business is very important. However, what's not often discussed is that this applies just as much to individuals as it does to a business.

What is somewhat easier and more accessible than purpose is meaning. Meaning is a more active and subjective idea that evolves alongside us as we move through life, and it's something that we can find in even the smallest crevices of our day.

The difference is that, while finding a personal purpose is hard, finding meaning is easier. A real meaning is something that is highly personal to you. You are the only one who needs to even talk or think about this part. The meaning that you derive from your life is just for you. That realisation is very freeing. You don't need to compare your meaning with someone else's. You don't need to tell me about it. You don't need to advertise it on your social media. Sure, if you really want to, go ahead, but the important thing to remember here is that meaning is personal.

The second question that we need to answer in order to Work Backwards concerns our life outside work. Just as we need to find some meaning in our jobs, we also need to find meaning in our everyday activities, relationships and the way that we live. The question you need to ask yourself is: *What meaning do I get outside work?*

I don't blame you if you just recoiled slightly in fear. On the surface, this seems like one of those questions that gets asked in therapy, but this is often easier to answer than most people realise. The trick is to ask yourself an alternative, easier question first: *What are you proud of?*

The answer to this question might evoke a litany of responses, such as:

I'm proud of the students I teach.
I'm proud that my child is happy and content.
I'm proud of my writing.
I'm proud to have gotten through this hard week.
I'm proud of my close relationship with my husband.
I'm proud of a sculpture I just created.

Whatever it is, vocalising what you are proud of takes you outside of a work mindset, and gives you a rounded, holistic view of who you are as a person. If purpose is the final destination on the road to figuring out your life, which only some people reach, then pride is the first stop that's accessible for all. And right now, with our ways of working on the precipice of breaking down irreversibly, a first step that's going in the right direction is a good step. To Work Backwards, you have to define at least one thing you're proud of. That will face you in the correct direction, ready to head the way you want to go.

If I were to answer this question, I would say that I'm most proud of, in no particular order: the books I've written that help people better understand complicated subjects in simple ways (especially this one); the websites and businesses I've created; the community of leading independent digital publishers that I started; my close relationships with my husband and family; and how I've been able to angle my life in a way that's rewarding and fulfilling in almost every aspect.

The common theme in the things I'm most proud of is that I get so much satisfaction from building and growing communities, which is one of the things I adore most in the world. No matter how far I get pulled away from it, that thread of wanting to unite people to achieve a common good is something that brings real meaning to my life.

In the IRL section, I'll help you answer these questions in order to identify what meaning you get outside of work, giving you complete clarity over where you find meaning in **IRL exercise 3** on page 110. Most people never get the chance to look introspectively at who they are and what motivates them before diving headfirst into work, and that's one of the core reasons they end up overworked, disengaged and apprehensive.

Now that we've clarified what we find meaningful, let's dive into the second part of creating a MAP: the anchors that are most important to you.

Anchors

S ome people have the antiquated idea that you have a 'work self' and a 'personal self', and the two are completely separate personalities, as though you're Hannah Montana, Miley Cyrus's teen character who famously switches from being an ordinary teenager to a pop star just by wearing a different wig. Your 'work self' is meant to be calm and professional at all times, and then when the weekend hits, your 'personal self' can finally drop the facade, wear the clothes you want to wear, and express yourself as you really are. Thankfully, this concept has gone the way of the fax machine – these days, most of us are able to bring our full selves to work and be the same full selves at home.

However, there are still some parts of our lives that we tend to concentrate on at work, and ignore as soon as we begin our commute home. I can almost guarantee that every workplace has got their corporate values figured out – not always well, but bad values are still better than no values. While businesses have understood the power of corporate values for a long time, most of us are yet to apply those lessons to figuring out our own personal set of values.

To separate them from work values, I call these 'anchors', and they are some of the most important things to identify if you want to understand how to live a life that's fully connected to them. An anchor is something that tethers you to reality. Sometimes known as core or personal values, your anchors are the qualities that make you unique. Just like a company's values, there's little to differentiate between individual values themselves, but it's your unique combination that sets you apart.

Your anchors follow you through life. They develop during your childhood and adolescence, are tested and pushed during your early adulthood, and are generally set by the time you join the workforce. Your anchors can be affected by your friends, your community, your religion and everything around you. Your anchors define who you are. You take them home with you, bringing the same set of values into the workplace the next day. Trying to separate the two, as though you highly value a behaviour during the day, but not at night, is not sustainable. If we want to get clear on how to find meaning outside of work, we need to get super clear on what our anchors are. Our core values connect our work and non-work domains, and some researchers have proposed that congruence between these two areas can positively influence how much meaning we find at work.[1]

Knowing your anchors is a key aspect to Working Backwards, and gives you a filter through which you can run your activities, goals and how you spend your time. Your anchors should be things you closely identify with, and that just make sense once you've nailed them. They are also something that people close to you, who really know you intimately, should be able to agree with. In fact, that's a good litmus test for the three or four anchors once you've narrowed them down: tell your partner, close friend or colleague what you think your anchors are. They should vehemently agree with you. If they don't, there could be a disconnect between how you want to be perceived and the way others are perceiving you.

Anchors are forged from birth, and are a combination of internal and external forces. Your parents have the biggest role to play in helping to set your anchors. Kathryn Dekas published a report with Wayne Baker, professor at University of Michigan, which confirmed that your parents are the single most important factor in determining how you think about work.[2] The closer your bond, the more likely you are to follow their lead. 'It's like many things you get from your parents, good and bad,' Kathryn says. 'A lot of things get passed on through socialisation from parents to children, like work values ... One of the inspirations for the 2013 paper is that my parents have very similar relationships with work as do I.' Kathryn's dad, an ex-professional athlete, and her mum, a clinical psychologist, passed on their positive views of work to their daughter. 'They have very different kinds of work ... but both are very, very passionate about their work and also saw it as more of a vocation, not a job. So I grew up with the assumption that I would have that same relationship with work but I would probably figure out for myself what type of work that I landed on.' Kathryn points out that parents can affect your work orientation in a positive way when they model behaviour that you learn from and try to emulate, as well as providing a repellent in showing you how you don't want to live.

When we know what our anchors are, we know when we're not living the life we should be. Steph Clarke is a facilitator and futurist who helps teams and organisations prepare for what's next. A few years ago she left the stability of her role at a large professional services firm to work for herself. Before transitioning away from full-time work, Steph spent time defining the core values that represented the way she wanted to live, and kept returning to the twin drivers of freedom and creativity. They were two things she wasn't always getting in her role at a large firm. 'I never felt like

I had enough annual leave anywhere I've ever worked,' she says. 'And I wanted to be able to pick and choose the work that I wanted to do. I felt like I was spending twenty per cent of my time doing interesting, valuable stuff, and eighty per cent of the time servicing the organisational debt of bureaucracy and paperwork.'

Steph moved away from full-time employment by working four days a week at her day job, and spent the rest of her time leaning into her anchors of flexibility and creativity to see if she could find a way of earning a living with them at the core of what she does.

She now works for herself and loves combining her 'work self' and 'personal self'. She relishes the freedom to be able to take extended periods of leave to travel, and the creativity of learning new skills like graphic design, writing and podcasting. 'Once you've worked for yourself, in some ways you're kind of invincible,' she says, explaining that if she took up a full-time job again, she wouldn't have to worry as much about job stability, knowing that she could always return to working for herself if she needed to. By identifying that she wanted to weave her personal and professional values together and live a life that had flexibility and creativity at the centre of it, Steph is a living example of the power of knowing who you are.

Know your anchors

Uncovering what your anchors are generally goes one of two ways. For some fortunate people, it's as easy as reading through a list of the most common anchors until you come across the two or three that immediately jump out at you. *That's me!* you scream, underlining them and knowing, deep down, that you've identified your anchors. For the rest of us, it might take a few more exercises to narrow down your anchors, but it's still a minimal time investment for something that can have such a huge impact. Knowing your anchors is one of the simplest things you can do to help you lean into the life you could be living. You should ideally have three to four anchors, or core values, that you live by.

Sometimes you can identify what's important to you just by looking at it, but you won't know until you see it. Read through this list of the 50 most common anchors slowly and thoughtfully. Consider carefully if each one is something that you value highly when it comes to how you want to live your life.

50 most common anchors

- Accountability
- Achievement
- Adaptability
- Adventure
- Altruism
- Assertiveness
- Authenticity
- Boldness
- Community
- Compassion
- Courage
- Creativity
- Curiosity
- Dependability
- Discipline
- Empathy
- Fairness
- Faith
- Family
- Freedom
- Fun
- Flexibility
- Generosity
- Gratitude
- Growth
- Hard work
- Honesty
- Independence
- Integrity
- Kindness
- Leadership
- Love
- Loyalty
- Optimism
- Perseverance
- Reputation
- Respect
- Responsibility
- Security
- Selflessness

- Self-reliance
- Self-respect
- Service
- Spirituality
- Stability

- Sustainability
- Trustworthiness
- Uniqueness
- Well-being
- Wisdom

It sometimes helps to read over the list slowly for a second time, really pausing after each one to reflect on whether, intrinsically, that is a value that defines you. If you're fortunate, some of them might have jumped out at you instantly.

My personal anchors are optimism, fairness and community, three values that underpin almost all of the emotions that drive me. They are certainly something that's been passed down from my parents to myself and my siblings.

If none of these anchors grabbed you immediately, don't worry. These are just the most common – there are many more that you can add to that list. In the IRL section of the book you can complete **IRL exercise 4** on page 112 to help narrow down your anchors.

Anchoring yourself

It takes time to fully understand what motivates you. It took Nisha Dass years to process and break free from an unhealthy relationship with work. She was obsessively checking her emails, even when she was on holidays, and was in a state of constant, chronic stress. She made important life decisions, like turning down holidays with friends, because her work came first. And whenever she went home to visit family in California, her body would succumb to sickness. 'It's almost like my immune system would break down by the time I actually took a vacation,' she says. 'I saw that this was not sustainable.'

So in 2018, in an effort to reclaim control of her well-being, Nisha started her own consulting business where she could set her own hours and decide which clients she wanted to take on. That's when she came across vChief, a staffing firm that helps senior executives find quality consultants to help them do their jobs better. Founded by Madeleine Niebauer, vChief has around 300 workers on their books who have all built their lives around prioritising themselves ahead of their job. The company was in a fast growth phase and Nisha joined as the Chief of Staff to the founder.

One of the business's guiding principles is that productivity is measured in output and outcomes, instead of hours worked. They give their workers unlimited time off – once agreed with their manager – and the ability to work fully remotely, as well as help pay for the set-up of home offices. The consultants work anywhere from 5 to 40 hours a month for their clients, and then log off their computers to return to their lives. The vast majority of people who work for vChief are parents. 'I think because of our benefits and our structure, we attracted more experienced employees for the positions that we were hiring,' says Nisha. 'It really helped us grow because you have people who aren't learning how to build a plane as they fly it.'

Nisha worked closely with Madeleine and her team to create a workplace environment that lets people bring their entire lives to work when they log on from anywhere in the world. They have different office chat channels dedicated to pets, children, travel and recommendations. 'We wanted to create a culture where if you're going to take time off in the afternoon to go to parent-teacher conferences, you should be able to celebrate that and post about it. You shouldn't feel like you need to hide it and call it a doctor's appointment or just say you're out of the office. You can be transparent and we will absolutely support you.'

Nisha's view on work has evolved a lot since 2018. One of the main changes has been a cognitive reframing of how she thinks about it. She previously thought of her job as achieving excellence at any cost, which was an unsustainable and unhealthy model of leadership. She now champions modern work values and believes that can have a positive impact by ensuring more workplaces create conditions where their teams have the ability to give their relationships, bodies and minds the same level of importance as the work that they do.

Kat Norton's discovery of what motivates her also happened during the Covid years, and forced a swift U-turn of her entire life. Kat was in her early twenties, living at home and working for a US company doing securitisation reviews for American banks. She had a pretty typical career path before that, going to university, studying an MBA at Binghamton University in New York and starting her career with an internship in 2015. She slowly climbed her way up the company, spending most weeks flying to a different US state to work with local offices.

Then the pandemic hit, and she found herself stuck at home, back in her childhood bedroom, struggling to adjust to the sudden change. One night, in April 2020, Kat went into her family living room and declared something strange to her parents. 'Mum, I'm going to be rich and famous soon,' she said with a straight face, 'so I need you to prepare your nervous system for that.' Her mum took one look at her and responded, without missing a beat: 'Kathleen, go clean your room.'

Kat returned to her room, where she got out a sheet of paper. On the paper she wrote down all the things she loved doing, such as passing on knowledge, mastering programs like Microsoft Excel, and dancing around for fun, and then tried to figure out a way to combine them all together. She also wrote out her simple monetary goal many times: 'My side hustle makes me $5000 a month' she repeated over and over, like a mantra. If she could just make $60,000 a year from a business on the side of her main job, Kat thought, she might be able to make a proper go of it.

After adjusting to the sudden change in work, Kat had a lot of extra time on her hands to reconnect with some of her interests. One of those, strangely, was playing around with Microsoft Excel. As anyone who's been forced to spend time among the devil cells will know, Excel has a unique way of frustrating even the most patient person with its confusing formulas and pivot tables. Taking cues from social media's energetic and relatable style, Kat called herself Miss Excel and made short, snappy videos that used popular music trends, cultural moments and awkward dance moves to show off easy hacks. 'I really went into it with no expectations,' she says. 'I just thought I'd have some fun.'

That fun translated into instant reach, with her fourth video, in which Kat explained a new Excel data-searching feature while dancing to a rap song, receiving over 100,000 views in just a few days. By the end of her first month of posting daily content, Kat had more than 100,000 followers on TikTok.

As Kat's audience grew, she thought that people would pay money for longer online courses that used some of the principles of micro-learning, where people learn things in short, sharp bursts. She built a digital course on how to master Excel, with each lesson five to ten minutes long, infused with as much creativity and entertainment as possible. 'I'd never made a course before,' says Kat, 'but it was just a natural melding together of my love for Excel, my love of teaching and my love of creating.' Kat mapped out that it would take her around 40 to 60 hours to create it. She figured she could either spread that out over months, or just buckle down and do it in one go, so she took two weeks off her job to script, film and edit all the content, and The Excelerator Course was born.

A few months after starting her social media page, Kat launched her course to her growing audience, with the goal of reaching people and earning extra money. People loved the energy, style and content of her course, and within two months she was bringing in US$15K a month in passive income – more than her full-time salary. Kat got out the piece of paper where she'd written down her original goal: make US$5K a month. With a sense of pride, she drew a little tick next to it, then wrote out a new goal: 'My side hustle makes me $25K a month.'

Buoyed by the instant success, she quit her job, moved out of her childhood bedroom, and travelled around America for the next year and a half, spending about a month at a time living and working from places like California, Arizona, Miami, Texas and Hawaii. Armed with a six-foot ring light, Kat and her partner Mike moved from Airbnb to Airbnb filming videos, growing her audience and creating new online courses.

What started off as a fun project during Covid quickly became an extremely profitable business. Kat, or Miss Excel as she is better known, now has over 1.5 million followers on social media, earning her over US$2 million a year.[3]

But the best part of all her success? Kat works only 25 hours a week. She has a small team around her now, including a virtual assistant, video editor, social media manager and graphic designer, who do most of the heavy lifting in getting the content out to her audience. This leaves Kat with most of the week to travel, spend time with her family, and think of new ways to engage her audience.

The biggest difference, however, is the deep connection she has to the core values that fulfil her. Through this process she has discovered that her anchors of authenticity (she really loves Excel, okay?) and service (she also adores helping people) have allowed her to connect with the work she does on a deeper level than ever before. 'I did love my previous job and the people I worked with, however my happiness and fulfilment level is now through the roof,' she says. 'For the first time in my life, I wake up truly happy each day. I am beyond grateful that I get to do what I love every day, which is to create and serve my community.'

Kat still has the original pieces of paper that she used to plan her ideal work life. They've been updated many times since she first started, each time with a bigger goal of reaching more people. 'This was the magical piece of paper,' laughs Kat. In reality, the magic was in the confidence and clarity it gave Kat to know she could go out there and create her ideal working life around her strengths, something she's now doing one TikTok dance at a time.

Priorities

Every single weekday, without fail, Eugene Tan's alarm goes off at 5.30 a.m. Known to everyone as Uge (it rhymes with huge), he jumps out of bed, grabs his camera and heads a few hundred metres from his house to the white sand crescent of Sydney's Bondi Beach. There he photographs early morning beach life and its inhabitants, as he has for the last 25 years. 'He never misses a day,' his wife Deb says over a coffee in a busy Bondi cafe where barely a few minutes pass without a local interrupting to chat with her and Uge. They are local celebrities in the beachside suburb, which Uge has documented from every conceivable angle.

Their story begins in the mid-1990s when Uge, an early riser and frustrated creative director, began taking photos of his neighbourhood. He sent the best ones to friends, and soon realised there was an appetite for a simple daily email with a photo of the day. 'This was back when you didn't get many emails, so you only got a handful and read everything,' laughs Uge.

His daily email, Aquabumps, rapidly gained an audience, with thousands of people signing up to receive a fresh photo from Bondi every morning. It didn't take long before readers began asking if they could buy prints of his shots. The email list kept growing, and

Uge opened his first gallery in a tiny Bondi shopfront in 2004. It was this space that Deb, an experienced sales executive, walked into a few years later, attempting to negotiate on the price of one of Uge's artworks. A first date quickly followed, and 20 years later they're married with two young children.

Uge and Deb's relationship with work is complicated. At times it's 'very smooth, where we have the lifestyle that everyone wants', says Uge. At other times, they face the tough realities of running a small business. They point to a constant labour shortage, navigating fixed costs and a shifting partnership market as some of their biggest challenges. Having a physical store selling prints in Bondi means their options for remote working are more limited, but Deb still aims to spend at least two days a week working from home. 'In my old job,' says Deb, 'I'd be schlepping to the city office in the morning.' Instead, she's often out swimming and surfing with her kids before heading into the shop.

Uge, who has been waking up before sunrise for over two decades, still manages to find joy in the details of his art. 'I love the craft of making the photos,' he says. 'I still love shooting in the water and in helicopters, but it's just trying to get those absolutely unique moments that no one else can capture. That's all I try and think about when I shoot.'

Swapping his previous life of working every day in the city for large multinational companies so he could prioritise his three passions of photography, surfing and the internet hasn't always been easy. In fact, there have been many moments when it's felt easier to give in to the constant difficulties of trying to run a small business than push through them. But even on those tough days, when Uge is in the water as the sun peeks over the Pacific Ocean and bathes the sandstone cliffs in golden red hues, he knows he wouldn't trade this path for anything else.

The way we are working is relatively new in historical terms. Sure, our parents, and our parents' parents, worked in similar ways, but there is nothing traditional about the way work has bustled its way into the prime position of our lives. In 2019, US writer Derek Thomson coined the term Workism to describe our modern fascination with sacrificing ourselves on the altar of work. 'Workism is making Americans miserable,' he wrote, describing it as 'the belief that work is not only necessary to economic production, but also the centerpiece of one's identity and life's purpose; and the belief that any policy to promote human welfare must *always* encourage more work.'[1]

For most of human history, we viewed work in polarising ways. The First Agricultural Revolution around 12,000 years ago saw the transition from nomadic culture to a more settled civilisation, paving the way for farmers, crop growers and hunters to emerge. The Ancient Greeks viewed work as something of a curse. Their word for work – *ponos* – translates roughly as sorrow or hardship. Work was a painful, but necessary, process that was never intended to bring meaning or joy. The philosopher Aristotle devised a distinction between 'work' and 'leisure', surmising that you couldn't have one without the other. The Romans viewed work through a similar lens, adding inequity to the equation with lower-class slaves performing the most arduous work, so that the ruling class could enjoy their leisure time. During the Middle Ages, around 400 to 1400 CE, work was primarily a way of feeding your family and yourself. But then came the first industrial revolution in England in the mid-eighteenth century, bringing the creation of machinery that increased production, output and our ambition exponentially.[2] From that moment on, work irreparably changed.

It's from this era that the concept of balancing work with other parts of our lives began to emerge, but the terminology we use today, that of the work–life balance, didn't emerge until the 1970s and 1980s.[3] Even then, it was a small trickle, with fewer than ten research studies on work–life balance published each year up to 2000. From 2003 onwards, there was a dramatic explosion in the number of studies published.[4] And with it came two of the biggest errors that we're still trying to address to this day.

The first is the notion that work–life balance assumes that work and life are equal, which they are certainly not. Work is the labour you're paid to complete by achieving tasks set out by your employer. If you work for yourself, or run a business, work is everything you do to establish a consistent revenue stream, solve a customer's problem or engage others to do so on your behalf.

Life, on the other hand, is a wide cornucopia of activities that make up the bulk of the reason we are here on Earth. We're not here to just work, although sometimes that's what it feels like. Our life consists of many areas, the most important being our relationships with our family and friends, and what we do to keep our mind and body engaged. Within that are areas such as the communities that we're part of, our spirituality and our hobbies and interests, but each of these layer up to our relationships with others, and what we do to keep ourselves fulfilled, interested and happy.

If we were to draw a pie chart of how a typical work–life balance would look, it would be something like this:

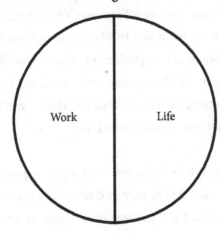

Work–life balance implies, by its very name, that work and life are two equal measures, each sitting on either side of a scale, fifty-fifty, each as important as the other. And that is the original sin: 'work' and 'life' are not, and should never be, equal. Your life – what you want to do, who you want to be, how you want to spend the small amount of time you have on this planet – is infinitely more important than any work you will ever do. We are more than our jobs.

The second error is one that makes me wish I had a magic wand I could have waved in the 1970s when the terminology was being popularised: we need to swap the labels around. Instead of talking about 'work–life' balance, with the priority given to work, we should be calling it the 'life–work' balance. Through this simple reframe we are reclaiming life as the most important part, which should always be addressed first.

Life-work balance

In its purest form, we can distil the ways we spend our time into four core elements:

Work: We labour for several reasons. Of course, the money work brings in to fund our lifestyle is at the top, but we also work for personal accomplishment, and to feel like we're part of something that's bigger than just ourselves. For a typical worker on a standard schedule of five days a week, work takes up about one-third of our lives.

Relationships: When we're not working, we spend time with other people, like our family and friends. This might include your partner and kids, parents or siblings, or anyone else who you consider to be in your unique family. Your friends also fall into this category, from those you've known your whole life to the new acquaintances you want to get to know better. An important aspect of forming and keeping relationships are the communities that you're a part of.

Mind: You are the only keeper of your mind, so it falls squarely on your shoulders to do whatever you can to maintain the best mental health. This includes anything that you do to keep yourself engaged, busy, fulfilled and happy. It might be playing cards every week with your friends, reading books or watching documentaries to learn more about the things that interest you. Your mind also includes your spirituality and beliefs, such as organised religion or meditation.

Body: We each only have one vessel we use to live, breathe and move. What we feed it and how we use it is individual for everyone, but health, nutrition and exercise are key factors in our lives. Some would argue that how long our body will last, and the condition it's in, are the only factors we should care about, as these supersede everything else. You can be firing in every other category, but if your body gives out then nothing else matters.

There are some crossovers, but the four simple categories of work, relationships, mind and body capture most of how we spend our time. Watch a movie to relax? That's to recharge your mind. Play competitive squash? That's for your body. Heading out to dinner with your family? You're spending time on your relationships.

One reason the phrase 'work–life balance' has caught on is because it's catchy, but if we use the same visual depiction as earlier, this is what it looks like if 'work' and 'life' are evenly balanced, with life broken down into its major components:

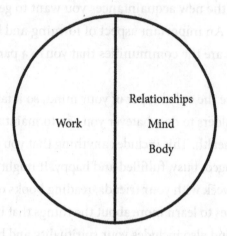

When you position it like this, you can instantly see the problem with our typical way of thinking about life–work balance. We're trying to squeeze way too much of life into one side in order to balance out work.

Full circle

There's a real clarity that comes from distilling our life down to its purest form. 'Balance rarely comes from increasing efficiency. It usually involves reducing responsibilities,' said Adam Grant, Professor at Wharton School of the University of Pennsylvania.[5] 'It's better to do a few things well than be overwhelmed by many.'

By focusing on just four core elements of how we can spend our time, we're cutting out the noise and committing quality time to what really matters. Of those four elements, most of us have focused too much on the first element, work, often to the detriment of the others. This has led to an overworked, disengaged and apprehensive workforce.

The obvious solution is to work less, something few of us need to be told. But how much less? What does the science actually say? And what is the optimum amount of time we should be spending on everything else if we want to live a happy and fulfilled life? To answer this, I spent a lot of time questioning experts around the world, as well as people who have reprioritised their lives to put themselves and their happiness first. Although zeroing in on an actual number wasn't an easy task, a consensus soon began to emerge.

Some of the most compelling research comes from a German study by Dr Christian Kroll and Dr Sebastian Pokutta, who published their findings in 2013 investigating what a 'perfect day' looked like for working women.[6] Building off seminal research in an area of study called subjective well-being, which reconstructs what an ideal day would look like, they concluded which activities would make up our time if we optimised it for happiness during a typical 16-hour day.

The list of things we can do each day is broad, ranging from eating to exercising, meditating to intimate relations, shopping to housework, and the results of the study showed just how little time most of us would allocate to work if we could. Based on their research, the ideal amount of time allocated to working was just 36 minutes a day (plus additional for commuting and computer time), compared to 56 minutes to going shopping, 82 minutes to socialising, 78 minutes to relaxing and 75 minutes to eating. In other words, for most of the working women they researched, work was something that they had to do, not something that they *wanted* to do.

'Overall, comparing our results with the actual way people spend their time, the implications for higher wellbeing include spending a little more time with friends, a lot more time with relatives, and a lot less time with the boss and coworkers,' they wrote. 'The results show how a paradigm shift away from a focus on increasing Gross Domestic Product towards greater wellbeing at the macro level could play out at the micro level with potential consequences for how we might live our day-to-day lives.'

If you take each of the activities in the research and fit them neatly into the four core categories of relationships, mind, body and work, the percentage that is scientifically optimised to happiness comes out to spending roughly 30% of our waking hours on our relationships, doing things like socialising and spending time with our children, 25% of time on our mind through activities like relaxing and meditating, 30% on our body, including exercise and preparing food, and the remaining 15% on working, computer time and commuting.

The point of their research was not to be a reflection on the practical feasibility of working for just 36 minutes a day. Instead, wrote Kroll and Pokutta, 'this paper takes the rather radical view to explore what a day in the life would look like if the highest possible [subjective well-being], or more precisely net positive effect, was the aim of somebody's existence ... If these results are taken at face value, they show that in order to maximise wellbeing it is likely that working and consuming ... might play a smaller role in people's daily activities compared to now. Instead, we would hypothesise that the things that matter most to our happiness – in moderate amounts for each activity – may then get more emphasis.' That is the politely worded research way of telling us that our current way of living and working is leading us down a path to unhappiness, as it's so grossly out of line with what actually makes us happy.

All of this brings us to a way of rebalancing our activities to be more in line with the direction we should be heading in. Instead of prioritising work ahead of everything else, we need to take a more holistic view, aiming for a full-circle life where each of the four quadrants of work, relationships, body and mind are all given roughly equal time and attention.

This is what that looks like:

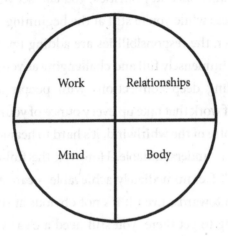

In an ideal full-circle life, each of the four core elements are equally important, and should have similar time dedicated to them. Assuming that we get eight hours of sleep each night, we are awake for 112 hours each week. This means we have 112 hours every week that we can spend how we choose, based on what we prioritise.

At certain times of our lives we will have more choice over how to fill these hours. In your early-career stage of life, you generally have a lot of spare time. It might not always feel that way when you're in the thick of it, but these precious early years typically have the least responsibility attached to them. Early career is usually pre-family, mortgage, caring for others, loans, high stress and other things that slowly compound the longer we live. During this stage, you should have a lot of agency over your schedule and how you allocate your time, meaning that angling your activities around your priorities should be more achievable. However, the naivety of this period means it can be easy to simply drift unconsciously through it without knowing what your priorities are. You can get distracted, pushed and pulled in other people's directions unless you actively fight against this. But by creating your own MAP, detailing your meaning, anchors and priorities, you can set yourself up for a lifetime of success while you're still at the beginning.

By mid career, the responsibilities are adding up. Life might feel exciting, tiring, immensely full and challenging as you juggle starting a family, building deep connections with people and managing intense bursts of work that take up every ounce of your energy. When you're in the centre of the whirlwind, it's hard to hear anything above the noise. That is understandable. However, the full-circle model – even if it doesn't feel immediately achievable – can still be an ideal situation to aim towards. Even if it's not obvious at the start exactly how you're going to get there, you still need a clear vision of where you're headed. The tools that we'll run through in Step 3 can be used to give you back more time, and at this stage, every small action that helps improve your balance counts in a big way.

As you enter your late career, the pressures should begin easing back slightly, and your years of experience will help you better understand yourself and what brings you joy. You can apply these insights to decide how best to use your time, and where you should be focusing. When your career time winds down, this model can still be used as a framework for how to spend your time to maximise your satisfaction, fulfilment and happiness.

A full-circle life is made up of internal and external ways of spending time. The internal half is when we spend time on our mind and body, and the external involves spending time working and on our relationships with those around us, including friends, family, children, colleagues and our community.

In a perfect week, we should be trying to devote equal time to each of those four areas: work, relationships, our mind and our body. Consciously deciding how to spend our time makes us hyper-aware of our priorities. Of course, these are ideal hours that will vary according to your individual circumstances and the stage of life that you're at, but it's a useful exercise to help you narrow down what you value most.

However, let's be honest here. There will be times in your life when things aren't well rounded. The ebb and flow of your priorities will change depending on your life stage, but you should still have something to aim towards.

Now, let's go into more detail about how to prioritise each area of your life.

Work

Based on data from 160 countries,[7] the average worker around the world currently works 43.9 hours a week. This differs greatly by location and occupation, with those in northern, southern and western Europe working the least (37.2 hours on average), and workers in southern Asia working the longest (an average of 49 hours). But how much *should* we work? It's something most people have never really thought about. For a century we've just assumed that working five days a week, from Monday to Friday, was a given. It's something we've rarely questioned.

But one researcher has. Around 15 years ago, Dr Brendan Burchell, a professor at the University of Cambridge, was invited to give a talk at Birmingham University on any topic he wanted. Brendan had always been interested in how work affects our well-being, especially when it comes to unemployment, job insecurity and work intensification, and as he pulled together his slides for the presentation, he had a particularly obvious question that he was trying to find an answer to: what is the optimal amount of paid work for employee well-being? Brendan was certain that someone must have a definitive answer to this question. But during the process of researching and presenting the seminar, he realised that nobody had actually figured it out.

There are lots of clear, and well-researched, benefits we derive from work. The main ones include economic gain, social status, social interaction, time structure and a sense of purpose or meaning.[8] But, Brendan wondered, how much work do we need to do in order to attain the positive mental health benefits we get from working? Brendan and his colleagues began researching this question, receiving funding from the Cambridge Political Economy Society. They called it the Employment Dosage Project, and used data tracking more than 70,000 British residents between 2009 and 2017, meaning they were able to follow individuals over several years as their hours or work changed, and to correlate this with changes in their mental health.

As he conducted his research, Brendan canvassed some of the people around him to try and guess what the results might be. 'Typically, people thought maybe working four days, possibly three, was going to be the peak wellbeing,' Brendan explained to me. 'I was thinking it would be maybe two or three days a week.'

The results surprised everyone, including Brendan. The initial research showed that working just *one* eight-hour paid day a week delivered the same mental health benefits as working five full days a week. 'I didn't believe it at first,' says Brendan, but the scientists went back to their data set, repeated it, checked and rechecked, and the results held up as a very robust finding that was equal for men and women. It turns out that we don't need to work as much as we think we do.

Brendan likes to explain his findings using an analogy to vitamin C. You only need a small amount of vitamin C to get all of its benefits. If you have less than that, you get scurvy and eventually die, but every amount above the small dosage that your body needs is not actually useful. 'Health food shops will try and sell you these massive doses that will be the equivalent of eating a hundred oranges each day. It doesn't do any harm, you just piss it all out, basically,' he says. 'And work is the same.' In other words, we all need to work far less than we think to get the positive mental health benefits it brings.

Of course, working one day a week isn't practical – mainly due to the economic gain that work gives us – but the outcome of his research was not to force a movement to work just eight hours a week, but to highlight that many of our preconceived notions about hard work are flawed. It also emphasises the desirability of ensuring that as many people as possible have some paid work, particularly those who would otherwise be unemployed.

The next data point for how much we *should* work, if we had a choice, came from a relatively obscure legal services company in New Zealand, which led the charge to champion a four-day work week. Our current model of a five-day, 40-hour work week has been the dominant model of working for around a century. While it's correct to point out that our earlier ancestors worked even longer hours, for the past 50 years there's been little progress in shortening our work week. As the architects behind Four Day Week Global, Andrew Barnes and Charlotte Lockhart have helped popularise the idea of a four-day work week when Andrew formally cut the working hours of the company he co-founded, and then released the results of the surprisingly positive effects it had to a global audience.

They've since worked with thousands of companies to help make a smooth transition to a four-day work week using their preferred '100–80–100' model, where workers get 100% of their pay for working 80% of their previous hours in exchange for a commitment to maintain 100% of their productivity. You'll meet Andrew later in the book in the Work section.

Fascinatingly, almost all the research coming from thousands of companies who have switched to a shorter work week shows that productivity does not drop when people work for 20% less hours.

One reason for this is Parkinson's law. Cyril Northcote Parkinson was a British historian and author who wrote an essay in *The Economist* in 1955.[9] He'd worked as a public servant for years and witnessed first-hand the stifling nature of bureaucracy. 'It is a commonplace observation that work expands so as to fill the time available for its completion,' he wrote, in a statement that's since repeatedly proven itself. We tend to work as hard as we need to for the time that we are allocated. There are obvious limits to this – you can't squeeze a full five days' worth of work into one – but so far, the overwhelming success of four-day work week trials shows that most employees are able to condense their usual workloads into less time without any drop in output.

Working for eight hours a day over four work days, including an hour's break for lunch and other small moments to refresh the mind and body, is emerging in various industries as one of the best tools we have to rebalance the role work plays in our lives.

We have 112 hours of waking time each week. Devoting a quarter of that time to working is the ideal ratio in order to live a happy, healthy life that leaves plenty of time for everything else.

Working 32 hours a week is the equivalent of four days of work. When you factor in a one-hour break for lunch and other distractions, you end up with around 28 hours of actual, focused, intense work time each week. If you're used to working 50-hour work weeks, this might seem wildly out of reach, but heading towards this level is what you should ideally be aiming for. There is independent research supporting this, too.[10] Data compiled by the Organisation for Economic Cooperation and Development found that the sweet spot of happiness for Australian workers was to work between 30 and 45 hours a week. Too much more or less than that and people tended to be unhappy about their lives and worried about their health. Dan Buettner, the American author who popularised the concept of 'blue zones', or the five places in the world where people live the longest, healthiest, happiest lives, has reviewed research on more than twenty million people worldwide through the Gallup-Sharecare Well-Being Index, and concluded that the ideal number of work hours we should be aiming for is 30 to 35 per week.[11] The most important benefit, however, is what this frees up for you outside of work. Every hour you're not working is an additional hour you can spend on other areas of your life – the things you're really going to care about on your deathbed.

Relationships

Our relationship with our family, friends, neighbours and community is an area that we don't tend to plan. Most of us assume that healthy relationships are something that just happen during the 'in-between' times, and that they will sort themselves out naturally. However, if we don't actively set aside time to nourish our friendships, family ties and connection with other people around us, they can be easily pushed to the back of the queue of our priorities.

The Harvard Study of Adult Development is the world's longest-running study of well-being. It has tracked thousands of people for 85 years (and counting), looking at which factors contribute most to living happier and longer lives.[12] Their sample size began with a cohort of 725 white men from Boston – it was 1938, after all – but has since expanded to include over 2000 people from diverse backgrounds. Every two years the participants answer detailed questions about their lives, covering everything from how much they exercise, what they're doing at work, how content they are, how much money they earn, and what they spend their time doing.

The research, now led by study director Robert Waldinger, showed that physical health has an obvious direct correlation to how long people live. It also found that the strongest predictor of who would be happy and healthy as they grew older boiled down to one primary factor: whether we have good relationships with other people. In other words, the sheer strength of our connections with other humans has a direct correlation to the quality and quantity of our years on Earth. 'It stands to reason that you'd be happier if you had good relationships – those two things go together,' Waldinger said,[13] 'but how could good relationships predict that you'd be less likely to get coronary artery disease or type 2 diabetes or arthritis?' The answer is that relationships protect our health by helping us to manage stress. 'Stress happens all day long,' Waldinger explained. 'What we believe is that if I have something upsetting happen, and I have someone to talk to at home or call on the phone, I can literally feel my body calm down.' In short, there is a strong relationship between deep relationships and well-being, and we should be doing everything we can to actively prioritise positive relationships in our lives.

When you live a full-circle life, the ideal amount of time you should spend on your relationships is 28 hours a week, spending roughly 4 hours a day with people that you care about. Four hours might seem like a lot, but there are myriad ways of going about this. This could involve everything from scheduling a regular date night with your partner, having a long conversation with a friend on the phone, playing board games with your family, having lunch with a colleague, or going for a walk with your neighbour.

Mind

This broad category encapsulates everything you can do to keep yourself mentally healthy. Alongside the body, it is the most personal of the quadrants – after all, it's inside our own heads.

This is the category that your hobbies fall into, whether it's watching films or completing complicated puzzles. Your mind includes your spirituality, too. That might be religion for some people, and meditation for others. What *doesn't* nourish your mind is social media, doom-scrolling on your phone or aimlessly flicking through TikTok videos. There is a place for a small amount of social media in helping to defrag your brain and in connecting to friends and family, but it's still ultimately a soulless exercise that brings diminishing returns the more time you spend doing it.

It's important to recognise here that these activities should be thought out and planned. Some experts, like Professor Cassie Holmes from the University of California in Los Angeles, believe that you should track your time. Just as you record your spending if you want to get out of debt, or keep a food diary in order to lose weight, she proposes that we should track every half hour of our time so we use it more intentionally. Her research found that we tend to have a 'sweet spot' of happiness in our days, which is around two to five hours a day.[14] If you have less than two hours of free time a day, you generally feel unhappy, while at the upper end, if you have more than five hours of free time each day, this begins to erode your sense of life satisfaction.[15]

'We often don't realise how critical time is for our happiness,' Laurie Santos, Professor of Psychology at Yale University, explains. An awareness of the impact of how we spend our time is gaining increasing traction with scientists, with several terms now used to describe how we feel about the time that we have.

There are two ends of the spectrum: time affluence and time famine. Time affluence is your subjective sense that you have some free time for yourself. This is when you feel like you've got time in each day to do the things you want to do: go to the gym, cook a good meal, or spend quality time with your family. The opposite of this is time famine, which Laurie describes as 'where we are literally starving for time'. This is a familiar feeling for many parents, carers, busy workers and anyone who fills their plate with too many demanding mental items. The negative effect this has on us is immense. 'We don't realise that time famine can cause such a hit to our happiness, and so we often don't invest in time,' says Laurie. 'If you self report as being time famished, that's as bad for your wellbeing as if you self report being unemployed.'

To live a full-circle life, the ideal amount of time to spend on your mind is 28 hours a week, or roughly 4 hours a day. This doesn't mean spending four hours a day meditating – the ways you can replenish yourself mentally are limited only by your imagination. They could include reading a good book, or watching a TV show that you adore. Sometimes, it might be just doing nothing, giving yourself room in your day to daydream at home. The important thing is, whatever way you choose to nourish your mind, it should be done consciously.

Body

Many people would argue that our bodies are *the* most important part of our life equation. Without a healthy body, none of the above elements even matter. Fortunately, there are tools available to us, which we'll explore in detail in the Work chapters, which can give us greater freedom to focus on our health. Changes to our work schedules since the pandemic have shown that. Research from Stanford University that looked at geolocation data near 3400 golf courses in America found that there were 278% more people playing golf at 4 p.m. on a randomly selected August in 2022 than on the same date in 2019.[16] In total, there were 83% more golf games played on weekdays in August 2022 than in the same period in 2019. That's a lot more people taking advantage of flexible working hours to hit a small white ball around a park.

To live a full-circle life, you should be spending around four hours a day on nourishing your body in some way. Of course, that doesn't mean four hours of exercise every day. An hour of that might be cooking something delicious and healthy that will nourish your body, spending extra time after a hot shower applying layers of moisturiser to your face, or walking your dog around the block.

One neat trick to help rebalance your life is to supercharge some elements by combining them. Playing board games with your family is working on your mind and your relationships (unless someone is inclined to throw a tantrum, in which case do *not* play board games with your family). Going running with a friend nourishes both your body and relationships at the same time. Even getting out of the office and having a walking meeting with your colleague, or taking a work call in the park, is a good way of combining different elements.

All up, we should devote around 28 hours every single week to our bodies in order to live a full-circle life. That might sound like a lot, but when you consider the fact that our body is the only vessel we have for our entire lives, it makes sense to ensure it's treated as a priority.

How we spend our time shows us our priorities. When we choose one thing over another, we're living out our anchors, and showing others, and ourselves, which values we think are worth acting on. Most of this is done without thinking, rushing from one thing to the next without ever understanding why we are doing it.

A full-circle life aims to spend an equal amount of time on each of the four core elements of life:

Work = around 4 days a week
Relationships = around 4 hours a day
Mind = around 4 hours a day
Body = around 4 hours a day

This is what that looks like:

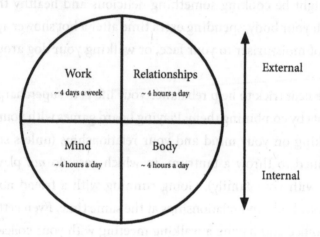

A full-circle life is not something that's easily achieved, but it's something to aim towards. Every small step in reclaiming some of your work hours is a step in the right direction.

It's important to point out here that the ideal number in hours cannot be achieved if we work on each of them in isolation. In fact, if we tried to spend a full day doing 7 hours of work, and then 4 hours on our mind, body and relationships in isolation, the combined 19 hours out of 24 would leave us very little time to get the amount of sleep needed to achieve each of them properly. That's not the way this is meant to work. We can only achieve the ideal hours by consciously combining activities, working any blend of the four quadrants together at the same time. For example, we could mix quality time on relationships with nourishing our body by joining a group fitness class with a friend, or combine mind and relationships together by playing card games after dinner. It is in these combinations where the magic lies, and thinking up ways of mingling areas together is one of the best ways of achieving your goal.

In recent years there has been a tangible, genuine global shift away from prioritising work as the most important thing in our life. For years we've been told that work should take the lead; it takes a lot to undo that wiring. Feelings of failure, letting people down, disappointment and accusations of laziness are just some of the by-products of questioning where work fits into our life. But making work your number-one priority means sacrificing things that are more important than work will ever be.

You can create your own vision for a full-circle life in **IRL exercise 5** on page 115 by creating a plan to begin the process of rebalancing life's important areas.

Coming full circle

Tiffany Farrington has nailed her life–work balance. It's not just a recent alignment, either – Tiffany has enjoyed almost two decades of what she calls 'bliss', leaning into her priorities at different life stages. Tiffany began her career as a publicist and event manager, but kept coming up against an annoying problem. She'd often spend months planning an event for a client, choosing a date and venue in advance, only to discover the week before the event that her biggest competitor was planning a similar event on the same night. This meant that invited guests, media and photographers had to run across town to attend multiple events on the same day.

So, for her next big event for Cartier in 2004, Tiffany emailed 25 of her public relations friends asking if any of them had an event on the same night to ensure it wouldn't clash. She soon began doing this regularly, until some of her friends asked if they could message the same group to check dates for their events too. Trying to be helpful, Tiffany gathered the upcoming dates of events into a single Word document and emailed it to her contacts every Wednesday. 'It's funny to look back at this time because it was never, ever meant to be a business,' she says. 'I was just trying to be helpful!'

The list ballooned to hundreds of people, and then came an online version, regular newsletter and a lot of wild, themed events. Social Diary is now a successful subscription business that provides a diary to avoid clashing events, a daily newsletter of media and celebrity contacts, editorial opportunities and influencer information. Tiffany worked very hard to build the business in the early years. 'Back in my party days, my work and social life were completely merged and that was heaven to me in my twenties and thirties,' she says.

Every day she builds the newsletter and sends it to her audience. 'I've always liked a different view out my window while I do it ... In 2009 I sent it from a yacht in the middle of the Caribbean, from a dance party in Barcelona at three am, from beach bars in Thailand and even from the only hotel in Cuba that had wi-fi, all whilst sipping on a Cuba Libre, naturally.' She lives by the saying that 'work expands to fit the time you have'. 'I can assure you, when you have beaches and palm trees out your window, you get your work done very fast!'

After living in big cities her whole life, in 2021 Tiffany moved to the country, and now lives and works a couple of hours north of Sydney in the picturesque wine-growing region of the Hunter Valley. 'It's simply calmed me in a way I never thought possible as I've always been so fast-paced and used to running around like mad,' she says. 'I love this new slow pace of life.' She's also been able to use tools such as flexible and remote working to be able to care for her parents when they became ill. 'I'm so lucky I was able to be bedside around the clock for when my dad was dying,' she says. 'I didn't have to take leave or ask a boss – I just set my laptop up in the hospital, which was everything ... I am so grateful to have been able to do that.'

Tiffany shows that you can build work flexibility into your life in the long term. She has built her business around her priorities, travelling the world, and now enjoys a full-circle life in the country with trees, wild animals, good wine and a great life–work balance that allows her to spend time doing what she loves. Of course, not everyone has a flexible business that allows them the complete freedom to do this, but you can still take lessons from the way Tiffany was able to consciously design her work around her life. For some people, this crafting might be just minutes or hours that you're able to claw back from your job using the tools we'll cover in detail in the third section. For others, it could be that by better understanding what your priorities are in life, you can use them as a filter to decide what to say yes and no to.

To Work Backwards, you need to start with your end goal. You do this by creating a MAP that indicates exactly where you are. The MAP shows you the meaning you want to get from work and outside it, the anchors that define you, and what your priorities are. These are the three things you need to know in order to put yourself first.

IRL Exercises: Life

Step 1: Create a MAP

Meaning

Meaning comes in many formats, and in order to live a full-circle life, you need to understand what meaning you derive from work and outside work, and how to increase each of those in small ways. Here are three exercises that you can do today In Real Life (IRL).

IRL exercise 1: Meaning at work

What meaning do you get from your job? There are many avenues to derive meaning from what you do, and you only need to find some meaning in one of them. Without any, work can feel dreary, monotonous and soul-destroying, but if you can clarify the meaning that you get from your job, you will become more aware of it and be able to lean into it.

For this exercise, mark how much meaning you get from each of the following areas on a scale. You can write your answers directly in the book, copy this onto a sheet of paper, or download free worksheets from WorkBackwards.com/IRL

The main categories where meaning at work comes from:

Relationships: The bond you build in a workplace with your
co-workers, clients, partners, students, mentors or anyone
else you interact with on a regular basis is a great way
of finding meaning. You all understand a similar work
language, and often go through some of the same ups
and downs. Even if you don't enjoy every aspect of your
job, you can lean on colleagues and those around you to

find happiness, camaraderie and empathy in the workplace.

Accomplishment: Many people find the act of achieving a goal, completing a task or getting to the end of a project very satisfying. It is this sense of accomplishment that gives meaning to what they do. It doesn't need to be a giant project, either. It could be the regular sense of satisfaction you get from doing a job well that gives you pride in what you achieve.

Prestige: Some workers find meaning from the status, power or position that their job gives them. They might be a police officer, security guard, senior manager or another role that other people look up to. In these cases, your work involves assuming a status in your company or society that brings you pride and satisfaction.

Community: When you feel like your job contributes positively to a community around you, this can help you find meaning. This could be the joy you get from helping others, contributing to a cause, or being socially responsible. Being part of something that's bigger than yourself can be very motivating.

Teamwork: We've been hardwired to want to work with others for thousands of years, building communities around similar interests. If you're a member of a strong team, you can find meaning and satisfaction from moving in a similar direction together.

Learning: Education and learning new things can be a strong way to find meaning at work. This might involve understanding more about the company you work for, its history and purpose, or understanding as much as you can about your customers and why they buy from you. Educating yourself so you can be better at your job is a good way to find meaning in your workplace as an expert on a topic.

Freedom: The ability to work autonomously can be very meaningful for some people. Not everyone likes to work this way, but if you're a self-starter who relishes a high level of agency where you get to decide how, what and when to work, then you can easily derive meaning from being your own boss.

1. Write down each area on a page.
Grab a blank sheet of paper and write down each of the seven areas:

1. Relationships
2. Accomplishment
3. Prestige
4. Community
5. Teamwork
6. Learning
7. Freedom.

2. Draw up a table.
Next to each of these headings, add a scale that ranges from 'No meaning' to 'Some meaning' and 'A lot of meaning'. This is what it should look like:

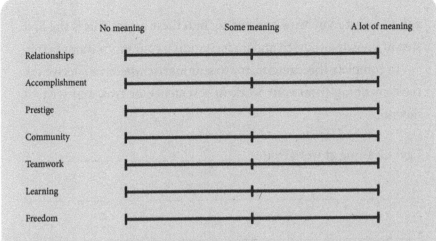

3. Mark where you are on the scale.

Go through each of the areas of potential meaning, and read the descriptions above. For each area, mark an 'X' on the scale indicating the amount of meaning you derive from this area. Do you get no meaning from it, some meaning or a lot of meaning?

4. Define what meaning you get from those areas.

For each area that you derive 'some' or 'a lot' of meaning from (i.e. if it's on the right-hand side of the scale), write out exactly what meaning you get. You don't need to write an essay, and you can ignore any area that you don't derive meaning from. An example in the Relationships area could be: 'I feel good when I'm around my workmates', or in the Community row you might write, 'I love helping kids feel connected to their neighbourhood'.

5. Summarise your answers.

Once you've written out some of the ways you find meaning at work, see if any stand out in particular. Where do you get the most meaning from? Circle the words or sentences that help identify your biggest sources of meaning. Understanding your sources of meaning allows you to invest more time and energy into these areas. This is the first step in knowing yourself and understanding your motivations better.

To complete this exercise, try to summarise where you derive the most meaning from your work in a sentence or two, and write it down:

I get meaning at work from: _____

_____

_____

IRL exercise 2: Job crafting

Job crafting is a scientifically proven exercise that can help you find more meaning at work. It involves adapting and shaping your role to include more activities you find meaningful, and fewer that you don't. This is not about shirking responsibility or not doing what's required of you, it's about crafting parts of your job to better suit you. It's a proactive approach to taking control of your own job satisfaction, and a tool anyone can use today. This specific job crafting exercise was inspired by the work of HR consultant Rob Baker.

There are three areas of your job that can be improved using job crafting.

Tasks: Actively deciding to take on more or fewer tasks to increase how you feel about your job.

Relationships: Altering interpersonal relationships by leaning into some and decreasing others to improve your work environment.

Cognitive: Changing the way you think about your job on a wider scale.

You can craft all of these areas, but it's best to do them one at a time. Changing your cognitive thinking is about mentally reframing your perception of a topic, so for this exercise we'll concentrate on crafting just the two areas of *Tasks* and *Relationships* at work. Let's start with *Tasks* first, then we can repeat the same exercise for *Relationships*.

1. Write a list of your most common tasks.

Create a list of the 10–20 most common tasks you do at work. Think of what you get up to during a typical week, and list the main ones. It can help to refer to your work calendar to remind you how you spend your time.

2. Draw a quadrant chart.

Create two long lines that intersect in the middle, like an even cross. If you're doing this exercise with a group, you can draw a quadrant cross on a whiteboard or large piece of paper. Label the ends of the horizontal axis so 'Draining' is on the left and 'Energising' on the right, and label the ends of the vertical axis with 'Short' at the top and 'Long' at the bottom. This is what it should look like:

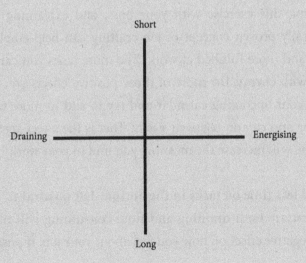

Each of the two axes represents a scale. The horizontal axis represents your energy levels when you are doing a particular task at work, and how it makes you feel as you're completing it. The vertical axis represents the amount of time it takes you to complete each task.

3. Populate the axis with each of your tasks.

Add each of the tasks that you do onto the axis, giving each of them a position on the quadrant chart that takes into account how long they take you to do ('short' vs 'long'), and how much energy they give you ('draining' vs 'energising'). Keep adding each task until you have a full quadrant that ranks all your tasks by those two elements.

4. Spend more time on tasks in the top-right quadrant.

The tasks in the top right-hand quadrant are those that are not time-consuming but give you a lot of energy back. The aim of job crafting is to be aware of which things you enjoy doing, so you can prioritise these.

If you can, aim to incorporate more tasks into your role that are on the right side of the quadrant that energise you. You can start by sharing this exercise with your boss, and explaining how the scientifically proven concept of job crafting can help employees be happier and more fulfilled at work. The more tasks you can do that fill you with energy, the more of those positive effects you will feel. Look at your upcoming calendar and try to add in more tasks that you enjoy and can do relatively easily. That is the sweet spot – that's where you will increase the meaning you find in your work.

5. Spend less time on tasks in the bottom-left quadrant.

Tasks that are both draining and time-consuming will ultimately have a negative effect on how you feel about your job. If possible, see if you can either do less of those tasks (after speaking to your boss, of course), or decrease the time that you devote to them.

This doesn't mean you should just stop doing anything you find difficult. It's about having an awareness of which tasks drain you, and figuring out if there is anything you can do to address that. One alternative is to make time outside your usual workplace to complete these 'heavier' tasks without the usual distractions so you can power through them quickly. Whatever method you choose, the mere act of being conscious about which tasks you do and don't enjoy can have a considerable impact on how you think about work.

6. Repeat this exercise for *Relationships*.

Once you've thought about how to craft your tasks better, you can move on to doing the same for your work relationships. To do this, draw up a quadrant chart with the following axes on it:

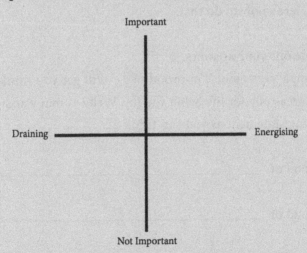

This time, instead of writing down all the tasks you do, make a list of the key relationships in your job. This should cover everyone you interact with on a regular basis, including co-workers, clients, bosses and mentors.

Start mapping each of your key relationships on the scale of how 'important' or 'not important' they are to you, and how 'draining' or 'energising' they feel. The people you have put in the top-right quadrant – i.e. 'important' and 'energising' – are the people you should spend more time with. Shape your working hours to include more time, both formally and informally, with the people who make you feel good. On the flipside, minimise the time you spend with anyone in the bottom-left quadrant – i.e. 'not important' and 'draining'. This isn't always practical, but it can still act as a useful guide to help you spend your valuable time at work in the best possible way.

IRL exercise 3: Meaning outside work

To Work Backwards you need to know what meaning you get outside work. One way of doing this is to create a list of everything you are proud of in your life that's not tied up with your identity at work. Here's how to do that.

1. Write out your answers.
The simple statement 'I'm proud of ...' will get you thinking about which areas of your life bring you joy. Write as many answers to the following statement as you can think of:

I'm proud of _____

I'm proud of _____

I'm proud of _____

I'm proud of _____

I'm proud of _____

Some examples of things you might be proud of include: how your kids are growing up, your relationship with your partner, how many countries you've travelled to, your recent home renovation, having the courage to do something big in your life, getting out of bed this morning, surviving through grief, saving money for a house deposit. Write out everything that comes to mind. It's okay if you can only think of one or two things. To have meaning outside work, all it takes is one.

2. Pull out a theme.

Now, read over your answers and try to pull out a theme. Where does your pride come from? That will tell you where you are currently finding meaning in life. If, for example, your responses centred on watching your child grow up and interacting with them, then part of the meaning that you derive in life is through them.

Read through what you've written and see if there's a theme that jumps out at you. Whatever links these things together is where you find meaning outside work. This might change at different parts of your life, but knowing what matters most to you right now is an important part of Working Backwards. This will help you ensure you spend more time doing things that align with what's important to you, and less doing things that don't.

To complete this exercise, try to summarise where you get meaning outside work in a sentence or two, and write it down:

I get meaning outside work from: _____

_____

_____

Anchors

Your anchors, or core values, are the things you really think are important. While each anchor is not unique, their combination and the order you put them in is. This exercise will help you identify what your anchors are, and put them into context so you can recognise and communicate them to everyone around you.

IRL exercise 4: Identify your anchors

1. Make a list of the biggest sources of meaning in your life.

If you're doing these exercises in order, read over your answers in exercises 1 and 3, where you clarified the meaning you get from work, and outside it. You can then take a tip from Wharton Professor Adam Grant and ask yourself why. This will help you narrow it down to the core value behind it. An example he gives is that you might say you derive meaning from exercise. *Why?* Because it's a challenge and you have to push yourself. *Why?* Because you value personal growth. Keep asking why until you get to the core value, or anchor, at the bottom of it.

2. Look to your heroes.

If you still haven't clarified the biggest sources of meaning in your life, answering these questions can help uncover your anchors:

Q. Who are your heroes?

Q. What are the qualities that you admire in them?

List some of the people you admire, from personal connections to celebrities, and see if you can figure out what it is about them that connects with you. If a clear theme emerges, that is a path to identifying what you see as important.

3. Pick out your anchors.

Often it takes seeing a list of anchors on a page before you can articulate the thoughts that are swimming around your head. Read over the list of the 50 most common anchors, or core values, on pages 71–72, to help you narrow it down. Ideally, you should have three anchors. Some people might have more, and others less, but three is generally the average.

4. Order your anchors.

Once you've narrowed it down to a few anchors, rank them in order of which is *most* important to you. This can be difficult, but it will help you understand your priorities.

5. SIT with it.

The last step is to let your anchors SIT for a while. SIT stands for the three elements that you need in order to let any idea percolate in your mind: Space (either mental or physical), Inputs (from other people) and Time (however long it takes).

Share your core values with someone who knows you well, such as your partner, family, close friend or colleague. Do they agree with you? Are there any that don't sit well with them? Your anchors should instantly resonate with you and anyone who knows you well. They are the things you value most, and it's important that you can communicate these values authentically to the people around you. Let them soak in for a while until you are super confident you've got to the core of what makes you, well, you.

To finish this exercise, write out the three to five anchors that describe your values and help define who you want to be:

My anchors:

_____

_____

_____

_____

_____

Priorities

To live a full-circle life, you need to give equal attention to each of the four core elements of mind, body, relationships and work. In this exercise, you'll begin creating a plan to regain some balance in your life.

IRL exercise 5: Create your full-circle plan

1. Draw a large circle divided into four parts.

Inside each of the four parts, write the headings *Work*, *Relationships*, *Mind* and *Body* in any order. This is what it could look like:

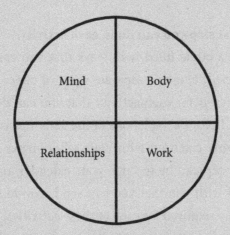

2. Think of how you can prioritise each of the four areas.

In an ideal full-circle life, you dedicate around the same amount of time to each of the four core areas. As a reminder, this is what the ideal time spent on each area is:

Mind: 4 hours a day
Body: 4 hours a day
Relationships: 4 hours a day
Work: 4 days a week

I can hear you saying that spending four hours a day each on your mind, body and relationships is almost impossible, but don't panic – these activities can and will overlap. If you go on a hike with a friend, you're working on your body, mind and relationships at the same time (which is one reason I seriously love hiking with my husband and our friends).

Think about each of the four areas, with particular focus on life outside of work. Inside each quadrant of the circle, write out just one thing in each area you can do today in order to spend more time on your body, mind and relationships. In the 'work' quadrant, write out how you can help rebalance your approach in a healthy way.

3. Write the first step you can do in each activity.

Once you have a circle filled with ways that you can begin living a more full-circle life, take a separate sheet of paper and write out what the first step is for each activity that you can do this week to get you started. If, for example, one of the activities you'd like to do is have a quarterly catch-up with your schoolmates to play poker, then your first step can be to open your calendar and find a good date that works with you that you can send around. By beginning with the first step required for each of these activities, you can break down a daunting list into something you can action this week.

4. Prioritise each of the four areas.

A priority forces you to select what you value above something else, so the final step in this exercise is for you to consciously choose and rank each of the four main areas in the order that you want to live them from here onwards.

Think about the areas that make up your life–work balance – that is, work, relationships, mind and body – and put them in the order that you want to prioritise them.

My priorities:

1. _____

2. _____

3. _____

4. _____

A full-circle life is an aspiration, and aiming towards it is the intention. No one has a perfect life, but we all need to be facing the right direction. By completing these exercises, you are creating a MAP to where you want to go, putting your life first and being super clear about exactly how you want to live.

Money

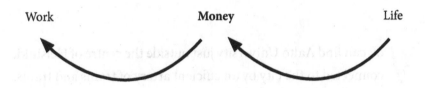

Work   Money   Life

'Happiness is a place between too little and too much.'

– Finnish proverb

Happy go lucky

You can find Aalto University just outside the centre of Helsinki, connected to the city by an efficient artery of trains and trams. Named after acclaimed Finnish architect Alvar Aalto, it was established in 2010 when the government of Finland merged three institutions of science and technology, business and the arts into one multidisciplinary university.

It's on this campus, on a sunny summer's day, where I meet philosopher Frank Martela, a lecturer at Aalto University and expert on the intersection between Finnish culture and happiness. We are sitting in his office, surrounded by rows of books and neatly titled folders containing his research. One of the walls is dominated by an intricate hand-drawn map of a fictional world, created by his eight-year-old son.

Frank was also a creative and thoughtful child. When inquisitive people asked him what he wanted to be when he grew up, six-year-old Frank would reply that he wanted to be 'a researcher of the world'. And several decades later, after a few wrong turns, that's where he has ended up, focusing most of his time trying to understand big topics like the meaning of life. 'I enjoy thinking about deep questions and what we should do with this thing called life,' he says.

One of the reasons he can do that is that Frank has lived his whole life in Finland, the northern European nation of five million people. Finland has traditionally been known for its modern architecture and deeply ingrained sauna culture, but there is a new export that fills the locals with quiet pride, disbelief and denial: Finland has repeatedly been named the happiest country in the world.

The World Happiness Report is published annually by the Sustainable Development Solutions Network, an initiative of the United Nations and Gallup research.[1] It looks at the state of happiness in the world, showing how science can help explain differences in personal and national happiness. Each year, over 100,000 people in 130 countries participate in the research. When the report was first released in 2012, not many people in Finland took much notice. In that first year, Denmark was ranked the happiest country in the world, with Finland in the top ten alongside other Nordic neighbours. Then over the next few years, as Switzerland and Norway took out the top spots, Finland rose in the rankings until, in 2018, it was officially named the happiest country in the world. It's a title that it has held onto for an unprecedented six years. 'There wasn't too much discussion about happiness rankings in Finland until the moment we were declared happiest country on Earth,' says Frank. 'Then suddenly everyone was asking what was the secret to Finnish happiness? And the Finnish people were like, "We don't have a secret, we didn't know that we were happy."' Frank explains that most Finns have 'a bit of a melancholic self-image' and think of themselves as relatively introverted and quiet. 'This idea that we were the happiest in the world didn't fit at all.'

So what's going on here? The first thing to unpack is the methodology. Most of the results that have made headlines were derived from a single question that was first devised by an American psychologist in 1965. Hadley Cantril created a simple visual scale, called the Cantril ladder, that asks people to imagine a ladder on which the best possible life for them is a ten, and the worst possible life is a zero. They are then asked to rate on which rung they think their life currently sits on the scale. It's a very simple question that helps researchers assess, and compare, general life satisfaction across different countries. In 2023, Finns rated themselves an average of 7.8 out of 10 on that scale – statistically, quite far ahead of second-place Denmark's 7.6. Despite its name, the World Happiness Report is not strictly about happiness. 'It's not about joyfulness or cheerfulness,' says Frank, 'but more about general life satisfaction.'

Frank, who co-authored a chapter for the 2020 World Happiness Report on why Nordic nations perform so strongly, says there are several overlapping reasons why Finland ranks so highly in life satisfaction. 'Countries with high-quality democratic institutions, free elections, free speech, low levels of corruption and so forth, tend to score high on these rankings.' He explains that Finland's strong welfare system, with relatively good unemployment benefits, labour regulation and parental leave, all contribute to a high safety net that gives Finns less fear about things like switching jobs if they're not happy, or returning to study to explore subjects that interest them.

Many Finns also have a unique way of thinking that they have inadvertently stumbled upon: most of them feel they have enough. Part of the reason for their high average score is the fact that there are so few people in Finland who score their life satisfaction in the low digits. 'So it's rather the lack of unsatisfied people that explains the high average rather than the presence of extremely happy people,' says Frank. In other words, Finns are not blindly optimistic happiness freaks who spend all day with smirks they can't wipe off their faces, they are merely content with what they have.

And what they do have provides a model for the rest of us: most Finns take the entire month of July off every year to enjoy the summer, as well as more time off throughout the year. Every child under school age has access to municipal day care, partly funded by income levels, meaning parents with young children can get some respite. 'The work–life balance probably is in quite better shape in Finland than in many other countries,' says Frank.

Finnish people are closely connected to nature, their community and themselves through their sauna culture, with over 90% of Finns having a sauna at least once a week.[2] 'It is quite an important part of many people's self-idea of what makes them happy,' Frank explains. 'It has this spiritual and communal dimension to it. It is also quite an equal space where it's hard to maintain the social rankings when you're naked. It puts everybody in an equal place.'

One of the secrets to Finnish happiness and life satisfaction is not that they are all wealthy and healthy, it's that they have enough of everything to keep them content. Other Finnish researchers have come to the same conclusion. A study published in January 2023 by Arto O. Salonen and Jyrki Konkka found that there were no happiness differences between Finns from different income groups; it didn't matter how much money they earned, everyone was relatively content with their lives.[3] Finns feel satisfied leading relatively straightforward, sustainable lives, with enough money to meet their simple needs. 'In other words,' Salonen and Konkka concluded, 'when you know what is enough, you are happy.'[4]

Work-and-spend cycle

Comedian Diane Morgan plays a deliciously deadpan journalist named Philomena Cunk in the Netflix series *Cunk on Earth*. It's a dry satirical show that humorously summarises the history of humankind, cutting uncomfortably close to the truth. In the final episode of the first series, she sums up modern society from the 1950s, pointing out the rise of television advertising that fooled consumers into always wanting more. 'They'd work hard to get money, to buy a car, so they could go to the shops and buy more things,' she explains, 'which they'd have to pay for by going back to work, which made them miserable, so they'd cheer themselves up by going out and buying more things, which they'd have to work to pay for.'

Professor Juliet Schor is one of the leading thinkers around this phenomenon, which researchers call the work-and-spend cycle. Twenty-five years ago she wrote *The Overspent American: Why We Want What We Don't Need*. It was a follow-up to *The Overworked American*, which looked at the effects of overwork on the US population. In that first book, Juliet theorised that longer working hours and increasing consumerism were catching people in a vicious, powerful spiral that had become pervasive. 'We are not merely caught in a pattern of spend-and-spend; the whole story is that we work-and-spend, and work-and-spend some more.'

One of the ideas she explained was the Diderot effect. It was named after French writer Denis Diderot, who wrote an essay in 1875 titled 'Regrets on Parting with My Old Dressing Gown'.[1] In this fictional story, Diderot wrote about receiving an elegant new dressing gown as a gift from a friend. At first, he was pleased with this kind gesture, until he noticed that all of his possessions – a straw chair, a wooden table, a rug, and even his art – looked drab next to the new robe. 'All is now discordant. No more coordination, no more unity, no more beauty,' he wrote. So he replaced each item, one by one, to match his new dressing gown. By the time he was finished, he wished he had never been given the well-intended gift. 'I was the absolute master of my old robe,' he wrote. 'I have become the slave of the new one.'

Yale Professor Laurie Santos hosts *The Happiness Lab* podcast, which has been downloaded more than 100 million times. Laurie's advice to anyone trying to break free of the vicious work-and-spend cycle is to stop and think about your life and what you're spending money on. 'Some people have an income where they're spending on the basics, right? They're just spending on rent and keeping the electricity on, and that's a cycle that's hard to get out of,' she explains. 'But if your spending cycle is about spending on new material possessions, like quick hits you think will get you some dopamine but you don't really need, I would suggest you look at whether or not those things you're spending money on are making you happy.' Laurie says that if you instead spent the money on getting back more time for yourself, or on doing something nice for other people, or even connecting with someone socially, then you'll most likely end up feeling better. 'The real question isn't just whether you're spending money, but whether the money you're spending is consistent with the kinds of things that will make you happier.'

Breaking the work-and-spend cycle depends on which life stage you're at: early, mid or late career.

Early career: At this stage of your life, it's natural to start off living from pay cheque to pay cheque, as you haven't had time to build up decent savings. You're probably not getting paid much, but you should also hopefully have fewer expenses and things to spend money on. At some stage, however, you have to stop spending everything that comes in. There are simple things you can do to help with this, like paying bills on time so you don't incur late fees, and avoiding a credit card for as long as you can. But the biggest change you can make at this stage is to be conscious of exactly where your money is going. You can then decide if it's being spent on areas of your life that align with your MAP, which we clarified in the first step.

Mid career: This is usually the stage of your life when you're earning the highest amount of money. Years of working hard, gradual job promotions, consistent saving, switching companies, pay rises, or the accumulation of bonuses or stock options are all common ways that you can shore up your finances to help you break the work-and-spend cycle. But the biggest thing you can do to smash your way out of it is actually easier than all of those: it's knowing what your 'enough' is, and being content with that. You can use your years of experience to better understand yourself and what makes you happy.

Late career: The work-and-spend cycle is tiring, and if you're still stuck deep in it at this point, it can be more difficult to break out of it. By this stage your lifestyle and life expenses are pretty baked in. However, just because it's the way you've always done things doesn't mean it's the way they always have to be. The best thing you can do is use your experience to your advantage, and deeply interrogate what has and hasn't fulfilled you up to now.

Currently, I am firmly in the mid-career stage of my life. I worked full-time for two decades straight, beginning at 18 and ending a few years after selling the media business I co-founded. After an intense journey that tested my own limits of how I liked to work, I needed a mental and physical break to reset my mind and my intentions. With international travel plans torpedoed by Covid, my husband and I jumped into a campervan and drove as far as we could, which ended up being the state border of New South Wales.

I'd never spent more than a few odd nights inside a campervan, and it was a shock to my system at first. We hired a large, seven-metre van built out of the core of a Mercedes Sprinter for a trip that was originally meant to be for six weeks. As more borders opened up and we drove through the long, boundless plains of Victoria and Western Australia, those six weeks magically stretched into six months as we fell for the freedom and simple pleasure of a pared-back life.

Living in a campervan is a deliciously simple existence. Like snails exploring, you carry all that you need on your back. Two sets of plates and cutlery, one frying pan and pot, two towels, a set of sheets and pillows, camping chairs and tables, and a few creature comforts to make it feel like home. When you're constricted by space you're forced to strip away a lifetime of accumulated stuff, and select only what fits inside a few boxes. The most surprising revelation is that, after a few months on the road, you discover you have everything you need.

My favourite part of campervanning was the evening routine. My husband and I fell into a familiar pattern. I'd set up an outdoor camping table and chairs and he would cook a one-pan dish, like chargrilled broccoli and beans, or fennel sausage and pasta. We'd eat early, before the sun went down, and enjoy each other's company, followed by a game of cards (Monopoly Deal was our usual go-to), a quick wash up and then the night-time closing routine.

A campervan is a collection of windows, shutters and curtains that all have a day and night function. In such a small space, everything has its final destination. The hand soap. The torch light. The remote control. The hand towels. The closing routine involved putting everything back to its rightful place, where it needed to be before we could rest. The front two chairs get turned around. The light blocker is snapped on. The windows are wound up and locked. The dishes are dried and returned to their hiding places. The fan is switched on. Our teeth are brushed. The lamp is charged. Each item is mentally ticked off, one at a time, usually in the same order. And then, once everything is in its place, we fall onto our surprisingly comfortable mattress, which we'd layered with our favourite sheet and pillows from home, and curl up with whatever book or magazine we're reading, lying in total bliss, listening to the calming buzz of the various campgrounds we parked in, as each camper plays out their own night-time routine in the vans and motorhomes around us. All content with having everything they need within reach.

Those months in a campervan, armed with the bare minimum that we needed to live a happy life, were some of my best. I soon learnt that I need a lot less than I thought I did, and with an open calendar and mind, I began playing around with different ways of working on the road. Could I be just as effective writing books, running workshops and consulting with businesses from the back of a campervan as I was in an office? I quickly learnt my first important lesson: collaborative work is only as good as your internet connection. You can only waste so many video meetings trying to connect and reconnect, endlessly repeating 'Can you hear me now?', before you just have to give up.

Next I considered the working week. Why confine ourselves to the shackles of Monday to Friday, leaving just two packed weekend days to spend time doing what we actually want? My husband and I decided to 'flip the week'. Instead of working five days and taking two off, we worked two days and took five off. Mondays and Tuesdays were for work. On those days, we'd park the campervan somewhere with good mobile coverage, or check into an Airbnb or hotel (for better wi-fi and, praise the gods, a washing machine). We'd plan meetings for these days, arrange workshops, video calls, interviews, whatever we needed to do. We worked smart and hard, batching our work and concentrating intently on different projects, and we ended up doing the amount of work we'd previously taken twice that time to complete. Then, from Wednesday to Sunday, we'd live our lives to the fullest: driving, travelling, swimming, exploring, hiking and more. Flipping the week wasn't perfect, and it's not what this book is about, but it was one of my first proper experiments with how, where and when to work.

We're not the only ones to use a motorhome as a vehicle to explore different ways of working and living. Caroline Clements and Dillon Seitchik-Reardon are a couple who often work side-by-side. Caroline is a writer and Dillon a photographer who also writes. In 2018 they published their first book together, an anthology of the best swimming pools, waterholes, rivers, lakes and beaches around Australia. *Places We Swim* became a local bestseller, inspiring a myriad of similar books and another edition that focused just on Sydney. To create their books, they would travel slowly for months at a time, returning to the city for contract work, and then hit the road again. 'Dillon and I got to a point where we felt like we were quite good at travelling together and working on these projects as a duo,' says Caroline.

Their 2024 publication, *Places We Swim California*, is their most ambitious project yet. It was the result of travelling around the US state for six months, this time with their two-year-old son, as they documented the best places to swim. 'The third member has definitely thrown things out, in a great way as well,' says Caroline. 'For the first two books we didn't know what we were doing but it kind of didn't matter because we had the time and it was just the two of us ... now we have to be way more organised and efficient.'

Caroline describes her life–work balance as 'kind of blurry', as they attempt to weave together book research, freelance work, travelling, writing and photography, catching up with family and friends and raising their son. She's certainly felt the shift in priorities that new parents inevitably experience. 'Your time, care, energy and love is going into another person ... you have to compartmentalise where you spend your energy. Maybe it doesn't all go into your work, it gets delivered to other places, but it doesn't mean that you can't be ambitious,' she says. 'It means you have to be more efficient when you're working.'

By taking time out from the usual path to success, they've been able to create lives for themselves that are sometimes nomadic, a little bit unstructured and always fulfilling. 'I love travel and I love taking photos,' says Dillon. 'Those two things together are some of my favourite things, and then doing that with my partner and with my child, it's kind of the perfect jump. There's challenges and there's complications, but I definitely think it's pretty close to my ideal situation.'

It also gives them time to think about and properly digest how they want to live, including what success looks like for them and their own definition of happiness. It's a topic Dillon has been considering for a long time. 'I think everybody has memories of when you were in your early twenties in uni, and were poorer than you ever were, but were super content and travelled a lot and had tons of time for friends,' he explains. 'And then we have this lifestyle inflation and we become disconnected when we have more, and then have to spend more time supporting that.'

Dillon and Caroline have questioned the traditional path and realised that it's not for them right now. 'For me my ambition is to earn the same amount every year, but be better at what I do and work a bit less,' says Dillon. 'I don't want to pursue endless growth for the sake of it ... I think just trying to be smarter about what we do really need to live, and having more free time, is better for us as individuals and as a family.'

You don't have to travel around in a motorhome to discover what's truly important for you. It is, however, a wonderful way of forcing you to pare life back to its bare essentials, and a stark reminder that you don't need to constantly surround yourself with more. You just need to know what truly fulfils you.

Know your 'enough'

Learn how much money, success and possessions you
need to be happy.

Handy man

Many years ago, legendary American writers Kurt Vonnegut and Joseph Heller were at an ostentatious party at a billionaire's mansion on Shelter Island in New York. They were both successful authors by then, Vonnegut famed for blending science fiction and black comedy in books like *Slaughterhouse-Five* and *Cat's Cradle*, and Heller predominantly for the wartime novel *Catch-22*. From the outside, the party's host appeared to be the epitome of success: he had a sprawling waterfront mansion, a supermodel wife, and more Picassos and Warhols than you'd find in an art gallery. Vonnegut was very impressed, and said enviously to Heller: 'Joe, how does it make you feel to know that our host only yesterday may have made more money than your novel *Catch-22* has earned in its entire history?' Joe didn't have to think too much about the question. 'But I've got something he can never have,' he responded.

'And what on Earth could that be?'

'The knowledge that I've got enough,' said Heller.

It was a line that Vonnegut repeated for years after Heller's death, every time he retold this story.[1]

'Enough' is one of the English language's most magical and revolutionary words. The very idea pushes back against ingrained capitalism, fear-based marketing and everything society teaches us about accumulating things, stuff, people and experiences. The most revolutionary action we can take is to accept that we have enough and that we are enough. It must be acknowledged here that 'enough' is a privileged statement, as it implies that all our basic needs have been met and we have the luxury of not wanting anything more than that.

The idea of challenging the traditional direction of my life first floated into my consciousness in my twenties, when I read a book called *Enough* by British writer John Naish.[2] *The Guardian* called it 'a cheerfully likeable manifesto for lifestyle change'. Each chapter ran through a different area of overwhelm in our lives; enough information, food, stuff, options, happiness and growth. It was an eerily prescient and fertile area of study that's been explored in more detail in recent books, such as Johann Hari's brilliant *Stolen Focus: Why You Can't Pay Attention*.[3] In his book, Naish explored the idea of being content with what we have; however, it was his chapter on 'Enough work' that really wormed its way into my head. That's also where I first heard about the work, and life, of Charles Handy.

Charles has been thinking about and critiquing the idea of work since he published his first book in the 1970s. His view of work is that we do too much of it; instead, he believes we should do a mixture of different things with our waking hours, like contract work, volunteering, education and fun activities. He coined the term 'portfolio career', which refers to working on multiple projects with different aims at the same time. Having a portfolio career means combining multiple streams of income from a few different jobs that you find interesting, always alternating between them to create 'a portfolio of activities – some we do for money, some for interest, some for pleasure, some for a cause … the different bits fit together to form a balanced whole greater than the parts.'[4]

It was the way that Charles Handy and his wife Elizabeth lived that sparked a firework of thoughts in me. This is how they lived the majority of their lives: at the start of each year, they calculated how much money they needed to fund their simple and satisfying life, and then did just the amount of work required to make that money. They worked as much as they needed to bring in that income, and spent the rest of their valuable time doing what they loved: hosting long lunches and dinner parties with interesting people, learning new skills and languages, helping for-impact companies achieve greater things, drinking great wine, reading books, learning and travelling. Elizabeth worked as a professional photographer until her death in 2018, and Charles wrote books about business and gave talks on his ideas. They worked only as much as they needed to live the life that they wanted. Charles describes how they arrived at this place: 'A few years ago we decided we didn't need to maximise our income; we wanted to maximise our life.'

Their style of living might not be for everyone, but it's worth interrogating to pull out some key learnings. We can't talk about the future of work, and in particular the future of *your* work, without talking about money. Let's be perfectly blunt here: a steady, regular salary is the main reason most people work. It's the fire hydrant of funds that enables us to keep a roof over our head, buy food, entertain ourselves and – if we're lucky enough – spend whatever's left over on ourselves or our long-term goals. Money is the enabler that allows us to live.

But instead of just taking an arbitrary salary that's determined by your employer, the Handys' model was to determine what your life costs and Work Backwards from there. This doesn't involve being frugal for the sake of it – in fact, it's the opposite of that. It's about figuring out what money you need to live the life that you want, down to the dollar, and then designing your work around that. The Handys achieved this by writing down everything they needed to have money for over an annual period, taking into account what brings them meaning. To ensure they weren't constantly worrying about money, they added a 20% buffer for safety. This calculation meant they had an awareness of exactly how much they needed to live the life they wanted. It demystified their finances and helped them align their money with their values.

There is a lot of science behind the positive effects of enjoying the little things in life. In one study of Belgian adults, individuals who had a strong capacity to savour the simple, seemingly mundane joys of daily life were found to be happier than those who did not.[5] And interestingly, the capacity to enjoy the small pleasures reduced in respondents who had more money. When you have access to every experience that you desire, it can undermine your ability to derive pleasure from the simple things.

The Handys' model of managing their money can give you some inspiration in finding ways to break the work-and-spend cycle. Once you understand *why* you are working and what life you want to lead, you can determine how much money you need to do that. The key is knowing what 'enough' means to you.

Money and happiness

C an money buy happiness? It's an age-old question that everyone seems to have an answer for, but there's a large amount of literature on it that reaches surprisingly conflicted conclusions. Perhaps the most quoted and infamous research is a 2010 Princeton study that found that money buys happiness up to US$75K, and then tapers off from there.[1] The finding reverberated around the world, powered by a hopeful narrative that wealth doesn't make you happy, and doesn't mean much once you exceed that amount. Many people have taken issue with this research, including writer Alan Trapulionis, who pointed out what he saw as major flaws in its methodology. This included that happiness was defined by the number of times people reported smiling on the previous day, that some wealthy 'outliers' were not counted, and that all the interviews were done over the phone from 9 a.m., which can skew data.[2]

'Scientists have studied the relationship between money and happiness for decades and their conclusion is clear: money buys happiness, but it buys less than most people think,' wrote Elizabeth Dunn, Daniel Gilbert and Timothy Wilson in their 2011 report 'If money doesn't make you happy, then you probably aren't spending it right'.[3] They explained that many of the links between money and happiness are due to the fact that money brings access to better nutrition and healthcare, more free time and meaningful labour, which are all important components to leading a happy life. 'Money is an opportunity for happiness, but it is an opportunity that people routinely squander because the things they think will make them happy often don't,' they wrote, adding that 'the relationship between money and happiness is surprisingly weak'. Their recommendations for how to get more happiness from your money included buying more experiences and fewer material goods, using your money to benefit others rather than yourself and buying many small pleasures rather than a few large ones.

Reuben Williams runs a podcast and a networking community that helps people get jobs in the sports industry. As the founder of a new start-up, Reuben has built his business, SportsGrad, on a subscription model with recurring revenue and less stress, but it's still been an intense ride. 'For the first two and half years I literally worked every single day because I had just lost my full-time job and had nothing to fall back on,' he says. During that time Reuben lived in the coastal town of Lorne in Victoria. 'This was the happiest period of my life,' he recalls. 'Things were simple, I was my own boss, with very few people involved. I'd ride my bike along the Great Ocean Road, come home and record a podcast, talk to some members, tinker with the website, then read a book and go for a walk.'

As the business grew, Reuben raised money from investors to grow his business and moved to Melbourne to be closer to his business partner and investors, but found that being back in a big city was overwhelming and less productive. One of Reuben's favourite stories is about a fisherman who starts off working in his beloved location, the beach. Over time he grows more successful, and moves further away from his beloved beach, until he ends up retiring back at the same beach where he first started out. 'Like the fisherman, part of me feels like I had what I really wanted from the beginning: the simple beach life,' he says. 'Now I'm trying to get back to that after a bit of growth in the city.'

While living in Lorne during those early days, Reuben would often walk to a lookout next to the Southern Ocean, watching the waves crash while considering what problems he had to solve at work. 'And nothing came to mind!' he laughs. 'It was bliss. My ideal working life is to get back to a state where the issues are minimal, I can help people, I'm near a beach, and I have a road bike.'

Prior to this, Reuben's goal was to 'scale the company to millions, own several houses, buy new rooms for my cricket club, open offices in every continent and several other material things'. But once he discovered how good 'a mental inbox of zero' felt, that became his new goal. 'As time goes on, my ideal working life keeps reducing in complexity. I just want to be able to help people online in between cycling beautiful parts of the world.' Reuben now travels to some of the top sporting events, creating content for his podcast and community. 'I didn't think a life like this was possible, but the fundamental reason those moments happen is because I have created more freedom to be who I want.'

Reuben knows what his version of 'enough' is, and everyone's version of that will be different. My 'enough' is different to your 'enough', and the same goes for your neighbours, colleagues, friends and family. You can spend a lifetime comparing yourself to others, or you can look internally to figure out what gives you happiness and be content with that. So, how do you do it?

Backwards Budget

To most people, there's nothing scarier than the word 'budget'. It generally implies sacrifices, restrictions and saying no to things you'd like to do. Some of that stems from traditional budgets being designed to limit what you can spend money on, as well as the complicated relationship that many people have with money. A lot of it has origins in what financial advisors call your 'money story', which is your approach to handling money. This tends to be passed down from your parents or other influences, and can define the way you think about the emotional side of your finances.

There are two main ways that businesses create budgets, and they each have learnings you can apply when thinking of your own. A top-down budget is when senior management creates a set of financials that are then expected to be adhered to, hence the name 'top-down'. The opposite of this is a bottom-up budget. This is where individuals, or teams, each create their own budget and forecasts based on the reality of what's going on, designed by those who are closest to spending the money. A bottom-up budget has a lot of advantages: it's generally more accurate, and it's co-created by the people who will actually use it.

To Work Backwards, we're going to apply the principles of a bottom-up budget, and tweak it slightly to create a Backwards Budget. This is one of the most clarifying and freeing exercises you can do to help you make better decisions and understand what 'enough' means to you. A Backwards Budget shows how much it will cost you to live a life that makes you happy, fulfilled and content. It is the bare minimum you need to earn from a salary or side hustle in order to be satisfied.

Creating your own Backwards Budget can be very illuminating. Some people discover that the ideal way they want to live and work is closer than they think. For others it's an eye-opener, revealing that they need to deeply interrogate what 'enough' is for them.

A Backwards Budget helps you understand the minimum amount of money you need to earn in whatever way you can. It could be a mixture of your salary, money from a small business, passive income from investments, or any other way you earn an income. The key here is that when you know how much money you need, you can then empower yourself by deciding how much work you have to do to achieve this. Knowing the minimum amount of money you need to live the life you want addresses the priorities you defined in the first step, and can be incredibly freeing.

Glen James is a former financial adviser, business owner and host of the popular *This Is Money* podcast. 'I like to teach about money doing a bottom-up budget because we've all got rent, we've all got a phone bill, we've all got food costs. We all have those basic costs, and if you can't pay for rent, then you're not on Google looking for an eight-day silent yoga retreat in India, are you? You have to build it backwards and find the amount that it costs you to wake up in the morning.'

A Backwards Budget works because you know where you're heading. If you've completed the first step in this book, you will already have a MAP. That is, you know what *meaning* you get from work and outside it, plus what your *anchors* are, and have your *priorities* in order. It's important that your MAP is clearly stated at the top of your Backwards Budget, as this will help you determine how your money should be spent. Your spending needs to be aligned with where you want to go. So that you're not constantly worrying about money, you should add a buffer into this, and also set money aside for the future. This type of budget is an awareness tool to help you understand how much it costs you to live the life you want, and to know what your 'enough' is.

Here are two quick examples from my own life. I have enough clothes, and I buy new clothes just a few times a year. I like to buy clothes that are well made and last a long time, but I have reconciled myself to the fact that buying new clothes does not bring me particular joy. As long as they are good quality, durable and simple styles that I can mix and match with most of the other items in my wardrobe, that's enough for me.

The same goes for transport. I haven't owned a car in almost a decade. In that time, I've used a car-sharing service in my local neighbourhood whenever I've needed one, borrowed cars from family members and hired cars for weekends away. I still enjoy the beauty and safety of a nice car, but I don't *need* it. I know my version of enough, and it doesn't include clothes or cars.

Just so that I don't come across as a complete martyr here, I do have a soft spot for beautifully made homewares and well-designed furniture that will last a generation. My husband and I tend to snap up most of these when we travel to exotic locations, and they are then dotted around our house to remind us of each experience. However, my biggest pleasure, and where I spend most of my money, is on experiences. I adore travelling to new places, learning new things on educational tours and tasting all the local delicacies in each location. If I had my last $100, I'd spend it at a market buying delicious fare. These choices reflect my own priorities and how I want to live. Your 'enough' is unique to you, and you should never judge someone else's.

But it's important to figure out what yours is. Create your own Backwards Budget by listing how much money you want to spend each month on every area of your life. It can be as precise as you'd like, but there's a real benefit in using it as a way of determining how much it costs you to live a life that's aligned to your anchors.

Nathan Thomas knows what his core value are. Growing up in a household that had, in his own words, 'a very poor relationship with money', he watched his father work seven days a week in his plumbing business, partly to keep up with his mother's constant expenses. 'If spending was an Olympic sport my mum would have been a gold medallist,' he laughs. 'I think it added a lot of stress on my father, who just had to keep working around the clock to stay afloat.'

He saw first-hand the stressful effect of a work-and-spend cycle, and it inspired him to have a savings mindset from a young age. When Nathan and his sister were given a $500 budget to each buy a new sound system for their rooms, his sister pleaded with her parents to buy something more expensive, but Nathan did his research and settled for one that was around half the budget, which was enough for him. 'I was under 10 years old and I was conscious of the cost,' he recalls.

He began working full-time straight from school, studying at university at night, to save to buy his first apartment. Nathan worked as an accountant, sometimes putting in 70 hours a week in a high-pressure environment, often eating dinner in the office to try to keep up with the constant workload. 'I had let work control everything, to the detriment of my relationship and sleep and my health.' He woke up one day and wondered what the heck he was doing with his life. 'Was this the life I dreamed of as a kid? I knew I had to take drastic action.'

It was around this time that he discovered FIRE, or Financial Independence, Retire Early. The FIRE movement was kickstarted by Joe Dominguez and Vicki Robin, two pioneers of the sustainability community who wrote *Your Money or Your Life* in 1993. In it they promoted a new way of creating a lifestyle that consisted of intense saving periods of living within your means, and investing rapidly to build up regular income streams without having to work as hard. It's now one of the biggest financial movements in the world, and has inspired millions of people to rethink their relationship with money and work.

Nathan's entry point into this philosophy came via Peter Adeney, a Canadian author who writes under the name Mr Money Moustache. When Nathan discovered him, he fell into a dizzying hole, reading all 500 of his blog posts in a fortnight. 'I was obsessed to the point my husband said to me I am sick to death of hearing about Mr Money Moustache,' he says. Despite the fact Nathan was very well educated financially as a tax accountant by trade, he found Peter's clear and witty writing style addictive. 'His message is super simple,' explains Nathan. 'Spend way less than you earn, invest the rest into ETFs (Exchange Traded Funds) and make enough passive income to buy your freedom. I also love his ethos of DIY and learning to do things yourself.'

Emboldened by a desire to work less and live more, Nathan and his husband Maikol thought about what was important to them. They wanted freedom to be able to work from anywhere, and also ways to incorporate their passion for sustainable living. Their solution was to leave their corporate jobs and start their own recruitment business together.

When I speak to Nathan, he and Maikol are travelling around Australia in their electric vehicle. In four months, they paid only A$130 in fast-charging electricity costs the entire time. They recently bought some land in Port Lincoln, South Australia, with sweeping water views where they plan to build an eco-home. 'We now do what we want with our life – we have freedom and this is what success feels like to me,' he says. 'I now get to choose what I do with my time.'

But it's their understanding in knowing what 'enough' is for them that has been their biggest lesson. 'I can live with less,' Nathan says. 'Living with less is easier, faster, less stressful.' They also proved that they can work from anywhere. 'I will never go back to working nine to five. It just does not suit our lives anymore.'

Nathan loves talking about the pleasure he gets from knowing that he has enough. 'Maikol and I are low-impact people these days. We buy less, we consume less, we reuse, repurpose and recycle. We have more than enough now.' He is deeply passionate about the link between living within your means and living sustainably. 'On a finite planet we can't all continue to endlessly and mindlessly consume. Something has to give, and we would be all better off if everyone started to be more conscious in their consumption and not buy shit that they don't need and doesn't make them happy.'

Nathan and Maikol have learnt what makes them happy: they know their version of 'enough', have crafted a way of living aligned to their values of freedom and sustainability, and have tailored their work and lives to bring them joy and contentment every single day.

It all starts with Working Backwards by knowing what you are aiming for first, and how much it will cost you to get there. To help you create your own Backwards Budget, in the IRL section I list all the categories of expenses you should include in **IRL exercise 6** on page 148. You can also download interactive worksheets, including a spreadsheet, from WorkBackwards.com/IRL.

Once you have completed your Backwards Budget, you will know what it costs you to live the life you want. This is a fascinating thought experiment. Does the figure scare or surprise you? Is it higher or lower than you thought? No matter what it is, having a clear handle on the minimum amount you need to live your desired life can be amazingly refreshing.

Let's say your Backwards Budget tells you that you need $6500 a month to live your life. That's $78K a year in after-tax income that you need to earn to cover all the basic bills you've set out. Everything above that is a bonus, savings, or additional money to help reduce your earning requirement in the future.

Knowing this number is freeing because it shows you what to aim towards, as well as provides you with an incentive to work less if your amount is easily achievable. Remember, this number is not set in stone. It's to be used as a guide as you Work Backwards to take control of your life.

IRL Exercises: Money

Step 2: Know your 'enough'

IRL exercise 6: Backwards Budget

A Backwards Budget is how much it costs you to live the life you want. It will give you a guide to how much money you need to bring in to cover the things that are important to you. You can earn as much money as you want above that, of course, but it's illuminating knowing what your base level is. Think of it as an awareness tool to help demystify your finances and better understand how what you spend matches up with the things that are important to you. Here's how to create your own Backwards Budget.

1. Remind yourself of your MAP.
The first thing to do, before you even get to thinking about dollars, is refresh yourself with the MAP you created in Step 1. Write out your MAP – that is, the meaning you get from work and outside it, your anchors and your priorities – at the top of a page. How you approach your money should line up with all of those, and they should be front and centre when it comes to thinking about how to spend your salary.

2. Think of a typical month.
Every month is different, but for this exercise, we're going to take an average month in your life and think of all the expenses you have to cover in order to live a satisfied life. We're trying to capture every dollar that goes out of your bank account for a month. You can write these answers down wherever you want, but to make it as easy as possible, I've created a free template that you can download as a

spreadsheet or PDF document. This way you can fill it out quickly without having to worry about anything except your responses. As an added bonus, if you use the free spreadsheet it will even add up your expenses for you. You can download interactive worksheets, including a Backwards Budget spreadsheet, from WorkBackwards. com/IRL.

3. Add up your expenses.

To create your Backwards Budget, download a few months of your bank statements and use them as a guide to how much you actually spend on these big categories. Then add them up into the following categories:

- **Accommodation:** how much do you spend each month on rent or paying off your mortgage? Wherever you live, this is most likely the biggest cost in your life.

    $ _____ per month

- **Bills:** Estimate how much you spend on regular monthly bills like gas, electricity, water, internet, phone, etc.

    $ _____ per month

- **Food and drink:** How much do you spend each month on groceries, dinner parties, lunches, coffees and going out with friends and family?

    $ _____ per month

- **Entertainment:** How much do you spend on keeping yourself amused, from Netflix subscriptions to movie, concert and theatre tickets each month?

    $ _____ per month

- **Personal:** Estimate how much you spend on yourself – things like haircuts, grooming, nails or any other type of personal care.

  $ _____ per month

- **Getting around:** How much do you pay to move around your city, including cars, Ubers, petrol, flights, public transport or whatever ways you use to move?

  $ _____ per month

- **Insurances:** Add up what you spend on insurance, such as car, health, pet and life insurances, depending on what you have.

  $ _____ per month

- **Loans:** Do you owe any money, such as a credit card, or a bank, car or personal loan?

  $ _____ per month

- **Kids:** Add up your kid-related costs, such as childcare, school fees and anything else.

  $ _____ per month

- **Clothes:** How much do you spend buying new or second-hand clothes, shoes, accessories, etc.?

  $ _____ per month

- **Pets:** How much does your pet cost a month, including food, vet, dog-walking, etc.?

  $ _____ per month

- **Health:** Estimate how much it costs to keep you in good health, such as gym membership, medications, doctors, dentists, chiropractors and more.

  $ _____ per month

- **Hobbies:** What does it cost you to indulge in hobbies that you really love to do, from hiking to kite surfing, playing chess to dance lessons?

  $ _____ per month

- **Education:** How much do you pay each month for learning, either formally or informally?

  $ _____ per month

- **Holidays:** How much do you spend on putting towards holidays and travel that you want to do each year? Think of flights, hotels and other prepayments.

  $ _____ per month

- **Fun:** Ensure you're putting aside an amount each month to just have some fun and spend it on things not covered in this plan.

  $ _____ per month

- **Savings:** How much money do you want to save each month for your longer-term goals?

  $ _____ per month

- **Giving:** Do you want to put some of your money aside to support causes and people you care deeply about?

  $ _____ per month

- **Additional:** If something isn't covered above, put it in here:

  Description: _____

  $ _____ per month

  Description: _____

  $ _____ per month

  Description: _____

  $ _____ per month

  Description: _____

  $ _____ per month

  Description: _____

  $ _____ per month

Once you've included all the costs, as specific or general as you like, add them up so that you have the total monthly cost for the lifestyle you want:

TOTAL: $ _____ per month

Then multiply that monthly total by 12, giving you the annual amount:

TOTAL: $ _____ per year

This is how much money you currently need to bring in each year to live your life. Everything above this is a bonus, which you can either save, or spend on things that give you meaning or line up with your anchors and priorities.

4. Consider your version of 'enough'.

Now that you know the annual amount of money you need to pay for the life you want, this is a good moment to pause and reflect.

Then it's time to think about what your version of 'enough' is. Does this Backwards Budget reflect your MAP, i.e. where you get meaning from, your anchors and your priorities? Now that you have an annual total, are there any categories that you think you could reduce? Is there anything you don't really need? Look at how much you are spending each month and consider if there are some areas you can tweak to better align with the MAP of where you want to go.

5. Think about how much money you currently earn.

Is the amount of money in your Backwards Budget higher or lower than your current annual after-tax salary? One of the reasons I love doing this exercise is that it's incredibly freeing to know how much income you need to be aiming towards.

If your current income level is below your Backwards Budget, you need to think about either reducing your expenses or increasing your income. If your current income level is above your Backwards Budget, that gives you more options, such as considering if it's possible to work less and still achieve everything you want to get from life.

Remember, this is just a guide. I'm not a financial adviser, and there are many in-depth resources that can help you plan what to do with your money after you earn it. The point of a Backwards Budget is to give you more clarity on how much money you need to live a meaningful life that aligns with your values and priorities. Arming yourself with this knowledge is one of the most important steps when you Work Backwards.

Work

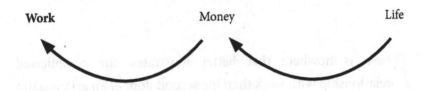

Work   Money   Life

'Nothing will work unless you do.'

- Maya Angelou

Ceiling cracks

There is nowhere that better illustrates our complicated relationship with work than the second floor of an art museum and performance space in Mexico City. Carved out of white marble hauled in from surrounding Mexican quarries, the Palacio de Bellas Artes stands proudly in the centre of the capital's historic zone. Thousands of visitors arrive each day to see some of the country's most celebrated artists tell stories through vivid art, most of which is painted directly on the interior walls of the building. Ascend the grand staircase and you'll come face-to-face with duelling murals, squaring off to tell the story of the past, present and future of work in competing narratives.

An 11-metre-long mural dominates almost the entire western wall of the second floor. Painted by Diego Rivera in 1934, *Man, Controller of the Universe* depicts the twin forces of capitalism and communism pulling at a sturdy, blond man in the centre of the mural. Dressed in a factory uniform, he controls a machine as iconography swirls all around him. You could spend hours interpreting each of the symbols and decoding the faces in the artwork. The forces of capitalism are depicted on the left-hand side as the technology of warfare, such as poison gas, warplanes and machine guns. Charles Darwin appears among the crowd, pointing to a monkey holding a small child's hand. On the right, the spirit of communism is brought to life with dozens of workers and the forces behind their movements – philosophers such as Karl Marx, Leon Trotsky and Friedrich Engels – huddled around revolutionary banners. Painted almost a century ago, it's an optimistic take on the contrasting views of labour and capital, which the artist saw as being as directly opposed as good and evil.

The most striking thing about the artwork, however, is that it was not meant to be here. In 1933, Rivera – who was twice married to Frida Kahlo in a complicated relationship – painted the same painting on the wall of 30 Rockefeller Plaza in New York City. Commissioned by the Rockefellers themselves, the original artwork had an even more obvious title of *Man at the Crossroads*, and Rivera spent months painting it on the interior wall of the building's foyer. At the last minute, Rivera decided to add a portrait of Russian politician Vladimir Lenin among the faces, which proved very controversial. When he refused to delete Lenin from the image, Rivera was paid for the mural and returned home to Mexico. The artwork remained unseen for the next year until, in February 1934, it was peeled off the wall and completely destroyed. In retaliation, Rivera recreated the artwork on the wall in Mexico City, even adding a new portrait of John Rockefeller Jr, a lifelong teetotaller, drinking a cocktail with a woman. Above their heads is a Petri dish of the syphilis bacteria.[1]

As Rivera was painting his mural in 1934, directly opposite, on the other side of the grand foyer, another mural was taking shape. *Catharsis* was the first public mural painted by José Clemente Orozco after living in America for seven years. Compared to Rivera's perceived optimism across the hall, Orozco's interpretation is a dark fever dream of nightmares. It's a dystopian vision of excess, greed and machines reflecting a world of conflict, vices, decay and destruction. In the upper left-hand corner, amid burning flames, a twisted cog from a machine appears to have grown an arm, wielding a sharp knife that threatens to kill frightened humans. Taken at face value, Orozco's mural is a warning, from a hundred years ago, that machines and robots will eventually rise up and destroy the very beings that created them.

The two artists, Rivera and Orozco, admired and despised each other in equal measures,[2] yet for a few months in 1934 they worked opposite each other, painting their prophetic artworks at the same time. Legend has is that when Orozco finished his mural, he crossed the hallway carrying his wet paintbrush. He handed it to Rivera, who took his time perfecting his paintings. 'Maybe this will help you to finish,' he said.

The two competing murals symbolise our ongoing, fractured relationship with work. On one side are the seesawing emotions of Rivera's work, highlighting the tension between capitalism and communism, with neither side being a perfect solution, littered with benefits and drawbacks in equal measures. Over the ensuing century since the mural was created, capitalism has been the clear victor. It's become the overarching system that governs our working lives, and clearly overpowered the balance Rivera depicted in his work. On the other side of the grand staircase, Orozco's fear that machines would eventually destroy humans is visceral. His prescience at diagnosing the looming threat (and opportunity) of artificial intelligence may have taken a hundred years to come to fruition, but decades after the paint dried, neither mural could have been any more prophetic.

These early depictions of our feelings about work show we've had a complicated relationship with it for a long time. In 1822, one of the world's first office buildings opened in London. Charles Lamb was one of the early adopters of the modern office, and each day he commuted to East India Company's new open workspaces. Was he excited to be at the forefront of a new type of working style that would soon spread like a virus around the world? Not quite. Lamb wrote a letter to a friend in the spring of 1822: 'You don't know how wearisome it is,' he wrote, 'to breathe the air of four pent walls, without relief, day after day, all the golden hours of the day between ten and four … oh for a few years between the grave and the desk! They are the same …'[3] Okay, so clearly Lamb wasn't a huge fan of going into the office, but his dour feelings didn't stop the march of history, as more and more white-collar workers were squeezed into cubicles and open-plan desks.

Our struggles with work are as old as work itself. The history of labour is a long, protracted battle between classes, social systems, technology and ideas that goes to the very core of who we are as human beings and how we should spend our time. Jim Stanford, the founding director of the Australia Institute's Centre for Future Work, sees our relationship with the working week as a symbol of our struggles, as workers fought their way from working 12 hours a day, 7 days a week, to getting Sundays off, then Saturdays, then annual holidays, paid parental leave and more. 'None of those things came about because employers said, "Oh, my workers love it and they're going to work harder",' he says. 'They all came about because workers organised, and demanded, and fought for those things.'

As our modern relationship with work has become more strained, constant cracks in the surface have become visible all around the world, with each flare-up a sign that something dramatic needs to change. During the pandemic years, many workers threatened to join 'the great resignation' and switch to better employment. *Crack!* On TikTok, younger workers celebrated the art of doing the bare minimum at work, calling it 'quiet quitting'. *Craaack!*

In France, the government enacted a 'right to disconnect' law to quell workers' dissatisfaction with being contacted at all hours.

Another crack! In the UK, protests disrupted politicians' plans to increase the pension age, despite the heavy price of inaction. *Crackkkkkk!* In South Korea, the government was forced to reduce the cap on working hours in 2017 from 68 hours a week to 52 – comprising 40 hours a week, plus up to 12 hours of paid overtime – due in part to hundreds of people dying each year because of overwork, or *gwarosa* (many activists believe the official number of deaths attributed to heart attacks, industrial accidents and sleep-deprived driving are just the tip of the iceberg). And when the South Korean government floated the idea of bringing back a 69-hour work week in 2023 – the equivalent of working 8 a.m. to 10 p.m. for five days in a row – this was met with fierce opposition and protests, predominantly from younger workers.[4] *Another big crack!*

Overall, attitudes to work have soured so much that entire movements have sprung up questioning the very notion of working in the first place. One of these is 'anti-work', and its rise is a fascinating insight into the extreme end of this global phenomenon. The history of anti-work – literally refusing to work – began as a criticism of capitalism. The movement is rooted in Marxism and anarchism, and the belief that everything needs to be, sometimes literally, burnt to the ground and society rebooted without forcing anyone to do anything. In 2013, a forum called r/antiwork began on Reddit as 'a quiet corner of the internet to discuss radical leftist ideas about ending work',[5] complete with a tongue-in-cheek slogan: 'Unemployment for all, not just the rich!' By 2019 it had attracted around 13,000 members, a motley crew of contributors who mainly griped about their work and shared tips on how to avoid doing it. Then the pandemic hit in 2020, upending many people's workplaces and forcing them to rethink their relationship with work. Over the next two years the number of users on the antiwork subreddit ballooned to over 2.7 million, an increase of over 20,000%.

Instead of just hosting rants about how to not work, the forum became the focal point for a movement of people to discuss how to leave their jobs, complain about capitalism, or just feel a sense of community where they could share their growing discontent with work in general. *Craccccck!*

The cracks will keep adding up until something shatters. They are manifesting themselves as three main emotional states, which most of us will recognise inside ourselves in some way.

1. We are overworked

Geoff McDonald began his career as a school teacher in South Africa before landing a job at Unilever, one of the largest consumer goods companies globally, best known for household brands like Dove, OMO and Rexona. His first job was to travel to universities around Africa recruiting graduates, and he spent the next 25 years working his way through the ranks in London, Sydney and other parts of the world. He eventually became Global Vice President of HR for the company, which boasted 170,000 employees in 90 countries.

It was an intense, busy and high-pressure role, and on 26 January 2008, Geoff's world came crashing down. It was his daughter's thirteenth birthday, but the day would instead be seared into Geoff's memory for a different reason. Early in the morning, Geoff woke up in the grip of a massive panic attack. It was an experience unlike anything he'd felt before, and his first thought was that he was about to have a heart attack. He tried to calm himself down, but his mind went down a dark path, catastrophising for hours about all the things that might be wrong with him. When his daughter bounded into his room at sunrise, he mustered whatever energy he had left to quietly beg his wife to take her and her sister downstairs and then to school. A few hours later, still unable to get out of bed, his wife convinced him to go and see a doctor, where he was officially diagnosed with anxiety-fuelled depression. As a high-functioning executive at the top of his career, those were not the words he expected to hear, but Geoff calls that experience his 'crucible moment'.

Geoff had never had any serious mental health issues in the past, and had no idea what depression really meant, but he decided on the spot that he would share his diagnosis with his wife, daughters, close friends, and some work colleagues. 'I'm not very good at masking my feelings or trying to be somebody that I'm not,' he says. 'You just need to look me in the eye and you'll see if there's something going on … If I had a physical illness and a doctor had diagnosed that, I would tell people what was wrong with me, so getting the diagnosis helped empower me to be open.' Geoff had a line manager at the time who had what he calls a compassionate relationship to mental ill health. 'There's a very big difference between compassion and empathy. With empathy, we put ourselves in somebody else's shoes, and we offer support and guidance, but with compassion, there's no judgment … He didn't judge me for the fact that I was sick with depression. In fact, he loved me and supported me through my illness.'

Geoff worked hard at his ongoing recovery, aided by a strong support network, and found that a sense of love and hope were the two most powerful ingredients in his recovery process. He remained in his high-powered role for another few years, navigating his way through the stresses and strains of senior leadership. The more he shared his story, the greater an impact he felt he could have. In 2014 he left his job to lean into his newly discovered sense of purpose to create workplaces, friendship groups and families where everyone feels they genuinely have the choice to ask for help if they are struggling with a common form of mental ill health.

Geoff is now on a mission. One is to destigmatise conversations around the negative consequences of stress and overwork. The other is to kickstart a wider conversation about the way society is built, and how businesses are incentivised solely on their financial performance. 'This leads to a real drive around short-termism,' he says. 'From this comes a drive for efficiency, reducing costs, taking people out of the system, replacing them with technology, and just putting more and more pressure on people to achieve the results.'

When Geoff goes into organisations now, the number-one issue that people want to talk about is the pressure they feel to work more. 'Everybody is talking about workload,' he says. And it's not just office workers who are overwhelmed – this is a trend that's repeated in every industry, from nurses to teachers, posties and waitstaff. In 2023, the world's most influential chef, René Redzepi, announced he was closing down his highly awarded restaurant, Noma, as the gruelling hours required by the chefs and hospitality workers to produce the quality their customers demanded were too much. 'It's unsustainable,' he said at the time.[6] 'We have to completely rethink the industry,' he said. 'This is simply too hard, and we have to work in a different way.'

And you know what? He's right.

2. We are disengaged

No matter which way you look at it, our tenuous relationship with work is leading to a generally disenfranchised workforce who no longer feel that the sacrifices are worth it. International forecaster Marian Salzman says one of the biggest shifts she predicts in the near future is a rethinking of the cornerstones of modern life. 'We are questioning everything,' she wrote in her influential annual trend report.[7] 'In the work world, employees (younger ones, especially) refuse to make the sacrifices earlier generations considered standard ... The notion that worker drones should devote their lives to pumping up the profits of corporate executives and investors is increasingly less accepted at a time when spending decades climbing the corporate ladder to grasp the golden ring (or watch) at journey's end is no longer on offer.'

Gen Z, born between the mid-1990s and 2010s, are the most disengaged of the generations. 'There's an illusion with work that everything you give up now – the stolen time commuting, working overtime, checking your email and Slack notifications after hours – will somehow earn you freedom and capital in your later years,' wrote Amil Niazi, summing up the dislocated feelings in 'Losing My Ambition' for *The Cut.*[8]

When we're connected to the work we do, this gives us a sense of purpose, helps us through difficult times and enables us to work better and more efficiently. Our current disconnection from work needs to be addressed before the impacts truly set in.

However, there's also the argument that work doesn't need to provide engagement, and we're looking in the wrong place for meaning. Dr Michael P. Leiter is one of the world's leading experts on burnout. He's been studying it for over four decades, writing two books with Dr Christina Maslach. Dr Maslach co-authored (with Susan Jackson) the Maslach Burnout Inventory in 1981, an instrument used globally to assess the experience of burnout. Michael co-authored the version of the assessment that is used most often in the workplace. Their research together shows that burnout is a workplace problem, not a worker problem. It occurs when there is a mismatch between employers and employees in one or more of the following areas: the amount of control a worker has, fair treatment, a sense of community, workload levels, the provision of rewards, or company values.

Michael is now a Professor Emeritus at Acadia University in Nova Scotia, Canada, an academic institution he's worked at since

1978. He argues that when it comes to engagement at work, we're sometimes looking in the wrong direction. Of course we can tweak parts of our job and environment, but it's a fallacy to think that a lot of our emotional needs can be fulfilled at work. 'Workplaces are designed primarily to get some tasks completed that need to get completed in order to run the shop,' he says. 'But people are coming in with a whole lot of psychological motivations, needs and aspirations about how to connect with people socially, about dealing with accomplishments, and feelings of advocacy, of feeling they have some sense of control and agency and autonomy with their work. They're coming in with all this stuff, all these psychological motives are active and the workplace is a main arena for these things to work out ... I think there's a real limit to how much workplaces are designed with the idea of really being fulfilling places for people.'

Michael's take is a refreshing antidote to modern management mantras that say your job needs to fulfil you, and that you're a failure if you're not fully engaged at work. As we explored in the first chapter, even small amounts of meaning derived from work, as well as outside of it, are important, but if you're looking at your workplace for all the answers to your psychological needs, you're looking in the wrong place.

Burnout isn't a new phenomenon, with the earliest records of it appearing in the 1820s, but its rapid rise to familiarity is. Deep disengagement with your work makes it more likely you will exhibit signs of burnout at some stage in your career. 'I look at it more as an existential crisis,' says Michael. 'I don't think of it so much as a mental health kind of thing, though it gets framed that way a lot. It's really a crisis of meaning, a crisis of who you are within the world in which you're operating.'

Researchers have identified three interlinked dimensions to burnout: occupational exhaustion, depersonalisation, and a decrease in feelings of personal accomplishment.[9] The first is where work drains you so much that you need to recover from it, both physically and emotionally. It's the kind of complete exhaustion that not even sleep can resolve, as there are deeper factors behind it than just tiredness. Depersonalisation means that you care less about the people you work with, the end result being that you feel less compassionate towards them. That feeling you sometimes get when your colleague really pisses you off and you couldn't care less what you say to them? That's a sign of depersonalisation. The last component is when you feel generally 'blah' about what you're achieving at work. When you feel good, that can help balance out the first two components, but when not even that is working, you could be on the path to burning out.

3. We are apprehensive

We have many reasons to worry. In the UK, around one in six adults say they have experienced a 'common mental disorder', such as depression or anxiety, in the past week.[10] The exact reasons for this are obviously complex and multi-layered, but with work being such a major focus of our lives, some of the blame has to lie with it.

There's also climate anxiety, a growing fear that our planet is in a perilous state that is generally being ignored. A study of 10,000 16-to-25-year-olds around the world found that almost 60% were very or extremely worried about climate change, with more than 45% saying these feelings were negatively affecting their daily life and functioning.[11]

The history of work is punctuated by advancements in technology, from the printing press in 1455 to the telephone in 1876, personal computers in 1972 and the internet a decade later. Each new technology has come with a shifting of the sands on which employment is built. Sometimes this takes a while to happen, while at other times it's more swift.

For years we've been told that, with a few variations, robots were coming for our jobs. The Jetsons heralded this in the 1960s, and *Back to the Future* dramatised it in the 1980s. For most of the twenty-first century, automation and artificial intelligence felt like something far off on the horizon – something that would impact the future workplaces of our kids, and our kids' kids. 'AI, like most transformative technologies, grows gradually, then arrives suddenly. Headlines make AI feel abrupt and singular when it's compared to a tidal wave, revolution or tectonic shift. In actuality, foundational work in AI has been going on since the 1950s,' Reid Hoffman, the co-founder of LinkedIn, wrote. 'With all the possibilities ahead, it's important to think beyond any one application, company, industry when it comes to AI, because I believe its impact will be on a much greater magnitude.'[12]

After decades of behind-the-scenes research and computer training, in 2021, new technology burst into our consciousness with the emergence of AI-powered software that was genuinely useful. OpenAI's ChatGPT (which stands for Generative Pre-trained Transformer, or a computer that's been fed billions of pieces of data to train it before being asked a question), Microsoft's Bing, Google's Bard, Ernie Bot from China's Baidu, DALL-E 2 and others all launched publicly in an inflection point that signalled a seismic shift and a new digital arms race. The rate at which technology in this space will directly impact the future of work feels overwhelming to many people. One report estimated that automation will eliminate 73 million jobs in the US by 2030[13] – and that's just the beginning of the revolution that's going to dramatically alter how and why we work.

Make no mistake, artificial intelligence will change our lives. It will eliminate basic, repetitive tasks, slowly working up the ladder of advancement until it can do a lot of what we currently call 'work'. It will have an immense impact on the meaning we get from our work, and is moving at such a rapid pace that our current frameworks – legal, moral and ethical – are struggling to keep up.

One group of academics, futurists and technology experts wrote an open letter to the US President warning of the dangers of technology. The 'cybernation revolution', they wrote, would create huge increases in productivity, with computers performing so many tasks that the country would soon face record-high levels of unemployment, leading to 'a separate nation of the poor, the unskilled, the jobless'. The US Secretary of Labor agreed, saying that new 'thinking machines' now have the skills 'equivalent to a high school diploma' and would soon take over the service industry.

Sounds scary, huh? What if I told you that this letter was actually written in 1964, when people were worried about machines taking the jobs of workers? As humans, we are programmed to have an underlying desire for control. When new technology like a two-wheeled bicycle became popularised, there were 'scientists' who linked it to an increase in cases of insanity.[14] When 5G made phones faster and more connected, hordes of people believed the invisible beams were affecting our health, with some even claiming the technology increased our susceptibility to Covid.[15] Now, with AI, there is more of the familiar scaremongering, but how much of it is real? The list of jobs most vulnerable to being replaced in part or entirely by AI range from those that involve higher education, such as programming, law or journalism, which are at the greatest risk, through to jobs that don't require tertiary education or apprenticeships, which are the least at risk (for now). Research from the University of Pennsylvania and OpenAI concluded that around a fifth of workers could see at least half of their tasks automated.[16]

Technology has always moved fast; we went from the first recorded flight by the Wright Brothers in 1903 to flying to the moon by 1969, in the blink of a single lifetime. We've survived many waves of technology that have restricted entire swathes of the economy. It's been estimated that in America in 1890, nearly one in 12 adult males was involved with the railway industry, before new technology superseded it. But now technology is accelerating so rapidly that we're seeing massive changes taking place over a single decade. The speed at which this is happening is dizzying, and it will change our relationship to work exponentially.

All of this is leading to a growing apprehension about the future, and our role in it. In 2015, long before ChatGPT was a glint in a programmer's eye, the Chapman University Survey on American fears found that technology-related fears were the second most prominent type of fear that people have[17] – and now that fear has been supercharged.

Paul Graham, one of America's leading venture capitalists, said that 'one difference between worry about AI and worry about other kinds of technologies (e.g. nuclear power, vaccines) is that people who understand it well worry more, on average, than people who don't. That difference is worth paying attention to.' And there is reason to feel fear. When asked, around half of 738 machine-learning researchers gave a probability of an extremely bad outcome, and a separate poll of 44 people working in AI safety suggested there was a 30% probability of something terrible happening.[18]

Fear of technology is not new, but our growing apprehension that things are moving too fast and could soon spin out of control, with massive effects on how we work, is mounting. Of course, there's a lot of optimism about the potential opportunities that technology will bring, but in a workforce that's already feeling overworked and disengaged, it's just another nail in the coffin of the way we're currently working.

The way we are working is leaving us overworked, disengaged and apprehensive. It's a hard place to come back from, but we can do it – we just need to find a way through some of the noise. To do that, we have to understand what is fact and what is fiction.

Myths and realities

For decades we've been told that the path to success is simply to work hard. Anyone can reach their goals, earn more money, buy more stuff just by knuckling down and working more. Spend longer inside your gleaming office tower or wading through your endless streams of emails and, eventually, if you work hard enough you'll progress up another rung of the corporate ladder.

But all of that was a big, juicy lie that was blown apart during the pandemic years, the biggest global experiment to happen to the workforce in a century. Those few years of new routines exposed lots of myths about how we work:

Myth: People work less when they work from home.

Myth: Everyone needs to be working at the same time.

Myth: You only get ahead by climbing the corporate ladder.

Myth: We're most productive Monday to Friday, 9 a.m.–5 p.m.

Myth: Employees have to be in an office to get work done.

Let's break each of these myths down, and show the fallacies they've been hiding behind this whole time.

Myth: People work less when they work from home.
Reality: Workers actually work for longer, and with fewer breaks, when away from the office.

There was a time, not too long ago, when most workers rarely worked from home. The right systems weren't in place, there was little trust, and a lot of managers assumed that 'working from home' was basically a euphemism for 'doing nothing'. Data from 20,000 people surveyed by Australian digital news publisher *The Daily Aus* showed that before the pandemic, only 16% of their audience of 18-to-30-year-olds had ever worked from home.[1] After the pandemic, the rapid shift in working styles was extraordinary and long-lasting. Just two years later, 70% of respondents said they worked from home more than one or two days a week.

The pandemic introduced a lot of new trends – think baking sourdough, online yoga, home workouts – but Google search data showed that most people returned to their baseline interests once our lives returned to normal.[2] Remote working was different. Not only did interest in 'remote jobs' continue to rise after the World Health Organisation declared the approaching end of the pandemic in 2022 and we resumed 'normal' activities, but roughly half of all job applications on LinkedIn at the end of 2022 were for remote work positions.[3]

Although it's still new and will continue to ride waves of popularity up and down, remote working in some form is here to stay. One of the most surprising effects to come from the shift from the traditional office to a home office is that instead of decreasing productivity, this actually did the opposite. Data from remote workers in 27 countries[4] found that not having to commute to work saved people an average of 72 minutes a day, and they spent around 30 minutes of that extra time doing additional work. That added up to around two hours a week more work than if they went into the office every day.

Remote work as we know it today is still relatively new, but a lot of the research points to things never going back to the way they were.

Myth: Everyone needs to be working at the same time.
Reality: Once trust has been established, there are lots of different ways to work.

Since modern offices were created, most knowledge workers have done synchronous work. This is when multiple workers all work together at the same time, for the same hours, and are generally contactable and available to each other during those hours. For most office workers, synchronous work has been the only option available. If you've ever sent an email to someone in your office, and then walked over to their desk to ask if they received the email you just sent them, then you're a synchronous worker. It's been long assumed that having everyone available at the same time was the best way of working, for ease of communication, and that the only way to build a culture is by working collectively at the same time.

The alternative to this is asynchronous working. This style doesn't require all workers to be available or immediately responsive at the same hours of the day. Instead, asynchronous working relies on transparency, as each employee is empowered to complete their work in their own time and in their own way. This shift in focus to output instead of input requires trust in both directions, and requires strong communication, handovers and structures. Fortunately, an entire software industry has grown around asynchronous work, with programs designed to smooth out the process so everyone can be aware of who is working on what.

This style of working takes into account different lifestyles, ways of working, locations and flexibility, giving more people the ability to contribute their best work, and their best time, to achieve a team's goal.

Myth: You only get ahead by climbing the corporate ladder.
Reality: There are many better ways of defining success.

The generations before us thought about their jobs and career as something they would do for a lifetime. Many of our parents and grandparents began a job in their late teens and continued to work for the same company until retirement. The idea of success, for many, was to slowly crawl up the career ladder, one rung at a time, until you got as close to the top as you could.

Thankfully, that way of thinking is now outdated. The average person will change jobs every two years and nine months, and go through three to seven different careers before they retire.[5]

Success is no longer about inching to the top of a work hierarchy. It is about so much more than that, including personal achievement, potential impact, learning and happiness. Just judging someone by their job title or outwardly perceived success no longer cuts it.

Myth: We're most productive Monday to Friday, 9 a.m.–5 p.m.
Reality: Let's face it, we're not. Productivity and output are personal and varied.

Despite everything else that's changed around us, the traditional hours that most of us work have stubbornly remained the same for the last hundred or so years. Growing mainstream acceptance of flexible work hours means you no longer even have to be online at the same time as someone else to work on a project together.

It's early in our experiments with these new ways of working, but research is fast accumulating that backs up alternative working styles. Every worker is different, and the time of day when we're most energetic, our concentration levels, learning styles and methods are all unique to us. The days of forcing everyone to squeeze their lifestyle into a workplace's demands are fading. The more studies and real-world experiments that show flexibility is the key to employee well-being and productivity there are, the sooner every workplace will adopt their own flexible practices.

Myth: Employees have to be in an office to get work done.
Reality: Different types of work require different environments.

Offices are usually social, loud, interactive, fun places to meet, plan, argue, chat and gossip with your colleagues. An office environment is important for certain activities, but it's not the only place to get work done. When we spend every working hour in an office, we'll overachieve on some collaborative tasks, but generally underachieve on work that requires long, uninterrupted time to strategise, be creative or solve complex problems. These tasks are better performed outside a traditional office.

In fact, you don't even need to be in the same country to work closely with a team. Andy Miller is the CEO of non-alcoholic brewery Heaps Normal. He currently lives in Thailand, while his leadership team is spread across three Australian states, with the rest of the staff across four. The company is a hybrid workforce that was established from the start to be flexible. 'The geographical separation has forced us to think more critically and be more creative about how to work together effectively as a team. And I think, overwhelmingly, that's been a positive thing.'

The traditional belief that a company that sells physical products, such as beer, needs in-person interactions with their suppliers was blown out of the water during the pandemic years. 'The unwritten rules of our industry said that those relationships needed to be built face to face,' says Andy, 'and that you can't bring on a new customer if you aren't standing in front of them handing them a physical sample of the product.'

The pandemic forced Andy and his team to sell the product in a different way, posting samples to potential customers and following up on the phone. It's a new format that's now been integrated alongside personal interactions, and prompted a lot of thinking about how to build a business in a rapidly changing world. 'For example,' says Andy, 'as a very small team, we didn't have the kind of overheads that a lot of other businesses in our situation may have had, and so therefore we were able to invest early in better employee benefits.'

Andy acknowledges that the future of work is not always even. 'You can't remotely brew beer,' he laughs, before adding that they are constantly experimenting with different ways of making sure the entire workforce, from marketing to sales to the brewers, can still incorporate some of the benefits of flexibility into their roles. There are drawbacks, of course, such as the financial and environmental cost of travel, and as CEO, Andy often finds himself staring at a computer for 12 hours a day, managing his team through a digital screen. 'I have to be really conscious of being present, not only for my team remotely, but also being present in my own physical location of Bangkok so that I can actually leverage some of the positive things about being remote, like being inspired by a different culture and being able to filter out distractions when more focused, deep work is called for. The things that help me contribute a unique perspective to my team.'

But the benefits are dramatic. The team get added flexibility in their lives, and Andy is able to live and work in a foreign country with his young family. Andy's partner is a diplomat who sometimes has to travel and live in different locations for years at a time. 'I've often said to my partner that this is just unbelievable, that somehow she can have a job that requires international travel for long periods and I can also still contribute productively to something that I love at the same time.'

With all these myths being overturned with exciting realities, the main question now is: How we can take advantage of this brave new world of work that we have entered?

Your future of work

There's a scene in Chloé Zhao's profound movie *Nomadland* that hits you deep in the chest. The movie follows Fern, played by Frances McDormand, as she aimlessly wanders the forgotten landscape of nomadic American workers. The scene comes early in the film, and features Merle Redwing, a real-life nomad, telling a story about one of her co-workers. 'I worked for corporate America, you know, for twenty years,' she says around a bonfire in the Arizona desert. 'And my friend, Bill, worked for the same company, and he had liver failure. A week before he was due to retire, HR called him in the hospice, and said, "Now, let's talk about your retirement."' The orange fire flickers over her weathered face as she tells the story. 'And he died ten days later, having never been able to take that sailboat that he bought out of his driveway. And he missed out on everything. And he told me before he died, "Just don't waste any time, Merle. Don't waste any time." So I retired as soon as I could. I didn't want my sailboat to be in the driveway when I died.'

Each of us has a vision of how we would really love to work if we had the choice: How often? From where? Doing what? And how, exactly? Until recently, for most people this vision was nothing but a mirage on the horizon that they could never reach. Very few people, aside from a few fortunate solo operators or wealthy individuals, could design how they wanted to work.

Until now, that is. We have more tools at our disposal than ever, so it's about deciding which of these tools can best help us lean further into meaning, our anchors and priorities.

Everyone's idea of their future of work is unique. Some people want a way of working that leaves room to spend quality time each day with their loved ones. For others, their vision is to spend the least amount of time working and the rest of their time exploring hobbies and things they adore. While a few of us have a vision to travel the world and log in to email and video conferences each morning before spending the afternoon swimming and napping on the beach.

The future of how you work is not, however, some far-flung fantasy. The future of work is here, right now, and it's up to you to take advantage of it. You just need to know what tools are available, and how to use them properly.

Work Backwards Step 3:
Use the right tools

Understand all the extraordinary ways we have to work better, and how to best use them.

The upside-down swan

I f I asked you to conjure up what the ideal workplace of the future looked like, you might come up with something like this: a business where all decisions that affect employees, from the largest to the minuscule, are made openly and democratically; a company that's not built solely to make profits for shareholders and where every worker, from the CEO to the receptionist, all own equal shares in its future; a flexible workplace where people aren't tied to one set desk or location and are free to work at their own pace from wherever they want; an ideas-led organisation where creativity is passionately debated by everyone, allowing the best ideas to rise to the surface collaboratively; a corporate structure that treats everyone like adults, and prioritises shared, ethical responsibility for everyone inside and outside the company. And, of course, if we're creating our dream workplace from scratch, it should also make lots of money, and grow its revenue by double digits every year so that everyone feels proud and engaged with what they're doing every day.

It sounds like a fantasy, right? Well, if this is your idea of the future of work then I hate to tell you this, but the future has already happened. The dreamy vision detailed above is a real company that was founded three decades ago, and its rapid rise and gradual fall is a cautionary tale of what can happen when idealism meets the harsh thud of reality.

The 1980s was a strange and wonderful time to be in business. In glistening office towers, ideals of greed, excess and corporate worship grew to new heights, and many industries became dominated by large multinational companies that aggressively acquired smaller companies that showed any signs of promise. This was especially evident in the advertising and marketing industry, where hungry holding companies acquired and assimilated new agencies into their fold whenever they grew to a certain size.

It was into this world that a bright and curious young marketer, David Abraham, worked his way up through advertising agencies in Britain until he arrived at one with a reputation for creative work and attracting top talent. It was here he met Andy Law, a visionary leader who headed up the London office. Andy was a decade older than David, and they bonded over a mutual dislike for constant corporate growth and a revolutionary desire to shake up the system.

Their opportunity arrived when news broke that their company was being acquired by one of the large holding groups. David and Andy feared a loss of independence and creative freedom, and eventually negotiated to buy back their company from their new corporate bosses, meaning that Andy, David and around 30 staff members would form their own separate advertising agency.

Excited by the opportunity to create the company of their dreams, Andy and David locked themselves in a room with some trusted colleagues and fantasised about what an ideal workplace could look like. Through these long, messy, optimistic sessions, a vision slowly formed of a company that would take many of the emerging ideas about the future of work and give them a real test, all at once.

And so, in 1995, the creative agency St Luke's was born, named after the patron saint of artists. The agency took all the tools available at the time, and reinvented them for a rapidly changing world. They drew up rules for flexible, hybrid and remote working before we even had agreed names for these things. Where employees worked, inside or outside the office, was up to them to decide and manage themselves. There were no set desks in the office, and early versions of mobile phones gave individuals the freedom to work from wherever they chose, which was often in communal rooms set up specifically for each major client or project, to encourage collaboration.

They also reinvented their corporate structure. St Luke's was 100% owned equally by every person who worked at the company. Once an employee passed their six-month probation, they had the same amount of equity in the business as the founders. Every decision was made not by the usual management team or board of directors, but by a group of elected staff members. Their role was to ensure everything that affected the company was discussed, debated and decided collectively. A separate group, also made up of elected employees at various levels, had fiscal responsibility for the balance sheet and how money was spent. In short, they helped create the future of work in 1995 by using everything they had in their toolkit.

Almost as soon as they opened their doors, St Luke's became the hottest advertising agency in the world. *Fast Company* called them 'the ad agency to end all ad agencies'.[1] *Harvard Business Review* said it was 'the most frightening company on Earth',[2] on account of how it was pushing the boundaries of what a workplace could be. Channel 4 in the UK aired a national *Cutting Edge* documentary on the company in 1999 to shed light on 'the radical and idealistic experiment in how to run a business'.[3]

The workplace at St Luke's was loud, energetic and intoxicating. When curious visitors arrived at their inner-city London office, Andy would often give them a tour, showing off the new Ericcson phones, which operated like early mobile phones when you were inside the office. As he walked, Andy used the analogy of an upside-down swan to describe the company. 'Most companies want to be seen like the graceful swan which glides effortlessly and serenely about its business, whilst underneath, hidden, its feet are going crazy, working as hard they can to deliver the swan to its destination,' he'd explain. 'We are an upside-down swan ... Our feet flap wildly and energetically in people's faces every minute of every day and provide a charged, noisy, vibrant and fun atmosphere from which there is little escape. But underneath, the body of the company glides purposefully forward.'

Their visionary positioning and creative output drew media interest around the world, as well as clients who desperately wanted to work with them. In their first year, they billed £45 million of revenue, exceeding their annual target in just four months. They won clients like IKEA, Eurostar rail, Boots pharmacies and more. The future of work had arrived with a loud British clang.

I began my first job, fresh out of school, in an advertising agency in Sydney in 1999. The hyped buzz of St Luke's made it all the way down under, and I became enthralled by the breathless media stories about this impossibly hip agency on the other side of the world. I absorbed mountains of content about the St Luke's mythology, including media interviews, YouTube documentaries, and several of Andy's books, which documented every important conversation in minute detail. From the outside, St Luke's was a revolutionary workplace that experimented with traditional structures to show us what could happen if we questioned it all. 'A lot of people say this is Utopia,' said Andy in 1996. 'It is a different way of working, but it's not some kind of hippie, freeloading operation … We've created this company to live beyond us.'

However, just five years after its spectacular rise, having grown from 30 staff to 180, St Luke's began to implode. In 2001, co-founder David left the company for a job heading up Discovery Networks in Europe. Andy, by then the chairman, resigned spectacularly over a bitter dispute about the company's future direction. Many of the original employees, who just a few years earlier had been describing this as their job for life, began leaving, and the agency's billings halved from £90 million in 2000 to £43 million in 2002. This company that symbolised the potential future of work had flown too close to the sun, and came crashing back to Earth. I knew that the truth lay somewhere inside this mythology, and there was only one way to find out.

Almost three decades after he co-founded St Luke's as a visionary thirty-something, David Abraham's face beams in from London on a brisk spring Monday morning. David had a very successful career after leaving St Luke's, including seven years as the CEO of Channel 4, the second biggest commercial broadcaster in the UK, but his face visibly lights up when he reminisces about this seminal time of his life.

From the outside, it looked like a fever dream, so one of my first questions to David is 'What the hell happened?' 'St Luke's brought out the best in people, but it also exposed you to the worst,' he says. 'The whole story was like a rock band that shined very brightly for five years, and then it was unable to evolve as it got bigger, and as we got older and things got a bit more serious. But while it lasted it was extraordinary.'

According to David's retelling, the intentions that he and other co-founders had with St Luke's were genuine. They were young, wide-eyed and truly believed they were creating the future of work. Instead of tinkering with one or two elements of culture and structure, they changed everything all at once, accelerating a lot of experiments in virtual-office-type principles, just as the internet and mobile phones emerged. 'It was wonderful, really, we just did everything,' says David. 'For me, it was an example of how, if you get the culture right and if you're innovative in how you approach things, it does translate into the work.' The moment in time was like 'lightning in a bottle', where work was creative, enjoyable and confident.

Then the cracks started to show. The sense of ownership that staff members felt for the company began to backfire. 'People were passionate, but they often struggled with how to resolve decision making and strategy. It got difficult,' David says. The co-founders had copied the original articles of company constitution from a non-profit template, and soon found it restrictive to their growth. David, Andy and others wanted to continue tweaking the system they had created, such as adding bonuses for staff members who were particularly important for certain projects. However, whenever David brought this up, he was shot down by other employees who felt it went against their stated position of equality.

As St Luke's grew, it attracted a new generation who, in David's retelling, were attracted by the strict idealism and rules that were created to break free of the old system. Every time David tried to start a conversation about how to reform the model to adapt it to change, while still adhering to its core principles, the response was to just stick to the made-up rules. 'It became a little bit of a competition to see who could be more idealistic than everyone else,' he says.

St Luke's also tried to use every available tool all at once to rethink work, instead of introducing changes more gradually. This meant that some people felt that compromising on even a small aspect could be interpreted as a defeat. 'In my subsequent career, whenever I was managing change, I did it in a more gradual way,' says David. 'When I entered into more senior roles, I said that I didn't want to change more than half of it in the first year – even if things needed changing – because that's just too much disruption.'

David eventually left in the early 2000s, after his St Luke's colleagues rejected his vision to expand their remit into a new industry. Disillusioned with the inability of his co-owners to continue adapting, he left. Ironically, says David now, if he'd had a large stake in the business like a more traditional ownership structure, he might have stayed forever.

Two decades later, St Luke's still exists as an advertising agency in London, but it bears little resemblance to the wild and rebellious company it was born as. When many of the original co-founders left in the mid-2000s, two long-time staff members decided the original model was no longer working, and in 2010 they led a management buy-out to return it to a more standard corporate structure with shareholders.

So what can we learn from a business that tried to reinvent the future of work, only to end up showing that humans are more complicated than we think? Although it fizzled out quicker than anyone would have hoped, St Luke's shone so brightly for its time that it still holds many lessons today. 'It's hard to overstate the impact St Luke's had on the industry,' wrote *Campaign*.[4] 'There was an exhilarating, damn annoying, passion, energy and confidence at the agency that helped make the industry feel interesting, vibrant. It wasn't sustainable, of course.'

'Humans are creative, fun and inspiring, yet work for so many is monotonous, complex and dreary,' wrote Andy Law in *Open Minds*, the book documenting his journey in 1999.[5] St Luke's 'fired the opening volley of a revolution that aims to do nothing less than alter the DNA of business itself,' he wrote, to 'furiously seek a new, better, more fulfilling and fairer role for business in the lives of its employees.'

St Luke's tried to reinvent everything, everywhere, all at once. For a brief period, it modelled what could happen when a workplace goes all-in to empower its workers, co-create an employee experience and treat its staff like adults who can make their own decisions. They got out the toolbox and used every single tool that they could, all at the same time.

The company's ultimate downfall was its grand ambition to change everything about business, and its purity, which attracted people who believed so passionately in their cause that they couldn't see it properly. But their story shouldn't stop us from dreaming bigger. Instead, it should serve as a light, showing how work can be inspiring, creative and fulfilling for all staff. The opening volley of the revolution was fired many years ago, and we're only just gathering the army behind us now to back it up.

Reframing the tools

I t can be easy to get lost in all the noise around the topic of the future of work. There's an entire industry of scientists, human resources teams, thought leaders, writers, researchers and businesses who are trying to understand where it's going. Some of them even have skin in the game to try to influence what the outcome should be.

In the several years it took to write this book, thousands of pieces of research have been published around work and where it's heading. Trying to keep up with them, and their sometimes contradictory proclamations, is enough to send anyone mad, so it's not surprising that you're reading this book to get some clear directions.

But before we get to that, there's something else we need to do first. Instead of pursuing one definitive conclusion about what the future of work looks like, one that works for everyone, I want to smash through this speculation with a sledgehammer.

The future of work is here already; it's personal and it's messy. We need to reframe the notion that there is a single answer to this topic. What's important to one person might be terrible for someone else, and what's insignificant to me might be exactly the thing that you've been looking for.

You need to experiment with various ways of working to find the ones that work best for you, and reframe each of the options that we have as tools for you to use. And remember, like any good tool, they are only as good as your ability to use them. Unless you're an expert, the tools should be used one at a time, maybe two at a stretch. This is so you can properly play with them, learn from them and measure which is actually having a beneficial effect on how you work.

Here are some of the tools that are now available to work smarter and better:

- hybrid working
- remote working
- flexible working
- four-day work weeks
- career breaks
- collective time off
- artificial intelligence
- better meetings.

The future of work is an invigorating notion, filling us with hope and grand visions. In the future, we'll all be productive beyond our wildest dreams. In the future, we'll work just a little and be completely fulfilled because we're living out our purpose every single day. Sound amazing? Well, it's all crap. Sure, we can learn how to work – and live – better, but there's no silver bullet that will instantly transform how you live and work. The future of work is doing the work, thinking deeply about who you are and then testing, experimenting, iterating and repeating until it slowly gets better.

In this section we're going to break down each of the tools available to you, and show you how to properly use them. This final step is aimed towards both workers and managers, who will have to experiment with these tools together to figure out which work best for you and your workplace.

Tool: Remote working

T he three primary ways of thinking about how to work when you're not spending 100% of your time in a workplace might all seem similar, but they each have subtle yet important differences:

Remote working is when you work primarily outside of a typical workplace.

Hybrid working is when you work in different locations at different times.

Flexible working is when you work different hours to the standard working times.

Each of these is an important tool to create a better way of working that suits you, and it's important to understand the nuances of each. They are tools to be used at different times of your life, and can be combined to create the ultimate way of working that fits in with how you want to live.

If you're early career, these tools are exciting ways to imagine a lifetime of working in a new way, and you should embrace them with open arms. It's a thrilling time to start a career when, after decades, traditional ways of working are all being re-imagined.

For mid-career workers, some of these tools can address long-standing pain points, while others are just painful. The key is to realise that none of them is intended to be the *sole* answer to your prayers, so test them out and adapt the parts that work to your lifestyle. This is likely the first time in your career that you have the chance to do this, so try to appreciate it for that.

And if you're late career, then some of these tools might seem downright strange to you, as they probably go against everything you think you know about work. You need to think about how these tools can help with your remaining years, enabling you to spend more time doing what you want, and slowly transition to the next stage.

We'll begin with one of the most radical tools: remote working. This is when an employee sets up a work lifestyle designed around being in the office very little, and sometimes not at all. After the experimental years of the pandemic, many companies are building remote-first businesses, which are designed to work virtually for most of the time. Take Yelp, the app that recommends local restaurants and other businesses based on location and reviews. They tried hybrid work for employees before CEO and co-founder Jeremy Stoppelman came to the conclusion that it was 'the worst of both worlds'. In other words, employees were getting some benefit from working from home, and some benefit from being in the office, but called it generally 'the hell of half measures'. When Yelp asked their staff which option they preferred, more than 85% said they preferred to work remotely most of the time.[1]

A growing number of tech companies, including Atlassian, Slack and Airbnb, have instigated similar working styles. Airbnb's CEO Brian Chesky introduced a policy in 2022 allowing staff to work from anywhere in the country they are employed in without their salary changing.[2] They can also move anywhere in the world and will be paid the equivalent local compensation. In order for this to work, employees still had to meet regularly for in-person gatherings, and focus heavily on working in-sync together online.

Harvard Business School professor Prithwiraj Choudhury studied companies that went 100% remote before the pandemic, such as Zapier and Gitlab, and found that workplaces with elements of flexibility, such as remote and hybrid ways of working, had employees who were more productive, more loyal and less likely to leave. 'We will probably in ten years stop calling this "remote work". We'll just call it work,' he said.[3]

The benefits for remote working are various, primarily focused on the ability to properly fit work time around your ideal lifestyle. Want to live by the beach? Near your parents? Have a 20-second commute to work every day? Play games with your newborn every lunchtime? Then remote work could be the ideal way to claim back some of your life.

It's also a boon for genuine diversity and inclusion. 'Single mums with childcare responsibilities are able to do work because they can connect remotely,' says Dr Sean Gallagher from Swinburne University's Centre for the New Workforce, giving examples of who can benefit from this type of work: 'Those working in regional areas or those with a broad range of neurodiversity, or those with a certain type of disability that precludes them from going into an office.'

However, it must also be pointed out that there's still an inherent inequality built into the structure of remote working itself, given that it primarily benefits professional 'white-collar' workers who are able to work online, and disadvantages workers who need to be physically present to perform their job, such as nurses, cleaners and hospitality workers. During the first year of the pandemic, when remote work was at its peak, 50% of those with a graduate degree were mostly working from home, compared to just 10% of those with no formal education qualifications.[4] However, there are still some aspects of traditional 'blue collar' jobs, such as paperwork, research, finance and scheduling, that can be done remotely.

As well as giving people more freedom to work on their own terms, another surprising benefit of remote working has been increased productivity. Pre-pandemic research from 2012 followed the US Patent Office as they experimented with allowing patent examiners to work from anywhere. The outcome was a 4.4% productivity gain.[5]

A lot of remote teams work asynchronously, or at different times, which has both positives and negatives. The advantages are that it allows for flexibility, and for the business to potentially function at all hours. Most of the disadvantages centre on the increased potential for misalignment, demotivation, loneliness and slacking off that can come when you're working at your own pace without the guidance of other colleagues.

Kim McKay prides herself on being ahead of the curve. She has a knack for seeing around corners, shifting her working styles and business to trends that she can sense coming before they fully arrive. Kim's career has wound through radio, then the music and travel industry, culminating in her starting her own business, a digital-focused communications agency called Klick.

For years, Kim knew that everyone's productive hours were different. She was most creative late at night, so she'd sometimes start her day mid-morning and work unusual hours. She always tried to shake her team out of the nine-to-five mentality. Occasionally she'd book a meeting into everyone's diary, only to surprise them with tickets to a movie in the middle of the day. 'I just wanted to prove that the world doesn't end if you step away for two hours,' she says, 'and when you go back you're probably better.'

Many of the trends that the rest of the working world struggled to adapt to at the start of the pandemic had already been road-tested by Kim. In 2019, she 'blew everything up' by rethinking how her business operated. She'd been desperately trying to hire a new staff member, who said they couldn't join her team in Sydney as they were moving to Stockholm. Kim didn't want to settle for someone who could make it into the inner-city office every day. 'Something's wrong with this picture,' she recalls. So she moved her business to a hybrid workplace, giving up the lease on a large office and telling her staff they could come into the office whenever suited them. The trend, deliciously free of the forced changes that would occur worldwide a year later, showed what an organic work schedule might look like. 'No one came in on Monday ever,' laughs Kim. 'By Tuesday you could see they started to miss each other or wanted some face-to-face time. On Wednesday they'd be out at meetings and then on Thursday, Friday they'd pop in. It was really interesting just to watch, because we didn't force it, we said, "If we want people to act like adults, let's treat them like that and see what happens."'

The biggest revelation, however, was the change in thinking about the purpose of the office. 'We realised that an office is the last place you go to do work. It's where you go to hang out, collaborate and communicate. Actual concentration never happens in open-plan offices.' Kim now runs her business completely remotely, eschewing a traditional office for the ability to connect with a team of gun contractors all around the world on a project-by-project basis.

But being a predominantly remote worker is not for everyone, and some experiments fail. Dan Joyce was the Chief Growth Officer at a meat-alternative start-up working in a fully remote role from London while the rest of his team were based in Australia, the US and the rest of the UK.

Dan was successful at his job, but within a few months of working almost fully remotely he found himself unfulfilled and bordering on depressed. 'Whether you call that isolated from working remotely or just not getting all the little jolts of energy from an in-person team, I missed out on something that, as it turns out, is absolutely imperative to me to have a fulfilling job,' he says.

As a remote worker, Dan's days started early to be online for the Australian time zone, and finished late so he could do the same with his American colleagues. He got together in person with his UK colleagues about one day a fortnight, but he felt that wasn't enough. 'I spent so much of the days at home by myself, trying to find that internal willpower and motivation to do what I knew I should be doing and could be doing, but half the time being challenged with just not feeling pumped and energised about what I was doing,' he says. 'And I should have been. I was doing the most incredible work, in an incredible industry, dealing with the most incredible restaurateurs around the world, and just found myself incredibly flat.'

Dan does a 'wheel of life' audit at the start of each year where he looks at the key parts of his life, including friends, health and money, and gives himself a score reflecting where he currently is and where he wants to be. When he did this a few months into his new role it was instantly clear that the way he was working was not working. His health was the lowest it had ever been, he was sluggish getting out of bed in the morning, found himself uncharacteristically playing video games on his phone and spending too much time on social media. 'I was not recognising a lot of my behaviours and who this person was,' he says. The areas of health and work were both flashing red at the same time. 'That's when I drew the line between the two, that there was a connection and that maybe work wasn't giving me as much purpose as I would've liked.'

Dan quit his remote working job, with a better understanding of exactly how he prefers to work. After this experiment, Dan has realised that there are other tools that suit his core values and priorities more. From this failed experiment, he has learnt that his ideal schedule is working four days a week in an office, energised by in-person colleagues, with a month of full flexibility each year to work anywhere in the world. These tools are now at the top of his list for any work he wants to do in the future.

How to use this tool

Remote working is a tool that suits some people, but not others. Here is how to use this tool to help you work smarter and live better:

1. Start with your company values.

Every company has a set of values that model the behaviour of its workers. For some companies, these are giant words painted onto walls and seared into the memories of everyone who works there. But company values are more than just statements, they are designed to be lived, breathed and used.

In order to create a successful working environment regardless of the location, start by using your company values as a guide. Allow them to lead the way on how remote work helps staff live up to the values when they're not in the office. If one of your company values is autonomous work, use that to help institutionalise working independently from home. If your business values creativity, use time outside the office to start the creative process, and then supercharge it when you all get together in-person a few days a week. (I wrote an entire book, *Killer Thinking*, about how to do this properly.) If one of your company values is transparency or openness, then establish really clear lines of communication and processes for when people are working from different places.

Every staff member, no matter how junior, can have a say in how a company's values are interpreted and used. See how you can fit remote working into your company's current values, and if you can't, then start a conversation with human resources or senior management about how it can be incorporated into future values.

2. Set clear boundaries.

Perhaps the most important aspect of remote working is setting and adhering to clear boundaries. Without them, the benefits can quickly dissolve into overwork, underpay and increased mental strain in your home environment.

'Having boundaries is not selfish,' says Arden Evenson, a content strategist who's spent half her career working as a full-time employee and the other half self-employed. 'Boundaries allow you to do your best work. It is good for you to know what those boundaries are, and you also have to let other people know what they are too.'

Clear boundaries are something that can only be set – and enforced – by you. If you don't clarify to yourself and those around you what hours you'll be working, when you won't be working, and how much of the work you've been assigned that you can physically and mentally complete, then the boundaries will begin to slide until they are no longer there. 'The individual has to take some ownership over it,' says Arden. 'And it's hard! I know it's hard, but you have to create space and then communicate it.'

In order to really understand the people you work with, and to set and communicate clear boundaries, you should have a user manual. This is a short template that everyone in your team fills out, detailing who they are and how they like to work. The aim is to get to know each other's needs so you can learn what the ideal working conditions are for your colleagues. It has the added benefit of helping you become more aware of your own ideal working styles, so you can lean further into these.

We all work differently. Some people like to start working as soon as they wake, then power through to the early afternoon before turning into a pumpkin after that. Others take hours for their brains to warm up, and are best engaged at twilight. Remote workers tend to dive in and out of work remotely, based around their children's nap times, sacred family dinners, or gym classes. Friction at work is one of the biggest killers of productivity, cohesiveness and happiness, so anything you can do to encourage empathy for each other's situations, and forge clearer lines of communication, is a winner. This is especially important in a world where many workplaces have a mixture of flexible, hybrid and remote work, and clear communication can be the defining factor in a project's success. In **IRL exercise 7** on page 259, I'll take you through how to set up your own user manual for you and your team, to help you set and communicate clear boundaries.

3. Work in public.
One of the biggest traps remote workers can make is to fall into obscurity within your business. When they're not visible in-person each day in an office, it can be easy to forget about remote workers or, even worse, to assume that they are just not being productive.

You can ensure you remain top-of-mind by working in public. This means being highly visible to other workmates on whichever platforms your company uses. It might be Slack, Teams, Google Docs, Canva, Jira, email or whatever software your company uses to keep projects on track. Working in public doesn't mean just flooding these zones with mindless content, it means being readily available during your working hours to answer any questions, and consistently contributing value in any way you can. Examples include 'end of day/week' emails that summarise what's happened and what's coming up, or in-depth work in progress (WIP) documents that contain the latest updates on a project and are regularly shared. Whatever way you want to communicate, if you're working from a remote location, do it in public.

4. Avoid hospital passes.

A hospital pass is a slang sporting term used in Australia and the UK to describe a poorly executed throw to a teammate where the recipient is likely to drop the ball as a result. It's also a good analogy of what not to do in this new world of work, where the ability to properly hand over projects to remote work colleagues can determine the success or failure of a project.

Handovers are a small problem you can solve with potential for a big impact. A structured, regular, concise document that is easily accessible, linking off to all relevant information, should be a minimum requirement when working remotely. If you don't have a clear handover procedure between different remote workers who are starting and finishing their shifts, it's easy to create one. When there are lot of stakeholders and moving parts, a clear handover can decrease confusion and increase productivity.

Tool: Hybrid working

I n 1979 the BBC aired a report predicting that the future of work was almost here. 'The office worker of the future may have to face not only a change of work style, but a change of workplace,' began host Michael Rodd. 'That's because the office of the future, already called a workstation, is so self-contained that it can exist almost anywhere, provided there is a telephone and electrical supply,' continued reporter Judith Hann as she awkwardly picked up a futuristic screen and laid it out flat on a desk.[1] 'So the necessary visual display unit, the electronic keyboard, computer and printer can be set up in your own house, and far more of us could be working from home by 1981.'

It was a bold prediction that would turn out to eventually come true, albeit not for another 40 years. Up until that point, for many workers the idea of 'working from home' was an occasional, one-off proposal to be negotiated with a lenient boss that was ripe with the potential to be abused. Then the pandemic forced anyone who could operate from home to do so.

Now hybrid work, where employees spend some days working from home and other days in the office, is increasingly common. The percentage of American workers who said they worked remotely shot from 5.7% pre-pandemic to around 42% in 2020.[2] That's a seismic once-in-a-generation shift in the way we work that will be felt for decades to come. Almost two years on, the trend was cemented in, with Gallup research reporting that 45% of full-time US employees worked from home either all or part of the time.[3] Now almost two-thirds of workers say they want to work a hybrid mix, spending some days in the office and the others at home,[4] and they are getting the opportunity to do that. In 2023, American workers who can, for example, spend about one-third of their workdays at home.[5]

One of the big debates in hybrid work is how many days is best, for both employees and employers. This obviously depends on which type of work you do; however, a US Survey of Working Arrangements and Attitudes tried to answer this by polling workers and their bosses, concluding that workers wanted to operate from home about 2.8 days a week, while employers wanted them to work from home about 2.3 days a week[6] – so there's not a huge difference in the expectations from either side. The actual number will vary based on your personal needs, desires, life stage and personality, but there are some models you can follow. One example is Tata Consultancy Services,[7] an Indian company that has around half a million employees around the world. Their working model is that 25% of an employee's time should be co-located with the team in an office, but it's up to individual teams within the business to decide how to best use that time. The rest of the time, employees can work remotely from anywhere, as long as they get their work done well. Australian tech company Atlassian have a 'Team Anywhere' policy that allows its 5700 staff to work from any location in a country where they have a corporate entity, and they only need to attend their nearest office four times a year. In a recent year, the company's co-founder, Scott Farquar, only went into the office three times over a 12-month period.[8]

Working from home is still a contentious issue in some industries where there's an office tug-of-war, with companies such as Goldman Sachs[9] and Elon Musk's X demanding 100% attendance in the office.

Shannon Molloy is a writer and editor who aims to work almost entirely from home. Although he initially committed to working two days out of the office in a post-Covid world, he estimates that he's barely in the office one day a week. As his team is spread out all over the country, he jokes that when he's in the office he spends most of his time in a meeting room on Zoom calls, anyway. 'I loathe the idea of going into the office,' he says. 'I can't even imagine how I ever worked only in an office setting.'

It's a sharp turnaround for Shannon, who spent most of the previous decade and a half in newsrooms that couldn't be accessed from outside the building. 'At the onset of the pandemic, the company I previously worked for had to pivot quickly to remote working. It was a nightmare. The systems were slow, buggy and prone to crashing.'

Shannon has a young child, and working from home means that when he closes his computer at 4 p.m., he can be with his baby in minutes. 'Working from home allows me to be a more present parent,' he says. 'I still struggle to be away from her for too long without getting a little melancholy. Working from home means I can be near her. I'm a sook, I know. If I was to work from the office every day, I'd miss her in the morning because I'd have to leave before she wakes, and I'd lose an hour with her in the afternoons while commuting home.'

Although many of these changes came in rapidly at the start of the pandemic, Shannon doesn't see things ever going back to the way they were. 'We've seen the light,' he says. 'Things are working relatively well. I suspect the ratio of office versus home will change – three or four days in the office, two or one at home perhaps. But a full-time permanent return? I doubt it.'

There are many good reasons why working from home has now become lodged into the lifestyle of workers around the world. The obvious benefits include avoiding the hassle, time and cost of commuting to and from work every day, and fewer distractions caused by co-workers interrupting you every few minutes to show you the latest trending video on TikTok (okay, maybe that was just at my media company!). But the biggest shift that working from home can bring about is more time for you to do what you want, living your life on your terms and your timetable. This increase in well-being can come about from being in your home environment, spending more time with your family or friends, and decreased stress levels from avoiding a high-pressure office environment.

The flipside to this, according to Dr Sean Gallagher from Swinburne University's Centre for the New Workforce, are what he calls the three Cs: 'Connection, communication and collaboration have really suffered from remote working,' he says. 'There's some value in working at home a couple of days a week. But I think coming back into the office and being around people and being humans is super important.' Research showed that working from home two days a week can boost an individual's productivity by about 5%. 'Longer than that and there are diminishing returns, but also you're missing out on the value of being in a workplace,' says Sean. 'The home is increasingly the place for the worker in the employee. And the office is increasingly the place for the human in the employee.' Getting the mix of worker and human is integral to meaningful work.

Working from home also has differing effects depending on the stage of your life. For mid- and late-career workers who previously had no choice but to work from a common workplace, the abrupt shift to occasionally working from home was a welcome change that helped break up the monotony of years of work. Many of these workers were able to draw on their deep well of experience to work more effectively from home than anywhere else. However, for early-career workers who are fresh to the workforce, removing the ability to watch, shadow and learn from more experienced co-workers is a loss that's difficult to recreate on video calls.

Hybrid working opens up possibilities that were not previously available, like the ability to live in a different country to the rest of your workmates. That's what Georgia McDonnell-Adams does as the Vice President of Partnerships for Boiler Room, a music and content company that unearths new and influential electronic artists. While most of her colleagues live and work close to London, she lives in Paris. Every Wednesday she catches the Eurostar train to London, a two-hour journey, and spends two days face-to-face with as many colleagues as possible before catching the train back to Paris on Thursday night. The commute may be long, but 'it pays off,' says Georgia. 'My family is settled in Paris, and childcare and school is so affordable here that we can still live in the city centre and enjoy a pretty cosmopolitan life.' The ability to decide what city to live in for lifestyle factors, instead of workplaces dictating where employees have to live, is a game changer for her.

Steven Hatfield knows where work is going. As the Global Leader of Future of Work for Deloitte, a multinational advisory firm with over 400,000 staff around the world, he advises the company and its clients on where he believes it's all going to end up. He is also somewhat of a rarity among the experts I spent time with for this book, in that he firmly believes that, in the long arc of work history, most of the radical changes will turn out to be positive. 'I'm a real possibilist,' he says. 'I look at trends in the data sets and I string them together to see the possibilities. I have a very optimistic view of things, based on the fact that it's highly possible that we could achieve this future that we're talking about, where we connect the dots around doing work that's more meaningful, working differently and performing as humans more.'

When the pandemic curtailed travel, Steven and his partner spent lockdown in their home in the Berkshires, a highland region between western Massachusetts and northwestern Connecticut in the United States. From there, he's built a team of colleagues who he works with mostly virtually, ensuring that he makes time in the middle of almost every workday to swim. He's a big advocate for hybrid working, when it's done well, and thinks too much time is spent in the weeds trying to find a silver-bullet solution instead of focusing on the principles of hybrid workplaces first. 'It really depends on the work and the function,' he says, giving the hypothetical example of a large company that has different departments looking after manufacturing, research, sales, marketing, finance and more. There is no single solution that would fit all the different types of workers. 'Each one would need a different sort of recipe based on the actual demand of work, so to try to blanket them into a three-day week structured model in an attempt to bring equity isn't going to work.' His advice, which he continues to model and test with his own workforce, is to frame the options as 'boundary-less'. 'A lot of boundaries that are used to structure jobs and hierarchy and process are all starting to erode in a way that makes it harder for leaders to appreciate where to go,' he says. 'A lot of the workforce is taking it and running with it. You need to lean into it and empower it to some extent by providing principles around the right experience, managing risks and generating trust.'

How to use this tool

There are obvious benefits to hybrid working, but you also need to be aware of the pitfalls so you can avoid them. This is how to make hybrid work best:

1. Know your working style.

When it comes to managing work and non-work activities, there are broadly two types of people: segmentors and integrators. Researcher Christena Nippert-Eng has studied people who create rigid boundaries between their work and personal lives.[10] Segmentors clearly align with the statement that 'In my life, there is a clear boundary between my career and my non-work roles', while integrators agree with 'It is often difficult to tell where my work life ends and my non-work life begins.'

Kathryn Dekas, the former Director of People Operations – Future of Work at Google, argues that knowing which type of worker you are can help you decide if hybrid work is right for you. 'Hybrid work, or remote work in particular, can be really hard for folks who prefer a much firmer boundary between their work and personal lives, and we saw that during the pandemic,' she says.

There's conflicting evidence on whether being a segmentor or integrator is better for your well-being, but the consensus is that knowing which one you are can at least help you better understand how you like to work. To be a successful hybrid worker, you often need to mentally switch quickly from one activity into another, like being a parent, and integrate work into your home-life activities, for example taking a work call while you're cooking dinner. There is no right or wrong style, but having an awareness will help you determine if hybrid working is for you.

2. Over-communicate.

If there's one thing that determines the success or failure of a hybrid workplace, it's the level of clear communication between employees at all levels: worker to manager, colleague to colleague, boss to direct report, department to department. When locations are mixed, there's more danger of people not knowing what's going on, or who's working on what project and from where.

The key to overcome this is the principle of over-communication. There should be no doubt at any time about:

- who is working from where and when (have a clear shared calendar)
- who is online at what hours (have a clear schedule)
- how to contact anyone at any time (have a clear contact list)
- who is doing what (have a clear set of responsibilities).

By removing the unknowns in a work environment, you can clear the path for it to be sustainable and effective.

One of the best ways to ensure clear communication is to set up a RACI matrix. Pronounced 'racy' (which makes it seem a tad sexier than it is), it stands for responsible, accountable, consulted and informed. It's a simple and popular model used to clarify who is doing exactly what on any project that you're working on. RACI aims to avoid the messy situation where lots of people are working on a project, but no one has any idea what each person is doing, and you all end up doubling up on tasks and redoing things and hating everything and everyone around you.

Sound familiar? If so, it's time to get RACI. This can solve a lot of the problems associated with hybrid working and ensure there is no confusion. In **IRL exercise 8** on page 262 I'll show you how to create your own RACI matrix.

3. Focus on trust.

A determining factor in successful hybrid work is trust, both that the worker will not abuse the freedom of working from home, and that a business has set up sufficient structures for it to work. Trust at work is painstakingly developed, yet easily lost, and it is the essential building block for a hybrid workplace.

Pre-pandemic, a lack of trust was the primary reason hybrid working remained off limits for all but the most trustworthy of employees. The idea that someone could be sitting on the couch, in bed or at their kitchen table, and working as efficiently as they would in their office cubicle, was almost laughable. On the rare occasions that this freedom was allowed, it had to be earned over time. Now, after a few years of proving that it can be done, trust is still essential to effectively operate in a hybrid environment.

Hertta Vuorenmaa is the Chair of the Finnish Association of Work Life Research and Research Director of Future of Work at Aalto University. When I speak with her she is working remotely from her holiday house in Finland, using video conferencing to enjoy summer and work at the same time. 'We've had technologies to work like this since the nineties,' she tells me, 'but no one really took it seriously until the pandemic. 'It was never about technologies, it was always about trust.'

For the past five years, Hertta and her team have tracked many of the 50 largest businesses in Finland to identify what some of the most successful companies have in common in terms of managing the fast-changing world of work. This has involved longitudinal qualitative interviews with senior leadership to better understand how technology is changing the way they work, manage people and organise work-related processes. The companies that are leading the way in her research are those most adaptable to change. 'They are sitting people down and saying, "Okay, we're going to get a bunch of new tools. We already have a bunch of new tools. Your jobs have already changed, our business is going to change within a few years. So how do we rethink this together?"'

Before the pandemic, most organisations Hertta worked with told her that they had tasks that could only be performed face-to-face, like selling, or discussing highly sensitive issues. 'It didn't matter what kind of business it was, I got the same story,' she says. 'And now, actually, we realise that some of the things work so much better [in a hybrid world].' The businesses that are excelling the most, however, have been working towards adapting to the coming changes for years.

One of the ways you earn trust is by being honest and transparent. Ensure that everyone around you knows how you're dealing with your workload, when you've got capacity or roadblocks, and encourage an open relationship that prioritises truth over a facade.

4. Adapt and learn.
Like every potential tool to help you work better, sometimes a hybrid approach will work brilliantly, and other times it will be a hindrance. Hybrid working is new, and it's a style of working that has evolved so much over the last few years that it's become commonplace. It will also continue evolving, so just because something worked well in the past doesn't mean it will continue to work in the future. 'A lot of our assumptions about work have changed,' says Kathryn Dekas. 'I don't think people have developed all the skills yet. Managers haven't, organisations haven't yet … So as a society and working culture we have a ton of learning to do.'

Keep an open mind and treat it as a constant experiment. If you find the number of days you spend in any one environment is not working, then communicate the reasons with your colleagues and switch it up. It's only through adapting to different stages of your life and work projects that you'll master how to best use this tool.

Most of the lessons on how to use these tools can still be applied whether you're a worker, manager or business owner, and whether you work in a traditional office or on a worksite, in a hospital, a school or elsewhere. A lot of jobs have parts to them, such as paperwork, emailing and organising, that can be performed outside a set location. If you're a worker struggling to know how to communicate some of these new options to your bosses, start a conversation about which of these tools you'd like to experiment with. You might even want to pass this book on after you've completed it, and use it as a springboard to talk about new ways of working. The future of work is here, but you need to reach out and grab it.

Tool: Flexible working

lexible working is an umbrella term that tries to catch all of the different ways work can be bent to fit the employee, instead of the other way around. Flexible work might include changing the usual start and finish times of a job, taking time off during the day to do personal tasks like picking kids up from school, or working for a very short window of time.

There's a lot of data that backs up the benefits of changing a work schedule to suit individual needs, and this is quickly becoming a non-negotiable, with one-third of workers saying they'd sacrifice a pay increase for the ability to work a fully flexible schedule.[1]

So what does flexible working actually look like in the real world? Here are some examples:

- shifting from full-time to part-time work so you work fewer hours
- changing the hours you work to start early or late, depending on your needs
- job-sharing, where two or more people work on one job together
- shift work, working during different, variable hours

- getting time off in lieu for hours worked overtime
- working seasonally, or only during certain times, like the
  school or academic year
- incorporating a siesta, or break/sleep time, into your day, as
  is customary in countries like Spain, Italy and Greece.

Flexible working is not a new phenomenon. It has been pioneered by
working women, in particular, for a long time. Since the invention
of the modern office last century, women have traditionally left
their careers during some of their peak earning years to raise young
families. Their subsequent re-entry into the workforce often served
as early experiments in how to make flexible working a success.
Juggling naps, childcare pick-up and drop-off times, feeding times
and school hours meant that many working parents have had to
work irregular hours without affecting their output.

Flexible working can mean moving days around to suit your
preferred lifestyle. Ryan Jon is a 35-year-old full-time podcaster
from Melbourne. He was working as a radio announcer when he
started a comedy podcast with his friend, Toni Lodge. Within five
months of launching their show, the *Toni and Ryan* podcast had
been downloaded five million times, and in 2022 they signed a
lucrative multi-year sponsorship deal with Spotify.

They now produce five episodes a week, but work very flexible
hours and try to batch most of their work into the beginning of
the week. Mondays are for planning, and on Tuesdays they record
all five weekly episodes in one sitting. 'On the planning day, we'll
have a thirty-minute chat at about nine am and lock in what we're
going to talk about the following day,' explains Ryan. 'Each topic
is led by Toni or I, so whoever is leading a certain topic then has a
whole twenty-four hours to figure out how we're going to talk about
it.' They've learned that recording all of their weekly episodes on

the same day works best for them personally. 'I'm an introvert so I need to build up to getting "in the zone" and then I'm exhausted afterwards,' says Ryan. 'We also noticed that after doing one episode, we're all revved up and having fun, so why stop? Keep that momentum going!'

Ryan's schedule is flexible, and it needs to be. When his daughter was born in early 2023, he took comfort in knowing that most of the heavy lifting, planning and recording of their podcast was completed by Tuesday each week. During the rest of the week he and Toni can still have Zoom calls and meetings, but he is generally free to spend time with his child.

The reasons someone would want to choose flexible working are numerous. There are internal drivers like freedom, independence and the desire to choose where and when to spend your focus. And there are external forces that require attention during standard hours, such as young children, and disability or caregiving responsibilities.

Flexible working benefits employers as well. Zac Rich is based in Los Angeles and works in a senior legal role with energy drink company Red Bull. He leads a team of government and regulatory affairs professionals who guide the business through any issues that arise, and enjoys the option of a more balanced work model. This enables him to cast a wider net when considering new candidates. 'It means we can look further afield for a broader cross-section of people to join our team. From a diversity point of view, there's more room for primary-care parents who need to be home on certain days of the week, or to hire applicants who live further away from city centres. It genuinely increases our diversity, while attracting and retaining the best people.'

Alexa Sabberton has been working remotely from her home in Oxfordshire in the UK as the founder of Personal Publicity, now five years old, where she manages the public profile of actors. She describes her own relationship with work as 'a rollercoaster', but she can't see herself doing anything else. Before working for herself, Alexa worked with large teams, until work broke her. 'My mental health suffered hugely working at those agencies where the pressure was ever-increasing,' she tells me. Working for herself to manage her own pressure was the only option for her, especially when considering starting a family. 'It has been hugely rewarding, in so many ways, while definitely massively challenging also.'

Alexa now takes advantage of a very flexible work schedule, fitting work into her life as a mother of one. She works roughly four full days a week, when her child is in day care, and usually tries to pack her mornings with intense work so after lunch she can multitask at home – but inevitably, work does bleed into evenings and weekends. She has a love/hate relationship with working from home. 'I love the freedom of starting my day when I want and being able to get jobs done while I work, but it's incredibly easy to procrastinate and to fail to set boundaries or even leave the house in a day.' She says that working from home has been a 'game changer for her', but that balance is key, with her ideal schedule working from her garden-studio office at home for two to three flexible days a week and travelling to London around once a week to be with clients and attend meetings.

Ben Lucas is a 28-year-old strategist from Sydney, but he prefers to think of himself as a professional problem-solver, working with businesses to help them come up with better solutions. He works an average of three to four days a week. 'My perception of work as this nine-to-five thing that you do for one place has been broken by the changes to ways of working,' he says. 'I've always thought "I can't be a good strategist for eight hours a day" – do you know how mentally exhausting that is? Focusing on anything for eight hours becomes counterproductive at some point.'

Ben left his full-time job and took on a part-time contract role that paid his bills, giving him the rest of the time to work on projects that excited him, like side hustles or spending time reading, learning or just chilling out. 'Work now feels more closely aligned to my life, or what I want my life to be,' he says. 'The idea of work–life balance gives us this idea of evenly split scales, or for most people, a seesaw, but pitting work and life at opposite sides of the scales is the wrong approach, we should strive for work–life synergy, or work–life symbiosis. That feels more like what I'm building towards and, as a result, I'm very rarely stressed about anything now.'

Ben rents a co-working space 20 minutes from his home. He enjoys the relationships he's building there without the baggage. 'We're stimulated with conversation around the office without ever having someone ask you to do something for them. It's amazing.' To change up his environment, he splits his time between working from there and from home, sometimes even both in the same day to break it up. He also tries to keep at least one day a week just for himself. 'It's wild the energy you feel on a sunny Friday where you wake up, can exercise, go for a swim and then have the day to work on the ideas that keep you up at night. Even doing this one day a week, you can find a new sense of purpose in what you do. You don't feel like you have to live for the weekend, you can live for the week. It brings new excitement.'

How to use this tool

1. Centre the human.
Sometimes the mechanics of how to work best in a flexible way can take precedence over the actual impact it has on people. Workplaces often begin with the mechanics of it all: What hours should we work?

Where should we work? How many days should we work at home or from the office? What days of the week? Should everyone work at the same time? And on it goes. Of course, the details on how and when you should be flexible are important, but it is sometimes just noise that gets in the way of what is really important: the human at the centre of it all.

If you're going to successfully implement flexibility in your workplace, or lobby your bosses to run an experiment, you have to be flexible with some of the rules. Having hard and fast regulations that can't be broken goes against the spirit of making it a useful and productive way of working. Worry less about how many hours you should be working in each location, and think more about what that means for the humans that make up the workforce.

Go easy on yourself and your teammates, ensuring you still carve out time for enjoyable activities throughout your workday to keep yourself fresh. Geoff McDonald, the former Vice President of HR at Unilever, pointed out a fascinating fact from a research study that compared people who had suffered burnout during the pandemic to those who hadn't. 'You know what they had?' he asks. 'A dog! The dog forced them to go out for a walk during the course of the day, twice a day. It was one of the variables that had prevented that group from being burnt out.' It's important to schedule frequent breaks to remind you to keep the human element at the core of our thinking about the future of work. Do that, and the rest of the technical answers will flow a lot easier.

2. Learn how to laser-focus.

When you work flexibly, every hour is important. Flexible working generally means working fewer hours in bursts where you need to focus as intently as you can to get your work done. There are various techniques that can help you do this, so figure out which work best for you. Some examples include putting noise-cancelling headphones on, or playing music that helps you to concentrate, like chilled lo-fi beats or familiar music that your brain can tune out to. For some people, the sound of low-volume white noise, like when the fan in your computer starts blowing loudly, helps them focus. It could also be something visual, like a sign near your desk or on your home office door that tells other people that you're working, to help reduce interruptions and maximise your work time. Whatever it is, find a technique that can help you be as productive as possible during your working hours.

Boundaries around how you spend your time can also help you stay motivated when the line between when you are and aren't working is fluid. Laura Giurge is an Assistant Professor at the London School of Economics. She was a postdoctoral research fellow at Cornell University when she began carving out time to read uninterrupted and realised the benefit it had on how she worked. 'It was not something that was urgent, but it was very important for me to stay on top of research,' she says. 'I did that for at least an hour in the morning and I just saw the benefits of doing so in a consistent way.'

Laura formalised her idea into an approach she calls proactive time. It's a simple concept that means being intentional with what you're aiming to do during a certain time; a heightened version of concentration. You should block out time in your diary for specific tasks you want to complete that are important but non-urgent. These tasks are determined in a 30-minute check-in session that's usually held at the start or end of the week. During this session, you create a list of all your upcoming work tasks, listing them in order of urgency and importance, and you then book in proactive time, ideally in two-hour blocks, to work on each task. When the allocated time comes around, minimise distractions by turning your phone and emails off, and letting workmates know not to disturb you, then dive deep into the work. Some people find this easier to do when working from home without colleagues around to distract them in person. 'If you bundle things in specific hours and block interruptions from outside, you can do a lot more things in two hours and feel satisfied for completing something in one go,' she says.

Laura has done a lot of research into the effectiveness of proactive time. In one study with a consumer goods company, employees who used proactive time reported greater productivity compared to those who didn't, as well as reduced feelings of burnout if they stuck with it, especially across the span of at least four weeks.[2] Many others have confirmed the same findings, showing that advance intent, and a little bit of planning, can have a big impact. Proactive time is one way you can add boundaries to a fluid world that blurs when and how you work.

3. Borrow from history.

Flexible work is not a new invention – it has been around for as long as humans have worked. Learn lessons from the past, and incorporate them into the way you work. In many European countries, such as Spain and Italy, people work until lunchtime, then take a few hours off to eat, spend time with family and take a nap or a siesta. Most people then return to work in the late afternoon for a second shift.

It's a flexible working tradition that dates back over 2000 years to Roman times, when they used to count the hours of the day starting from sunrise. The sixth hour of the day, or *sexta* in Latin, was around lunchtime, when they took a break from their work, and the heat, to eat and rest.

Working parents have used flexible work arrangements for centuries to juggle home life with earning an income, and some of the tools they have forged can be borrowed. Take job sharing, a common tool used when a working parent returns to the workforce but can't work full-time. Instead, some workers will share the role with others in a similar situation, dividing up the hours and ensuring there are clear handovers between shifts. History has many cases of flexible working, where work has taken a second seat to other things in life. We should look to examples from the past to identify what we can integrate into our present.

4. Think beyond video calls.

One of the lasting legacies of the pandemic is the rise of video conferencing. Within a few months of 2020, the ability to see a colleague's face on a video call on Zoom, Teams or Google Hangouts superseded phone calls and became the default method of communication. There are amazing benefits to using video as a tool to better connect with people, instead of just audio, but just because it exists doesn't mean you always need to use it.

The automatic setting on most calendars now is to invite someone to a video conference – but it doesn't have to be. The reason it's the default option is that the makers of your calendar software, for example Google and Microsoft, want to keep you spending as much time as possible on their closed systems. Instead, you can actively fight against that and schedule a wide variety of meeting formats: in person, over coffee, at a bar. You can also utilise the old-fashioned mobile phone as a primary way of communicating at work. The ability to do something else, like walking around the city block, making lunch or driving home, while also conducting a meeting will give you hours back if you can replace enough meetings.

Video conferencing should be viewed as another tool that works well in certain situations, but not in every one. Not everything needs to be a video call, and changing up the format of communication is one of the hallmarks of a successful flexible worker. Make some meetings a phone call, do other things by email, send a private Slack message or meet in person if you have the opportunity. Always aim to use the right medium for the message.

Tool: Four-day work week

The promise of a shorter working week has been dangled tantalisingly in front of us for a long time. In 1956, then US Vice President Richard Nixon promised his fellow Americans they would only have to work four days 'in the not too distant future'. A few intrepid state governments experimented sporadically with four-day working weeks, like Utah in the early 1990s, which scheduled four ten-hour days for city employees. Iceland, always a progressive experimenter, conducted several large-scale trials a decade later, which they declared an 'overwhelming success'.

However, it was a legal services company from New Zealand that properly started a seismic generational shift to legislating shorter working hours around the world. The medium-sized company, Perpetual Guardian, was founded by Andrew Barnes, and in 2018 it tested a change in working hours for its 240 employees. That change ignited a global trend with the potential to change the way we work.

When I speak with Andrew, who now divides his time between England and New Zealand, he's just returned to his Auckland apartment after three months away. 'I am a great subscriber to "he who dies with the most passports wins",' he jokes of his transcontinental lifestyle.

Andrew's official title reads 'Architect of Global Movement Behind the Four-day Week'. It's a trend with so much momentum behind it that it's taken Andrew by surprise. 'This is not a journey I expected to be on. It's not arguably what we even set out to do.' As builders work around him to complete his apartment, he confides with a smile: 'You don't get many chances to change the world, and suddenly it looks like we're changing the world.'

Andrew originally set out to test the thesis that he could get better productivity out of his team if he reimagined the way their work was structured. His original aim was to simply test the productivity question: What would happen if he made a small tweak to the number of hours his employees worked? What would happen if he mandated that they worked 20% less? 'When I announced it in my own company, there was nobody in my leadership team, no board member, who supported it,' he says. 'The only reason it got through is because I was the principal shareholder in the company!'

Andrew pushed the trial through, and after two months was shocked to find that 78% of employees said they were able to successfully manage their life–work balance, compared to 54% the previous year. Their self-reported stress levels had decreased by 7%, and overall life satisfaction grew by 5%. Andrew announced their results to the world, adding that he'd seen enough to make the change permanent, and the resulting tsunami of publicity overwhelmed the small team. They stopped counting when they reached about 13,000 global news stories about their successful experiment, estimating that billions of people saw some part of their results. 'I didn't expect that this little experiment would get such a global reaction,' says Andrew, 'and the fact it did says I think we're ready for a rethink of how we work.'

Since then, Andrew and his partner, Charlotte Lockhart, are aiming to push it from a mad idea to a mainstream one, although the idea is still without universal implementation. Andrew and Charlotte now help coordinate thousands of tests in companies around the world, from Canada to Belgium, America to Romania. Workers in almost every country, when asked by researchers, have said they'd like to work from home or have shorter working hours – except in one country. In Bangladesh, researchers from Unilever were surprised when their results bucked the trend, signifying that workers would prefer to come into an office every day. When the researchers followed up with the respondents, who were predominantly young women, they discovered why. There was one thing in their homes that the women were happy to escape for a few hours: their mothers-in-law.

One of the reasons Andrew thinks four-day weeks are inevitable is because the way we are working is seriously broken. He runs through a shopping list of statistics: one in five people in the workforce will have a stress or mental health issue. In the UK alone, 17.9 million sick days a year are caused by work-related stress, adding up to a $56 billion hit to the economy. Decades of work have hardly shifted the gender pay gap. The share of care responsibilities disproportionately falls on women's shoulders. Our productivity is generally caught in a perverse trap of more work and less productivity. Andrew points out that countries which work the longest often have the worst productivity outcomes. A lot of these symptoms, he says, are 'a reflection of a world where everything has been sacrificed on the altar of work. What defines us is often not who we are, it's what we do.'

In 2022, the Australian government held an eight-month inquiry, chaired by Greens Senator Barbara Pocock, into the impact that combining work and care responsibilities has on the well-being of workers, carers and those who they care for. Over the course of 11 days of public hearings and 125 submissions, they produced a

262-page report that made dozens of recommendations on how to improve conditions for all workers, including a recommendation that the government review the standard working hours of all Australians.[1] 'The nineteenth-century social contract that provided workers and their households a living income in exchange for their work, is no longer fit for a world where so many workers have caring responsibilities and where so many women join men at work.' One of the conclusions was a recommendation that all Australian employees who could, should trial a four-day work week at full pay.

There is now more research emerging on the results of four-day week trials around the world, with one theme coming up repeatedly: 'When people experience these working time reductions, they don't want to go back,' says Brendan Burchell from the University of Cambridge. Every week, additional data becomes available from hundreds of companies with thousands of employees who are experimenting with working four days a week. The data shows that most companies choose to continue paying their employees the same salary as if they worked five days a week, and find that they can get the same amount of work done even with this 20% reduction in hours worked.

Results from nearly 3000 UK workers who completed 12 months of working four-day weeks concluded that more than 90% of the companies would continue it, mainly due to benefits like a 71% reduction in employee burnout levels and a 43% improvement in mental health.[2] Interestingly, data from these research studies shows that these positive outcomes are generally better for women than men, across factors like mental health, and life and job satisfaction. Other studies found benefits such as less stress, better sleep and more time to invest in other areas of your life.[3]

And if that wasn't enough to convince you or your boss, there's an environmental argument for it too. It's estimated that a worldwide shift to shorter work weeks could cut the total number of carbon dioxide emissions this century by a third.[4] However, Brendan points out that we're still at the very early stage of mass adoption. 'So far, most of the research has been done in small and medium-sized enterprises, and concentrated around professional-type work ... but we are now getting more diverse companies involved in manufacturing and the public sector, like hospitals.'

But there are those who caution the shift to a four-day working week. Dr Sean Gallagher believes that the pendulum will eventually swing back to employers dictating that their staff work five days a week. 'I personally don't see the four-day week working for three reasons,' he explains. 'For a start, the four-day work week is really only for knowledge workers for the most part ... The second thing is that we've become less efficient in the work that we are doing ... But the third point is that it's a bigger question here: what is the purpose of work? Is the purpose of work to just do productive output and only do that for four days of the week? Is it just that productive output? And that's all we do as humans? I think it devalues us as the human in the worker.'

Other critics also point to the Hawthorne effect, referring to learnings from a series of studies conducted by sociologist Elton Mayo at the Hawthorne plant of a Western Electric Company in America.[5] Mayo made small changes to the workers' conditions, like altering the lighting, food breaks and working hours, and observed that change affected productivity. It was the start of modern employee engagement, but many people argue that it also proved that when people know they are being observed, they perform better. Similar conclusions are being drawn regarding the positive results coming from research into the four-day work week.

However, despite the scepticism, most of the evidence is mounting up that there are countless positive benefits to working less and living more, proving that the four-day work week is one of the most powerful tools that we have to help fix a broken work system.

How to use this tool

Testing out a shorter work week is one of the best ways of rebalancing work and life, but it needs to be done in the right way.

1. Engage everyone at every stage.

The push for a shorter working week can come from anywhere. Some progressive employees and switched-on managers who follow the countless media stories around the topic might already be curious, but any worker who wants to improve their conditions can push for it. Share some of the mountain of research studies with your managers and encourage them to run an experiment to see if it could work in your workplace. If you do decide to implement a four-day work week, instead of focusing on the process, focus on the people who will help create the processes.

Andrew Barnes has helped more companies switch to four-day weeks than anyone else in the world, and his advice to managers is simple. 'At the heart of a successful four-day week implementation is recognising that you have to engage your employees as a critical part of the journey,' he says. 'A lot of this is not about process re-engineering, it's about attitude re-engineering and cultural change.'

If you're an employee, ask to be involved in the process so you can co-create it with your bosses to ensure that everyone has a say. This is not the type of change that should be announced one day and implemented the next without consultation. Everyone in the company should be involved far in advance in order to design the best programme together. There are lots of variations in what a shorter working week can look like, and everyone, from management to workers, should go into it collectively with a spirit of experimentation to give it the best chance of working.

2. Unclear is unkind.

This learning comes from one of my favourite lessons from Brené Brown, research professor at the University of Houston and best-selling author and speaker. 'Clear is kind. Unclear is unkind,' says Brené. This saying can be consistently applied to different aspects of work and life. 'Most of us avoid clarity because we tell ourselves that we're being kind, when what we're actually doing is being unkind and unfair,' she wrote.[6]

The same can be said about shifting to a new way of working. When there are unknowns, the best thing you can do is provide clear guidelines and open communication, and answer everyone's questions (even when the answer is 'I genuinely don't know'). There is always fear when doing something that hasn't been done before, but providing as much information as you can about how the process is going, and being clear on the expectations around workload and working times, can go some way to increasing the chances of success.

3. Trial before you dial.

I've helped several companies run experiments on four-day weeks, and it's always fascinating to observe how different people deal with change. The biggest learning from these experiences is that each team, business and industry is unique, and there's no one-size-fits-all when it comes to employees. That's why it's recommended that you choose a set trial period, usually from two to six months, to test it out with staff. Like any experiment, you should test and measure results before, during and after the period so you can see what effect it's had.

When I've introduced a four-day work week into a new business, this is how I continually measure it to see its impact. I set up a regular survey and ask the following questions of everyone in the company, getting them to assign their responses on a scale of 1–10 and watching how they change over time. You can also use them as a basis for measurement at your workplace, and suggest that senior management use these as a guide:

- If you had to assess your overall happiness (in both work and life) right now, where would it be?
- How would you rate your overall mental well-being right now?
- How would you rate your work productivity right now?
- How would you rate your connection with your work colleagues right now?
- How would you rate your satisfaction with work right now?
- How would you rate your ability to effectively work on side projects/hobbies/interests right now?

You should ask these questions before kicking off any experiment so you have a baseline level, and then track the responses on a regular basis, taking note of any changes. Before starting, you should also be clear about exactly what outcomes you're expecting, so that you can determine if the trial has been successful or not. One of the companies I helped successfully transition to a four-day work week is SYMO Interactive, the media company founded by Glen James from This Is Money. They are a small and focused team of around seven employees. We initially began with a three-month trial over a quiet period. There was some initial hesitation from staff members, mainly focused on the finer details of how it would work, as well as excitement at being on the forefront of a new way of working. But most of that doubt fell away quickly, with regular check-in surveys confirming that every element that we tracked, including happiness, mental well-being and satisfaction with work, all improved over the course of the experiment.

When I call Glen almost a year later to check how he's going, he is outside working on his 7.5-metre Sea Ray boat, which is parked in his driveway. He says that the transformation has been revolutionary, forcing them to rethink the way they operated. 'As a business owner, it really got me thinking,' he says. Glen says there has been no drop in productivity across the business, and it's encouraged him to focus more and get his work completed in a shorter amount of time each week.

He now spends just two days a week at his desk recording podcasts or having internal meetings. The additional freedom has allowed him to start an educational course two days a week, studying maritime operations, so he can lean further into his passion of boating. 'I don't think I would have done that if the rest of the team didn't have Fridays off,' he says. 'To be honest, doing those two days a week studying something completely different than my work actually makes me a better podcaster. I'm more engaged when I'm back talking about money because the next day I'm talking with people about boat stuff. The change has been wild.'

4. Think output, not hours.

The usual way that we measure how hard someone works is time. We've used the hours someone sits at their physical desks as a proxy for how hard they work. An employee who arrived early and left late was held in high esteem, as something to aim towards. The term 'presenteeism' was even coined to described being physically at your workplace and appearing dedicated, no matter how unproductive you are.

A shift to a shorter work week changes the focus from looking at the hours someone works to looking at the productivity and outcomes they can achieve during those hours. It's a large mental jump, and something that needs to be agreed at all levels of a company and modelled from the top down. It means new ways of measuring performance and rewarding effort that focus on what someone does, instead of how they do it. As long as a worker can perform all the tasks they are meant to as part of their job, they should be celebrated.

Although the four-day work week is still a relatively new phenomenon, and one that will take decades to properly cascade through our society, early research results suggest it is a one-way street, with some studies reporting that a whopping 90% of companies that complete an experiment are implementing it permanently.[7] It doesn't matter if you're a junior employee or run your own business, you can still play a role in introducing the future to your workplace.

Tool: Career breaks

There are myriad ways you can break up your working life so it doesn't feel like a never-ending slog. One of the most common, and effective, is a sabbatical, or a career break. Taking an extended period off work so you can properly rest and renew before tackling the next chapter is gaining popularity. Data from the Society for Human Resource Management shows that the number of people taking large chunks of time out of their career tripled from 2018 to 2022.[1] Much of that was driven by a reassessment of priorities due to the forced changes during the pandemic.

The finishing line for most workers is when they retire from full-time work. This is usually around 65 years old, with many governments around the world gradually increasing the official retirement age in order to reduce their growing pension burden as the global population ages. Retiring from full-time work is the ultimate goal, a date marked deep into workers' psyches as they crawl towards the finish line. But after they cross it, overnight they go from working five days a week to not working at all.

There are several problems with this. Firstly, switching off their earning capacity overnight is a massive jolt to the economics, and lifestyle, of the retiree. Secondly, it's a devastating 'brain drain' to think that we just switch off all the value and wisdom gained in four decades of work as we walk out the door on retirement day. The third problem, due to medical advances, is that this final stage of life can last for another four decades. That's an extremely long time to stretch out the retirement income we're meant to have saved.

When you distil our careers down to their most basic form, most people have three distinct stages: learn, earn and burn.

Learn: The first 20 or so years of our life are dedicated to education. Primary, secondary and senior school until our late teens, then maybe an apprenticeship, on-the-job training or some further study at university, colleges or other forms of higher education depending on vocation and desire. For most people, the learning stage comes to an abrupt halt somewhere in our twenties, when we move into the next stage.

Earn: We generally enter the full-time workforce in our late teens or early twenties, and work basically non-stop until we retire somewhere in our sixties. There is occasional time off this treadmill, most commonly to raise a young family, but we have four decades to earn as much as we can to set us up for the final stage.

Burn: After retirement in our sixties or seventies, we burn through the money that we've (ideally) saved during the earn phase, or that's paid by our social security safety net, depending on where we live. The rate of burn, how long it lasts and how much assistance you get from governments, charities and pensions during this phase vary a lot depending on the outcomes of your Learn and Earn phases.

In the early history of work, these stages were determined by our physicality. We worked on farms to hunt and harvest food as soon as we were physically able, then toiled for as long as our bodies would allow. The final phase, a prehistoric form of retirement, came on when our bodies forced us to stop. It was a simple system that only really evolved during the first industrial revolution. Since then, the three stages of Learn, Earn and Burn have dictated how we work and live. Moving through each of them in order is the default mode we've come to expect, following a straight path from one stage to the next.

This is what it looks like if we plot a typical life on a scale:

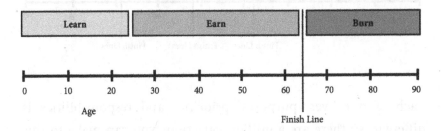

Seeing our lives laid out from birth to death – at around 90 years old for most people, slightly older for women – can be confronting, especially when you add your own position onto the linear scale.

Where are you on this scale? It might be a sudden jolt to realise that you're in the tail end of your supposed earning years. Or it could be a realisation that you're still near the starting blocks of a forty-year slog that lies ahead of you. Living life in a straight line with no breaks can feel stifling, boring and predictable, but it's the only model we're taught when we are in the pivotal transition period between the Learn and Earn stages of life.

The truth is that you can switch up the three stages as much as you want. If you were to insert two career breaks into your life, roughly ten years apart, to spend time travelling the world and learning a new language, then you would have a life scale that's peppered with multiple finish lines. Each of them would be within sight of each other, so it wouldn't feel like a lifetime of hard work just to get to the end.

This is what that could look like:

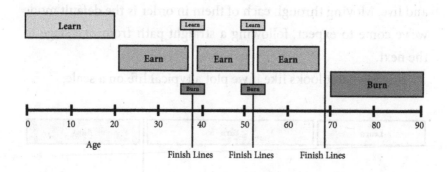

Each of our lives, purposes, priorities and responsibilities is different, so there are a million variations you can make to this life scale to personalise it. For example, another model is to overlap all of the stages, making the outcome less linear, with more integration between them. In this case, learning becomes a lifelong aim, earning capacity extends beyond a traditional retirement when your knowledge is at its peak, and you spread your spending across a longer time period with less emphasis on always wanting more, instead learning how to be happy with your version of 'enough'. This is the idealised model that I am now trying to live, where there's an enjoyment of each stage over your entire life, instead of automatically shifting between them with a defined start and finish.

If we were to draw this one, it would look like this:

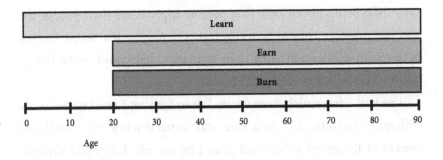

Rather than thinking of work as having a finish line, imagine there are several finish lines that you'll reach along the way. When you get to each one, give yourself permission to stop, celebrate the achievement, look back at where you've come from and properly recuperate before starting the next one. We need to normalise taking time out of the constant career climb to assess whether we want to keep going, or sit on the sidelines for a while and cheer other people on. In **IRL exercise 9** on page 265, you'll be able to create your own life scale, adding in whatever finish lines you like.

Arden Evenson is an experienced content strategist who's spent half her career working as a full-time employee and the other half self-employed. She's a self-described 'recovering overachiever' who spent lots of time during the pandemic rethinking her own relationship with work and helping those around her do the same. 'There's a certain definition of achievement and success that's about moving upward on a corporate or academic ladder,' she says, adding that most of the clients she works with, friends and colleagues are tuned to think this way. 'It's requiring us to do a lot of unlearning to re-navigate and figure out what our own definitions of ambition and success are.' Sometimes it's the little things you can change that have big impacts. 'I was talking to a lot of people who were really miserable in their job and in ways that felt in many cases not fixable, but there are always small things that can be tweaked,' she says. 'Maybe it's about how that person approaches their job, or the specific projects they're working on. Or maybe it's about having better communication with their manager that could make things better. Maybe not perfect but better.'

I've had a few finish lines in my life so far that I used to delineate different chapters. My first one was experiencing my childhood dream of living on a deserted island by myself. I detailed some of what happened in my first book, *Cult Status*, and I feel like my life can be divided into before and after that experience. I then spent over a decade building media titles like *Same Same, AWOL, Punkee* and *Junkee*. I had a clear finish line in mind for this period of my life: selling our company, Junkee Media. For years, my business partner and I would discuss what life might look like on the other side of running a demanding company. Selling it was a protracted effort that took a few years from the moment the board and shareholders agreed to put it on the market, to the moment we signed the contract. Even then, once the finish line was finally in sight, part of the sale hinged on myself, and other key staff, signing multi-year contracts to continue working for the new parent company.

I signed a three-year contract, which originally felt like an eternity, but at least I knew the next finish line had a firm date on it. What I didn't realise was that I would genuinely enjoy the challenge of learning how to work inside a larger company. It was a new set of obstacles and opportunities, and – after discussions with my husband to ensure our timelines aligned – I extended my earn-out period for an additional year. My first major finishing line was selling a company – something I'd dreamed about many times during the business journey – and it gave me the impetus to properly step back and reassess everything about my life.

You don't need to even put a final finish line in your plan. You can continue to derive meaning, identity and a sense of community from work for as long as you physically and mentally can. Take Warren Fahey, who at 77 years old is in one of the most productive periods of his career. Warren is one of the country's most respected historians, with a keen focus on Australian history and an encyclopaedic knowledge of most bush songs and poetry since colonisation.

Each morning at 8.30, Warren sits down at the desk in his wood-panelled home office, surrounded by some of the 30 books he's written and 900 music albums he helped bring to life. A former music executive and record store owner, Warren has the definition of a portfolio career. 'I'd go stir-crazy if I wasn't working ... I tend to work Monday to Friday, then it's not uncommon for me to do four hours on a Sunday and a Saturday if I'm enjoying what I'm working on.'

Where does his motivation to work so much come from? 'I have limited time left in my life,' he says. 'That's a clock that's ticking that I'm very aware of. I don't know if it's about leaving an imprint. I think it's more about getting projects that I've got in here' – Warren signals to his head – 'out of here and somewhere.'

Money is not the motivating force when you're in your late career. 'Everything I've done was for my own satisfaction. I get a real sense of accomplishment ... Nobody does what I do, and I feel almost obligated to get these things out.' That's the definition of work as a calling, something that Warren discovered over five decades earlier when he walked into the ABC studios at Sydney and asked if he could review books on industrial folklore. The radio station didn't quite know what to make of his bravado, so they said yes, and 50 years later he still appears regularly on the ABC.

Warren doesn't dwell on his work after he finishes it, bouncing quickly from one completed project to the next. 'I'm a bit like some of those animals, foxes and things,' he says. 'They have their kids and then say, "See you, piss off. Fend for yourself."' He doesn't listen back to his old recordings or revisit his books, he simply moves on to the next project on his to-do list. He'll continue to work for as long as he can. 'What else am I going to do?' he asks. 'Go play bowls or something? Not likely!'

How to use this tool

Taking time out from your career can be the mental and physical break you need to dive into the next stage. This is how to plan and execute it properly.

1. Decide which type of sabbatical you need.

There are different ways of taking a career break, depending on what you want to get out of it. Kira Schabram, Matt Bloom and DJ DiDonna have been studying sabbaticals for years,[2] and have identified three types:

Working holiday: where some work is combined with taking time off the usual pressures, often before rejoining your original profession.

Free dive: when you metaphorically dive deep into something completely different as a jolting change.

Quest: a sabbatical where you're seeking out something spiritually higher, taking time out to slowly heal and recover before exploring new areas.

It doesn't matter which type of career break you take, the benefits are broadly identical across the board, and almost everyone who takes time off from their busy, worn schedules to experience life outside of the confines finds the experience incredibly freeing, and the benefits long-lasting. Think about what you actually want to achieve by taking time off, and what you'd like to change at the end of it.

2. Plan ahead.

Taking time away from a regular salary is not something you can do without planning. There are always logistical difficulties – kids at school, renting apartments, visas and costs – but anything worth doing takes time.

Research and connect with people who have done it already (finding relevant Facebook groups can be very useful for this), and begin planning for a break as far in advance as you can. This will give you time to save the money that's needed, negotiate with your workplace if you'll be returning after the break, and start untangling the inevitable bureaucratic mess that comes from stepping into the unknown. While planning can't completely eliminate the hard parts of swapping your regular routine for something new, it can help ease some of the pain. And when you log out of your work email for six months of exploring new countries and endless lifetime experiences, it'll all be worth it.

3. Tell the world.

There was once a time when taking a break from the default mode was seen as something to hide, but career breaks are increasingly becoming normalised in professional environments. In 2022, LinkedIn added a new feature that allows users to add more context to explain gaps in their career history after a survey of 23,000 people showed that over two-thirds had taken a break at some stage in their professional career.[3]

Whether it's a break for full-time parenting to help raise a new family, extended time off to refresh a tired mind, carer's leave or a sabbatical to explore the world, there is no need to have an unexplained gap in your CV. You should be proud that you have the ability, and the courage, to step off the treadmill of life and try something new.

4. Use all the tools.

As this section of the book demonstrates, we have more tools available to us right now than ever before to integrate life and work into new shapes that are personalised just for you. If you do take a break from your career, take your time to find the tools that suit you, whether that's remote work as you can dial in from your house, flexible work to do parts of your job as the sun rises, working a shorter week, or having a long break from your usual career. The options to pick and mix to suit your lifestyle are endless, and you can even blend several of them together, like aiming to be a remote worker for six months during a 'working holiday' career break. The possibilities, and opportunities, are endless.

Tool: Sabbath time

The first thing you notice is the noise, or rather, the lack of it. The usual cacophony of city noises – clipped conversations, car horns, dogs barking – slowly dims along with the Friday evening sunlight until the streets outside are so quiet that you feel like you're the last people on Earth. And in a strange way, you are too. Your world shrinks down to the size of a single living room, filled with your family and closest friends; nothing else exists outside a dining table filled with food.

It's a scene that's repeated around the world in Jewish households every Friday night. In Tel Aviv, the majority of the city shuts down from Friday at sunset for 24 hours, with hardly a shop remaining open or anyone wandering the empty streets. The ancient Jewish weekly ritual of Shabbat encourages households to spend quality time together without the distraction of any work. It begins with lighting candles and attending synagogue, followed by a traditional festive Shabbat dinner with family and friends. Depending on the level of observance, over the next 24 hours everyone follows different rules, with the overarching one being to take a break from the regular schedule of everyday life, like working, cooking and cleaning.

The first time you experience the Jewish holiday in a mainly observant city like Tel Aviv, it feels like a veil is being slowly lowered over everything and everyone. Time slows down, your heart rate decreases, energy levels drop, and a deep serenity envelops the city. You really feel the unique energy that comes from this collective time off that allows the city's inhabitants to properly reset themselves for the week ahead.

A Sabbath is a day of abstinence from work, and is observed in many different cultures, with Shabbat the most common. In Christianity, a version of Sabbath is often observed on Sundays, although it's becoming less common as Western society secularises. From the outside, the weekly Jewish Sabbath looks like a day's holiday every week. 'But the Shabbat is a much more radical approach to rest than a simple respite from work and technology,' wrote Ezra Klein in *The New York Times*. 'Implicit in the practice of the Sabbath is a stinging critique of the speed at which we live our lives, the ways we choose to spend our time and how we think about the idea of rest itself.'[1]

While a religious style of Sabbath is not for everyone, taking regular scheduled time out from work, technology and the pressures of modern life can have a positive impact on the time we do spend working. Having at least one full day's rest a week, when we turn off computers, put down mobile phones and spend deep time with family and friends is a useful tool that we can all learn from. Think of it as a circuit-breaker to help interrupt the usual flow and reset our minds and bodies.

This is an idea that can be extended to regularly unplug from the external and reconnect with the internal. Without the noise of always-on digital channels, you give yourself space to think, digest and process the rest of the week. It's forced rest that anyone can adopt, regardless of your spiritual beliefs.

A trend in recent years is a 'digital Sabbath', or 'secular Sabbath', where certain days of the week – or hours, if that's too long – are reserved as time away from digital devices. Phones, televisions and computers are all switched off for a set period. It's an attractive antidote to digital overload. Proponents of digital Sabbaths point to the increased capacity to think and connect with others without the distractions of screens. However you want to do it, a digital detox is a great tool that you can use to help you concentrate better, be more creative and return to work more focused than before.

How to use this tool

There are many forms of taking short, regular breaks from thinking about work. Here are some ways to do it.

1. Divorce it from religion.

As soon as you start talking about Sabbaths or Shabbat, some non-religious people might automatically tune out, concerned you're going to start preaching at them. If you're religious, feel free to lean into the social and spiritual benefits that you personally get from your faith, but if you're not, please don't let that stop you from exploring the positive benefits you can take away from this.

I am not religious, but when I spent a month in Israel, I soon began to look forward to Shabbat every Friday evening. My husband and I would go market shopping on Friday morning, joining the throng of people stocking up on food for the weekend. As the sun set and Tel Aviv's mood calmed, we'd spend the night cooking up a delicious meal, playing cards, reading and watching a movie. With nothing open outside, it was a forced homely evening. On Saturday we'd have a long lie-in, then cycle or run around the neighbourhood, taking advantage of the quieter beach and streets. Every week, this practice gave us permission to slow down and go with the flow.

Religions like Judaism and Christianity have weathered the test of time. Their strong sense of community, combined with healthy rituals like weekly time-out, are some of the ways they have stayed relevant over thousands of years.

2. The more, the merrier.

One reason Sabbaths work so well in allowing proper downtime is that everyone does it at the same time. In Israel you can hardly find a supermarket or store open during the Sabbath, and this collective inaction is part of its magic. It wouldn't be half as effective if only some of the city took time off while the rest continued their regular, buzzing lives around them.

Laura Giurge from the London School of Economics and Kaitlin Woolley from Cornell University have run several studies on the negative consequences of working during time off. 'When Henry Ford introduced the five-day work week, it accidentally created the weekend, which is when most people wouldn't work,' says Laura. 'It allowed people to connect with others because everybody else was off, and so they could plan things with friends and family.' Their research showed that when people are working while others have time off, like on a weekend or a public holiday, it affects their intrinsic motivation to work. 'They start to think of better ways to spend their weekends or holidays and as a result begin to question whether they truly enjoy and feel engaged with their work,' she explains. 'There's even research showing that retired individuals experience greater happiness on the weekend because the majority of their friends and family have that time off and they can spend it together.'

You should aim to take a set amount of time to yourself each week. It could be an hour off social media, a night off television, or a weekend off work. Whatever it is, it's important that you communicate your intentions to your partner, friends and family, and encourage them to do something similar. It helps if you're all on a similar wavelength. If you're going to get bombarded with texts and phone calls when you're trying to switch off, it won't be nearly as effective.

There are variations of this you can use in a workplace. One example is to collectively agree with your colleagues – and, of course, your boss – that certain time periods should be no-go zones for communication. Perhaps everyone agrees that no emails, texts or Slack messages should be sent on weekends, or that no one is expected to read or respond to an email after 7 p.m. on weekdays. These might sound like simple, common-sense approaches, but if you don't have the conversation, it's easy for the lines to be blurred. When it comes to collective time off, the more people who are doing it at the same time, the more beneficial it is.

3. Set your own rules.

How you choose to adapt your version of a Sabbath is completely up to you. You can make a secular Sabbath, or forced time off, fit into your lifestyle in whatever way works best, there are no set rules you have to follow.

Instead of diving headfirst into taking 24 hours off working every week, you might want to build up to this slowly. If your version of Sabbath involves, for example, wanting to spend less time on your phone in the form of a digital detox, you can begin by going for a walk without your phone, then put it away for mealtimes, and work your way up to not using it for an entire afternoon, evening or day.

Once you've decided when you want to switch off, you then need to decide what you want to do with your time instead. You might want to choose a book to read, or a jigsaw puzzle to complete, or you might prefer to leave it loose. But one thing you should do is set your intention before you start: what's the reason you are doing this? How do you want to feel at the other end? By focusing on the mental state you want to achieve from each secular Sabbath, you have some way of knowing if it's working for you.

If you just do this once and then give up, you're not going to get much out of it. Stick with it until it becomes part of the way you defrag your brain and set yourself up for the coming week, and the effects will show. The only rule to follow is that there are no rules.

4. Lean into boredom.

We are so used to living our lives on a highly charged level, rushing from one thing to the next and ticking through our to-do lists, that it can be disarming to shut it all down and have nothing on your calendar. That is part of the appeal of using this tool – it can help calm your mind down. But one of the most common side effects is boredom.

We have built our lives to avoid boredom. Many of the unconscious habits we've developed – such as listening to podcasts as we walk, or scrolling our phones on the toilet – are to keep our minds busy every second of the day. Taking forced time off is one way of leaning into boredom, and reframing it as a positive experience.

There's a real beauty in boredom that many people do not properly experience in our modern digital world. It's in this space where creativity is fostered and problems are solved, as we give our minds permission to wander down whatever path they'd like to go down. It is here, in the dark pockets of boredom, that ideas can really flourish.

Finding a version of Sabbath that works for you can help you to work and live better by simply doing nothing on a regular basis. How easy is that?

Tool: Artificial intelligence

I n November 1980, Bill Gates attended a meeting that would have a massive impact on the future of humanity. Having taught himself programming at 13 years old, Bill was a few years into turning the company he'd founded into one of the most important technology companies in history. However, it wasn't until he sat down with a brilliant young programmer, Charles Simonyi, who showed him a graphical user interface for a computer, that Gates could see the future of computing ahead of him. This one shift, to make computers user-friendly and accessible, was what he had been searching for.

Gates would have to wait another 40 years to get the same feeling again. Computing technology progressed so much in those decades that it wasn't just the invention of a new technology that would impress him, it was how it could be used. Gates and his company, Microsoft, had been following a small company that was playing around with artificial intelligence (AI) since 2016. Originally established as a non-profit, OpenAI had made impressive, steady progress, and in mid-2022 Gates set the team a challenge: to see if they could build an AI machine smart enough to pass an Advanced Placement biology exam without having been specially trained for that purpose. Gates chose the difficult exam as you couldn't pass it by just regurgitating scientific facts, you had to think critically. He thought that such an impressive feat would keep the team busy for at least the next few years.

A few months later, in September 2022, he met with OpenAI again. Gates sat in awe as their newly built AI machine got 59 out of the 60 multiple choice questions correct, and then wrote six long-form answers from the exam that an outside expert gave the equivalent of an A or A+. 'I knew I had just seen the most important advance in technology since the graphical user interface,' Gates wrote in his essay, 'The Age of AI Has Begun'.[1] 'The development of AI is as fundamental as the creation of the microprocessor, the personal computer, the internet, and the mobile phone. It will change the way people work, learn, travel, get health care, and communicate with each other. Entire industries will reorient around it. Businesses will distinguish themselves by how well they use it.'

Artificial intelligence is one of the largest technology shifts in our lifetime, changing the way we live and work forever, but we have to ensure that we don't fall into its productivity trap. The near-future is one where AI performs in a matter of seconds many tasks that would normally take us hours to complete. Generative AI, or GenAI, uses computers to produce content such as text, images, video and audio that previously would have taken a long time to create from scratch. It's tempting to use the time saved to complete even more tasks, and that's the productivity fallacy we need to avoid.

AI will streamline our lives. It will take away basic, repetitive tasks to begin, slowly working up the ladder of advancement until it can also perform more complex tasks. The natural tendency for humans is to be scared, fearful, intimidated, and to find more things to do that AI can't do. But what if we saw AI for what it was – as a useful tool to give us some of our time back? AI can be one of the things that help us achieve a better life–work balance, but we need to use our regained time wisely.

There are sceptics who question the hype around how much new technology like ChatGPT will affect the way we work. Dr Jim Stanford splits his time between Australia and Canada, giving him a unique perspective on labour laws, working hours and how different governments approach the future of work. As the founding director of the Centre for Future Work, he's worked in union movements and universities for much of his career, studying the economics of how and why we work. He's also a tempering force on some of the hyperbole surrounding the AI movement. When I speak to him, he's in Vancouver, walking from one end of the sprawling University of British Columbia campus to the other. Occasionally our conversation is interrupted by the sound of drilling jackhammers and car horns as the institution expands its footprint. 'That's going to be some building named after some rich corporate donor,' he laughs.

Jim could be classified as a technology-realist, who sees parallels in history to the AI hype. 'The discourse around the future of work has been unduly obsessed with technology and devices, and the way that different specific innovations are going to affect people's jobs in the future in a technologically determinist way that I think is quite wrong,' he says. 'Of course ChatGPT, and AI in general, have lots of implications and we'll have to watch how it happens, and try to regulate how it happens, but the idea that all these changes are being driven by the inexorable forward march of technology I think really, really misses the critical social context of it all.'

There's been a lot of hype. Back in 2013, two researchers at Oxford University concluded that almost half of 702 different jobs that they studied could be done by machines. 'According to our estimate,' they wrote, '47% of total US employment is in the high risk category, meaning that associated occupations are potentially automatable over some unspecified number of years, perhaps a decade or two.'[2] One decade later, their worst predictions haven't happened yet.

AI is 'invented and developed and implemented and applied and managed by human beings,' says Jim. 'Technology isn't inexorable, technology isn't autonomous. What we call technology is just the cumulative human knowledge about how to do things using tools ... and I think those social relationships and power relationships are vital to understanding how technology evolves, and how its implications are managed, and how its costs and benefits are shared.'

Artificial intelligence is here, whether we like it or not. So how do we use it to our advantage?

How to use this tool

You have a choice: you can use AI to make your working life better, or you can ignore it as it seeps into every part of our lives. This is how to do the former.

1. Keep up.

AI is evolving at a rapid pace. Just two months after it officially launched, ChatGPT reached 100 million users, making it the fastest growing consumer application in history. Seemingly every week there is a new announcement, launch or technology being added to this space. While it's impossible to be across every one of these, if you don't at least try to keep up, it could soon outstrip your ability to harness its full power.

The best way to understand AI is to actually use it. Don't be afraid of it – instead, embrace it as the most useful tool to emerge in our lifetimes. There are countless ways you can use AI in your work and personal lives to help with some of the repetitive tasks that take up too much time.

As its name implies, most forms of 'artificial intelligence' will learn more from you the more you interact with them. Treat large language models (LLM) such as ChatGPT as another colleague – ask it questions and use its output to help you in your job. However, as a technology it is still not always reliable, so ensure that you continue to double-check its output to ensure its accuracy.

Another reason to stay on top of these new technologies is so that we can continue to lead them down the paths we want. Hertta Vuorenmaa, Chair of the Finnish Association of Work Life Research, is cautiously optimistic about the future. 'These technologies are complex and they challenge us in a whole new way. They are changing the logic of our work,' she says. 'One of the key things we need to understand is that technology needs to be our tool, and our slave, not the master,' she says. A way of ensuring this is by knowing – and continuing to critically evaluate – how the technologies can work in our favour, and which buttons we need to push to keep it that way.

2. Use your saved time wisely.

Steven Hatfield, the Global Leader for Future of Work at Deloitte, has a favourite robot called Flippy. Created by Miso Robotics, Flippy is a machine that prepares and fries food in restaurants, with the aim of eliminating dull, dirty and dangerous tasks in professional kitchens. The machine has now been incorporated in hundreds of food chains around the world. 'He's in the back flipping the burgers and testing the oil of the French fries,' says Steven. 'He is enabling that workforce to either elevate up to just managing the robots, or to be up front dealing with the customers in a different way.'

Flippy is just the start of the robotic revolution that aims to take some of the repetitive tasks off humans to save time and resources. 'They can't do the exceptional things, which is when you have to make a judgement call, but the worker ends up doing that and it's actually healthier for the worker and more interesting work,' says Steven. Plus, if AI can complete a task in a few minutes that a human would take a few hours to do, think about how you can use the time that's been saved. 'I have an optimistic view,' says Steven, 'that humans will start doing more interesting and better things. I hope we get to the point that we start thinking about connecting the dots with more personal time, leisure and wellbeing.'

Instead of mindlessly filling that time with more work, think about what your version of a full-circle life looks like, and how you can use the time to nourish other areas instead of automatically defaulting to work. AI has the potential to be the greatest gift to a healthy life–work balance, but whether we take up this opportunity and use the time well is entirely up to us.

3. Collaborate with robots.

There's a term used in the technology space, 'cobot', which is a portmanteau of 'collaborative' and 'robot'. It's a friendly way of describing what happens when humans and robots work together to achieve a common goal, and it's also a useful frame to think about where technology is heading.

Instead of replacing humans completely in an automated future, robots are able to augment the work that humans are already doing by completing some tasks within a bigger job. Dr Sean Gallagher from Swinburne University is also a Chief Investigator at the Australian Cobotics Centre. He uses the example of a production line, where robots pick up heavy items and hold them in place so workers can then paint and complete work on them. 'The future of work is human,' says Sean, who is a firm advocate for humans and robots working together. 'We shouldn't remove the human from the value-add processes because they have a lot of problem-solving skills.'

Of course, this doesn't just work on the factory floor, it applies to most workplaces. 'Fifty per cent of a nurse's time in North America is spent doing things that have to deal with admin,' says Steven Hatfield. 'So if we can digitise more and more of that, be that an AI tool or a robot, and free them up to go back to bedside care, that'll be a real boom to what ostensibly is already a looming shortage.'

Challenge yourself to think deeply about how you can work with a robot on any part of your job. Collaboration is always better than competition.

4. Embrace the anxiety.

Seemingly every week there is new data about the anxiety levels of workers regarding AI. A study released by Advertising Week showed that an overwhelming majority of Australians (75%) are worried about the impact of adopting AI at work.[3] They mainly cited fears like the potential to reduce creativity and the ability to apply human judgement, as well as surveillance and dependency concerns.

It is scary and unknown, and our concerns are only going to increase as technology becomes more powerful. So, we have a decision to make: we can either hide from it and hope it doesn't affect us too much, or we can dive straight in and confront our anxiety head-on.

As difficult as this path seems, acknowledging the reasons behind our fears, and trying to understand them, is the best chance we have of developing a healthy relationship with technology in the future. AI will change the way we work forever, and it's up to us to ensure that change is for the better.

Tool: Better meetings

O ur brains were not designed to attend back-to-back meetings for hours on end. In a revealing research study, Microsoft's Human Factors Lab strapped EEG monitors onto 14 people to track the electrical activity in their brains as they sat through video meetings.[1] They observed what happened when four half-hour meetings were held back-to-back – not uncommon in a typical corporate day – and discovered that the average beta wave activity increased with each meeting, suggesting a build-up of stress. For participants who took ten minutes between each meeting to calm down – in this study they meditated – their average beta wave activity remained largely 'cool' and steady over time.

You'd be hard pressed to find anyone who says they really love meetings, and this is mainly because we're doing them wrong. They might go on for too long, have too many people in them, not be relevant to all attendees, be unstructured, or have no clear outcome at the end. If any of that sounds familiar, then learning how to be better at meetings is one of the tools you can use to forge a better work life. Think of all the hours you'll claw back to spend on other things if you can get meetings under control.

The tyranny of meetings has been compounded by the rise of video conferencing, which means you can now sit in the comfort of your own home and stare at a bright green light for hours on end. The more we work from home, the more meetings we are having. In the first few months after professional workers retreated to their homes during Covid, the number of virtual meetings skyrocketed – so much that by the end of 2020, they had doubled. That growth continued, and two years later there were 250% more meetings in our diaries than before the pandemic.[2]

At the start of 2023, e-commerce company Shopify logged into the diaries of their 10,000 employees around the world and cancelled every recurring meeting that had three or more people.[3] This idea, often referred to as calendar bankruptcy, is a simple way to clear out all the existing meetings in your diary so you can start fresh.[4]

In my last full-time job, I had a wonderful executive assistant. Her primary job was to maximise every 15-minute block in my diary from morning to evening, aiming to squeeze as many people and meetings into a day until my calendar had no white space left. That's what I thought success was: making every work day as productive as I could by filling it with endless meetings. But it's not, that's part of the 'busyness' trap that many people fall into too.

Regaining control of who you meet with and how you do it is one of the easiest ways to improve your working environment. Small changes can have profound outcomes and save you hours of reclaimed time – hours that you can put to better use.

Andy Miller, CEO of non-alcoholic drinks manufacturer Heaps Normal, thinks about meetings a lot. 'I find a lot of tension in meetings,' he says, 'where there's so much pressure for them to be productive and also to be an open space for dialogue.' As a remote leader, Andy often finds the expectation that meetings – especially video meetings – are primarily for ticking through items on an agenda, instead of ways of connecting with people. 'I've reflected on the importance of creating moments that are not just about work, and making space for interactions with colleagues that are not work … it is often overlooked and it's difficult to achieve unless you're being quite deliberate about it.'

One of Andy's favourite quotes about meetings was written by American management consultant Mary Parker Follett in 1924: 'In the very process of meeting, by the very process of meeting, we both become something different.' This reminds Andy that meetings are sometimes messy and always social. 'I think it's just an academic way of referring to our need for a psychologically safe place to think out loud, have ideas, and to be prepared for your ideas to be challenged and to evolve through that process. Creating space for meetings to have that role in our team and in our organisation has been interesting and has had a really positive effect.'

How to use this tool

We spend a lot of our work lives in meetings, so here's how to make this tool work for you.

1. Declare calendar bankruptcy.

A lot of people are addicted to being busy. They squeeze as many meetings, calls, emails and work as they can into an already packed schedule, running from one appointment to the next. Like an addict, sometimes the best solution is to give in and go 'cold turkey' on your busyness.

One option is to declare 'calendar bankruptcy'. To do this, go into your diary and take a photo or screenshot so you still have a record if you need to refer to it. Then go into every appointment and delete them. Blow it all up. Tell everyone around you that you're officially declaring calendar bankruptcy. Then, once your schedule is perfectly clear, you can start adding things back, consciously, one at a time.

Before you put a new meeting in your diary, ask yourself IFF it really needs to go back in. IFF stands for:

- *Intention:* Is this meeting necessary?
- *Format:* Is this the right format?
- *Frequency:* Does it need to happen this often?

From then on, only put things in your diary if they are absolutely necessary.

2. Be crystal clear.

Think of a meeting as having three parts: before, during and after. At each of these stages you should be extremely clear with everyone around you about what is required from them.

Before the meeting, ensure there is a clear reason it's being held and that all attendees are aware of it. You don't need to circulate a formally written document, but even putting a quick description in the calendar invite laying out the aim and a rough outline of the meeting process will help.

During the meeting, try to stick to an agenda to keep it on track. The aim of this is not to create additional paperwork or bureaucracy, it's to value everyone who has given up their time to attend. You should never leave a meeting without asking three simple questions: *What are the next steps? Who should do them? And by when?* If nothing else is accomplished during the meeting, being clear on the outcome will ensure it's not time wasted.

After the meeting, the organiser, or whoever they appoint, should email attendees the answer to those three questions, for accountability. It's really that simple.

3. Have meeting-free days.

We all spend too long in meetings. It's estimated that there are 11 million meetings held in America alone every single day, and a survey of 1900 business leaders found that workers in large organisations of 500 or more employees spend about 75% of their time preparing, attending, leading and concluding meetings.[5]

If meetings take up too much of your time at work, one good solution is to implement an entire day of the week where no meetings can take place. Anyone in a team can suggest this, from a junior employee to the CEO, and you can always begin with just your department to test how successful it is. If implemented correctly, having one meeting-free day a week leaves an entire day that can be spent on deep thinking, problem-solving, strategising and higher-level work that requires few distractions.

4. Experiment with your toolkit.

All the tools we've run through in this final step are yours to use as you will, whether you want to experiment with improving your meetings, working more flexibly, introducing a four-day work week or taking some time off technology. Each of these tools can be used by themselves or in various combinations. To help you decide which tool is best for you, there is a simple exercise you can complete in the final **IRL exercise 10** on page 266 in the next section.

These tools are only as good as your use of them, but hopefully by now you've armed yourself with new information and fresh inspiration to pick some of them up and have a go. There has never been a better time to do that.

IRL Exercises: Work

Step 3: Use the right tools

IRL exercise 7: User manual

To understand how to get the most out of your work colleagues, you should have a user manual. This is a short template that everyone in your team fills out, reflecting who they are and how they like to work.

The aim is to communicate and better understand each other's needs so you can identify the ideal working conditions for your teammates. It also has the added benefit of making you more aware of your own ideal working styles. Each of our working styles is unique, and having the right tool to be able to clearly articulate that to your colleagues can be a defining factor in your happiness at work or a project's success. Create your own user manual first, then share yours to encourage others in your team to do the same. Here's how to do it.

1. Complete each of these statements.

To create a user manual, each team member should fill out a series of prompts that help you understand their motivations and preferred style of working. These are the main subject headings of a typical user manual:

About me: Describe who you are, some personal background, and share anything you feel comfortable with. This can be your favourite quotes, movies, meals or holidays.

When I like to work: Tell everyone about the life you prefer to lead so they can work within those hours instead of against them. When do you like to exercise? When's your best time for emails or creativity? What time do you take lunch? What time do you want, or not want, to be contacted? The more specific you are here, the more useful your user manual will be.

How I like to communicate: There are thousands of ways to reach people – which do you prefer? Phone calls, Zoom, in-person, WhatsApp, email, Slack, Teams or something else?

My superpower: It's important to know what your point of difference is. This doesn't need to be an Olympic level of achievement, just something unique to you. What is it that you can do better than others?

How I like to receive feedback: Are you someone who wants instant feedback, or would you prefer it's communicated in a regular weekly catch-up? Your manager and the people around you are not mind-readers, so help them out here.

How I like to learn: Do you learn best from written instructions, throwing yourself in the deep end or watching someone else do hard things?

What I need from you: How can someone get the best out of you? To answer this, think through the best boss or manager you've ever had, and verbalise what they did that helped to optimise your output.

What I struggle with: What are the biggest things that you dislike in a workplace or colleague? Be honest here.

Something about me that might surprise you: It can be fun to end your personal user manual with something personal and interesting.

You can mix and match the above, as well as personalise it for your team or your company if there are certain ways of working that are unique to it. Feel free to also add photos, quotes or emojis to really make it your own.

2. Create a presentation and share it.

Once you've agreed on the subject headings for your personal user manual, put each of them on a new presentation slide. Invite your team together and take them through the presentation, then encourage them to fill out their own. Give everyone at least a fortnight to properly think through their answers, then arrange a meeting where everyone presents their personal user manual to the team, one at a time.

3. Start a ritual around user manuals.

Whenever someone new joins your team, have them fill in their user manual and present it to the team. This can become a ritual to welcome people to your team and get to know them.

Put all your colleagues' user manuals in a public folder, and consult them regularly. It can be very useful for new team members to read over everyone else's user manual, invoking empathy and bringing understanding to a team.

A user manual is a brilliant tool you can start using with your colleagues today, and it's something that anyone can introduce to a team, no matter what level you're at.

IRL exercise 8: RACI matrix

RACI stands for responsible, accountable, consulted and informed. It is a helpful tool that should bring any issues to the surface around who is meant to be doing what on any given project. It also solves a potential problem, particularly in bigger companies, where you get to the end of a project and realise that your boss's boss, or even their boss's boss, hasn't been brought on the journey and could kill it all with a single email. This is how to do it.

1. Draw up a matrix.

A RACI is a simple matrix with a column across the top of the page for each person who is involved in the project. Running down the page are rows detailing each of the key tasks or deliverables.

On a blank page, whiteboard or spreadsheet, draw up a column for every person working on the project, using the example below as a guide.

	Person 1	Person 2	Person 3	Person 4
Task				
Task				
Task				
Task				

2. Fill out the matrix.

Gather everyone on the project and, collectively, fill out each of the columns, listing who is responsible, accountable, consulted and informed for each of the tasks.

Do that by writing the names of everyone on your team across the top, and then each of the tasks and deliverables for your project down the side. For each corresponding box, clearly allocate who is responsible, accountable, consulted and informed for each aspect of the project by adding one of those four labels inside each box.

Responsible: This person, or it might be a group of people, is directly responsible for the success or failure of this part of the project. It's their job to keep everyone on track, and really they should be the one setting up the RACI in the first place. The buck stops with them, and they are the engine that will keep everything going. You can assign responsibility to more than one person, but I've found that it's best to keep this list as small as possible, otherwise you risk having an entire cohort of people who are all designated as 'responsible' as a way of sharing the risk.

Accountable: This person – or again, it can be more than one – is generally the person the responsible person above reports to. That's not always the case, but the accountable person is someone who looks over the work that those with responsibility are actually doing, and ensures it's all on track. If the project goes off the rails, it's the role of the 'accountable' person to ultimately, well, be accountable for its success. The accountable person is usually more senior than those in the 'responsible' column.

Consulted: This is a person, or group, who is not directly involved in the project, but will be affected by it in some way. They might work in a different department or team, but will have valuable insights they can add into the process to ensure its success. People who are consulted are asked for advice and given regular updates, but are not responsible or accountable for the project. There's great benefit getting input from those who aren't as emotionally involved or close to the work, so this is a really important set of people who should be treated as such.

Informed: These are the people who need to be kept across the project at a high level, but don't have as much input into it. This might be an executive team, board or heads of departments who have some interest in the output and success of a project, and should be kept informed, but that's about it.

3. Document it.

Make sure you capture exactly what each person has been assigned, paying particular attention to ensure there aren't too many people in Responsible or Accountable. Once complete, circulate the document so everyone is across it. Refer back to it if the process ever falls down, and if someone isn't doing what they said they would, call it out. You will at least have an agreed document you can use to ensure the conversation remains productive and focused.

A RACI is a super useful tool that anyone can suggest and implement. It might be a small project involving just a few people, or a large company one that affects dozens of people. Often just the act of gathering everyone who's working on a project and clearly articulating who is doing what is worth it.

IRL exercise 9: Life scale

In this exercise, we'll create a personalised scale of your life, showing how you can combine the three stages of Learn, Earn and Burn, and where your ideal finish lines are.

1. Draw up a timeline.

Copy the below scale onto a sheet of paper. This scale represents your entire life, from birth to 90 years old.

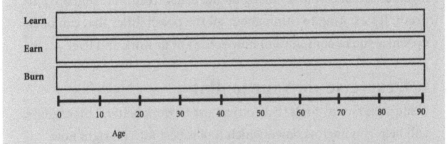

2. Mark your age on it.

Where are you currently sitting on the scale? Draw a line that signifies how old you are now. This might feel confronting, but it's a good way of getting some perspective on how much of your career and your life you have left.

3. Add in any proposed finish lines.

Instead of thinking about retirement at 65 as the only finish line you're aiming towards, consider if there are any proposed breaks you'd like to take throughout your career. Add them into your timeline at the age you'd like to take them. These might include overseas travel, raising a family, education, house renovations, selling a business, long-service leave or just some time off the default mode of working.

4. Shade in future stages.

Starting from your age now, shade out your planned periods to learn, earn and burn. This will force you to think about how your life is set up, and what you can do in order to get to a stage that starts blending them together. If you have any career breaks planned, think about what the mix of learning, earning and burning looks like during this period, and after it.

Once you've completed your ideal life scale you'll have lots of food for thought on how you can blend different parts of your life together, instead of just staying on the usual treadmill from birth to death. It's exciting to think about all the possibilities that can open up when you're conscious of how you want to work and live.

IRL exercise 10: Your toolkit

There are so many tools that you can use to work better. This exercise will help you narrow down which tool is best for you right now.

1. Understand each tool.

Ensure that you've read through each of the eight sections in the Work chapter that outline what the tools are, and how to best use them. As a refresher, the tools are:

- remote working
- hybrid working
- flexible working
- four-day work week
- career breaks
- Sabbath time
- artificial intelligence
- better meetings.

Keep in mind these are just some of the options available to you now. You can always add your own ways of working better to this list.

Then think about which ones you want to experiment with. Remember that each tool is just that, an experiment – it's not going to solve all of your problems straight away. But the right combination of these tools can have a big impact on how fulfilled, satisfied and happy you are, both at work and outside it.

2. Choose your tools.
Pick out which of these tools you think would work best in your situation, taking into account how your workplace, or bosses, will respond to any new ideas. A few of these things might be outside of your control, but you'll be surprised how open some managers and HR teams are to testing them out.

Decide which tools you think would work for you, and think about what your aim is in successfully integrating it into your life.

Tool: _____

Aim: _____

Tool: _____

Aim: _____

Tool: _____

Aim: _____

3. Plan how you can introduce these tools at work.

Every worker and workplace is unique, so how you actually go about implementing these tools depends on many factors. However, what they all have in common is that information is the key. You need to arm yourself, your co-workers and your bosses with as much quality information about the tools you want to use as possible, so that the evidence becomes overwhelming.

This book is a good place to start, as are the dozens of scientific studies, research papers and news articles in the endnotes on pages 273–284, which can help you explore these topics further. Use these to convince those in power in your organisation to commence a short-term trial, with yourself as one of the guinea pigs. When it's just a test, there's almost no downside for the business. The worst that can happen is that the experiment fails and you keep doing what you're doing. And the best case? You can prove that there are better ways to work.

Conclusion: The beginning

The way we are working is broken, and it's up to us to fix it.

One day it will be us lying helplessly on a hospital bed with no more chances to redo anything. It might be half a year, half a decade or half a century away, but everyone's time will come. And when it does, the piercing clarity of those final days will wash over everything that we've achieved throughout our life. We'll look back at the way we worked, how we lived and who we loved. The details won't be important, but the broad brushstrokes will be.

Did we live our life in default mode, spending our years on a spin cycle we could never get out of? Or did we smash the usual path and reverse our thinking so we could get the most out of our one wild and precious life?

Instead of falling into the usual trap of getting a job, then using the salary to fund whatever lifestyle we can afford, we need to acknowledge that this has led a lot of us down the wrong path, repeating the same mistakes every pay cycle until we retire.

The Work Backwards framework can be summed up in a single diagram:

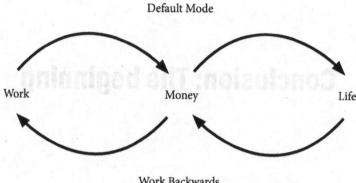

Default Mode

Work   Money   Life

Work Backwards

Life: Begin at the end result that you want, and consciously decide how you want to live, taking into account your passions, skills, happiness and the impact you want to have. You now know how to create your own MAP to get you there.

Money: Once you've defined where you want to go, you can use a Backwards Budget to work out how much money it will cost to get there and what 'enough' is for you.

Work: In the final step you've learnt about some of the tools we now have access to. The exact tools to use will change depending on your situation, life and career stage, but you should experiment with as many of them as you can to find the ones that work best.

To make this process as easy as possible, you can go to WorkBackwards.com/IRL and download all the worksheets, spreadsheets and resources for free so you can complete them in your own time.

There's a viral social media post that's been circulating since 2015, accumulating millions of re-shares. It depicts a thin and frail Steve Jobs with what it claims were his last words: 'In other eyes, my life is the essence of success, but aside from work, I have a little joy,' it reads. 'The non-stop pursuing of wealth will only turn a person into a twisted being, just like me.'

These are, however, not the Apple founder's last words. They are fake, put into Jobs' mouth by an anonymous writer. According to his sister, who was by his side, Steve Jobs didn't talk about work, or money, in his final days. All he cared about were his relationships. 'Before embarking,' she recounted at his funeral, 'he'd looked at his sister, Patty, then for a long time at his children, then at his life partner, Laurene, and then over their shoulders past them. Steve's final words were: "Oh wow. Oh wow. Oh wow."'

Oh wow.

I don't mean to be overly morbid, but there's a dead certainty that one day you'll also utter your last words. As you're lying there, surrounded by loved ones and reflecting on your journey, you might even think back to this moment that you're in *right now*, reading the final chapter of this book.

You might even realise it was a pivotal moment, a turning point, a beginning. This was the moment you were able to free yourself from the shackles of convention, and realise with piercing clarity that we've all been working and living backwards for decades. This was the moment when you recognised there is a growing movement of people all over the world, driven by shifting priorities and cemented in place by a pandemic, who are all striving for change.

So please, take the messages inside this book as your inspiration for change. We are overworked and disconnected, we are scared and excited by the future. In order to reset our lives and our priorities, we need to Work Backwards, one by one, to create a life that is full of meaning, satisfaction, joy and happiness. The future of your work is waiting.

Tim Duggan
hello@timduggan.com.au
www.WorkBackwards.com

Endnotes

Introduction: The end

1   Ray, J. (2022). *World Unhappier, More Stressed Out Than Ever.* Gallup.com. https://news.gallup.com/poll/394025/world-unhappier-stressed-ever.aspx.

2   Abramson, A. (2022). *Burnout and Stress Are Everywhere.* American Psychological Association. https://www.apa.org/monitor/2022/01/special-burnout-stress.

3   McKinsey Health Institute (2022). *Addressing Employee Burnout: Are You Solving the Right Problem?* www.mckinsey.com. https://www.mckinsey.com/mhi/our-insights/addressing-employee-burnout-are-you-solving-the-right-problem.

4   Shane, D. (2019). Jack Ma Endorses China's Controversial 12 Hours a Day, 6 Days a Week Work Culture. *CNN Business.* 15 Apr. https://edition.cnn.com/2019/04/15/business/jack-ma-996-china/index.html

5   Fuerte, K. (2021). *The 'Karoshi' Phenomenon Is Now a Worldwide Problem.* Observatory of the Institute of the Future of Education. https://observatory.tec.mx/edu-news/karoshi-phenomenon/

6   World Health Organisation (2021). *Long Working Hours Increasing Deaths from Heart Disease and Stroke.* www.who.int. https://www.who.int/news/item/17-05-2021-long-working-hours-increasing-deaths-from-heart-disease-and-stroke-who-ilo

7   Microsoft (2022). *Great Expectations: Making Hybrid Work Work*. www.microsoft.com. https://www.microsoft.com/en-us/worklab/work-trend-index/great-expectations-making-hybrid-work-work

8   Microsoft. *The Rise of the Triple Peak Day*. www.microsoft.com. https://www.microsoft.com/en-us/worklab/triple-peak-day

9   Gallup (2022). *State of the Global Workplace Report*. https://www.gallup.com/workplace/349484/state-of-the-global-workplace.aspx#ite-393218

10 Greenwood, S. (2023). *How Americans View Their Jobs*. Pew Research Center's Social & Demographic Trends Project. https://www.pewresearch.org/social-trends/2023/03/30/how-americans-view-their-jobs/

11 Qualtrics. *Return to Work / Back to Business Study, Part 2*. https://www.qualtrics.com/m/assets/wp-content/uploads/2020/07/Back-to-Business-Round-2.pdf

12 PWC (2021). *Hopes & Fears: Future of Work*. https://www.pwc.com.tr/hopes-fears-future-of-work

13 PWC (2022). *PwC's Global Workforce Hopes and Fears Survey 2022*. https://www.pwc.com/gx/en/issues/workforce/hopes-and-fears-2022.html

A better way

1   Kramer, H. (2017). *How Many Churches and Denominations Are There in America and the World?* The Complete Pilgrim - Religious Travel Sites. https://thecompletepilgrim.com/many-churches-denominations-america-world/

2   Teller, M. (2022). The Curious Case of the Ladder at the Church of the Holy Sepulchre. *Prospect* magazine. 14 Apr. https://www.prospectmagazine.co.uk/arts-and-books/the-curious-case-of-the-ladder-at-the-church-of-the-holy-sepulchre

3   Dickler, J. (2022). *63% of Americans Are Living Paycheck to Paycheck — Including Nearly Half of Six-figure Earners*. CNBC. https://www.cnbc.com/2022/10/24/more-americans-live-paycheck-to-paycheck-as-inflation-outpaces-income.html

The games we play

1   McLuhan, M. (1994). *Understanding Media: The Extensions of Man*. Cambridge, MA: MIT Press.

2   Hasbro (2015). *Monopoly History*. web.archive.org. https://web.archive.org/web/20150304181619/http://www.hasbro.com/monopoly/en_US/discover/about.cfm

3   Raworth, K. (2017). *Monopoly Was Invented to Demonstrate the Evils of Capitalism*. BBC.com. https://www.bbc.com/worklife/article/20170728-monopoly-was-invented-to-demonstrate-the-evils-of-capitalism

4   Russo, N. (2017). Propagandopoly: Monopoly as an Ideological Tool. *Works That Work* magazine. https://worksthatwork.com/9/propagandopoly-monopoly-as-an-ideological-tool

5   Landlords Game History, 'The History of The Landlord's Game & Monopoloy'. https://landlordsgame.info/

6   Pilon, M. (2015). Monopoly's Inventor: The Progressive Who Didn't Pass 'Go'. *The New York Times*. https://www.nytimes.com/2015/02/15/business/behind-monopoly-an-inventor-who-didnt-pass-go.html

7   Pilon, M. (2015). The Secret History of Monopoly: The Capitalist Board Game's Leftwing Origins. *The Guardian*. https://www.theguardian.com/lifeandstyle/2015/apr/11/secret-history-monopoly-capitalist-game-leftwing-origins

8   Pilon, M. (2015). *The Monopolists*. Bloomsbury Publishing USA.

9   Pew Research Center - U.S. Politics & Policy. (2022). *Modest Declines in Positive Views of 'Socialism' and 'Capitalism' in U.S.* https://www.pewresearch.org/politics/2022/09/19/modest-declines-in-positive-views-of-socialism-and-capitalism-in-u-s/

A life worth living

1   Bartlett, S. (2022). *Jimmy Carr: The Easiest Way to Live a Happier Life*. Diary of a CEO. https://www.youtube.com/watch?v=roROKlZhZyo

2   Sturgis, S. (2014). *Want to Be Happier? Try Walking Even Part of the Way to Work*. Bloomberg.com. https://www.bloomberg.com/news/articles/2014-09-14/want-to-be-happier-try-walking-even-part-of-the-way-to-work

3   NSW Police. *Police Prosecutions Command - NSW Police Public Site*. https://www.police.nsw.gov.au/about_us/ organisational_structure/units/police_prosecutions_ command#:~:text=Police%20Prosecutors%20prosecute%20 about%2095

We can't unsee

1   Gambuto, J.V. (2020). *Prepare for the Ultimate Gaslighting**. Medium. https://forge.medium.com/prepare-for-the-ultimate-gaslighting-6a8ce3f0a0e0

2   Dhingra, N., Samo, A., Schaninger, B. and Schrimper, M. (2021). *Help Your Employees Find Purpose – or Watch Them Leave*. www.mckinsey.com. https://www.mckinsey.com/ capabilities/people-and-organizational-performance/our-insights/help-your-employees-find-purpose-or-watch-them-leave

3   Woodbury, R. (2023). *https://twitter.com/rex_woodbury*. X (formerly Twitter). https://twitter.com/rex_woodbury/status/16 41837391529771014?s=46&t=iFuqxJ-RKg7XhOyIPRXoiQ

4   Dickler, J. (2022). *63% of Americans Are Living Paycheck to Paycheck — Including Nearly Half of Six-figure Earners*. CNBC. https://www.cnbc.com/2022/10/24/more-americans-live-paycheck-to-paycheck-as-inflation-outpaces-income.html

Make life work

1   Mervis, B. (2022). 50 Things We Love in the World of Food Right Now. *The Guardian*. https://www.theguardian.com/food/ ng-interactive/2022/feb/20/50-things-we-love-in-the-world-of-food-right-now

2   Department for Professional Employees (DPE) (2021). *The Professional and Technical Workforce: By the Numbers*. https:// www.dpeaflcio.org/factsheets/the-professional-and-technical-workforce-by-the-numbers

3   Zweig, M. (2012). Front Matter. In: *The Working Class Majority*, 2nd ed. [online] Cornell University Press, pp.i–iv. Available at: https://www.jstor.org/stable/10.7591/j.ctt7v7g0

Meaning

1 Achor, S., Reece, A., Kellerman, G. and Robichaux, A. (2018). 9 Out of 10 People Are Willing to Earn Less Money to Do More-Meaningful Work. *Harvard Business Review.* https://hbr.org/2018/11/9-out-of-10-people-are-willing-to-earn-less-money-to-do-more-meaningful-work.

2 Morris, M.L.-W., Bailey, C., Madden, A. and Morris, L. (2022). Why We Don't Talk About Meaning at Work. *MIT Sloan Management Review.* https://sloanreview.mit.edu/article/why-we-dont-talk-about-meaning-at-work/.

3 Wrzesniewski, A. and Dutton, J. (2001). Crafting a Job: Revisioning Employees as active Crafters of Their Work. *Academy of Management Review,* 26(2), pp.179–201.

4 Berg, J.M., Grant, A.M. and Johnson, V. (2010). When Callings Are Calling: Crafting Work and Leisure in Pursuit of Unanswered Occupational Callings. *Organization Science,* 21(5), pp.973–994. https://doi.org/10.1287/orsc.1090.0497.

5 Ghitulescu, B.E. (2007). *Shaping Tasks and Relationships at Work: Examining the Antecedents and Consequences of Employee Job Crafting.* https://d-scholarship.pitt.edu/10312/.

6 Lyons, P. (2008). The Crafting of Jobs and Individual Differences. *Journal of Business and Psychology,* 23(1-2), pp.25–36. https://doi.org/10.1007/s10869-008-9080-2.

7 Shanafelt, T.D., West, C.P., Sloan, J.A., Novotny, P.J., Poland, G.A., Menaker, R., Rummans, T.A. and Dyrbye, L.N. (2009). Career Fit and Burnout Among Academic Faculty. *Archives of Internal Medicine,* 169(10), p.990. https://doi.org/10.1001/archinternmed.2009.70.

8 Rosso, B.D., Dekas, K.H. and Wrzesniewski, A. (2020). On the Meaning of Work: A Theoretical Integration and Review. *Research in Organizational Behavior,* 30, pp.91–127. https://www.sciencedirect.com/science/article/abs/pii/S0191308510000067

Anchors

1   Brief, A.P. and Nord, W.R. (1991). The Meaning of Occupational Work: A Collection of Essays. *Administrative Science Quarterly*, 36(4), p.681. https://doi.org/10.2307/2393284

2   Baker, W. (2013). *Some See Work as a Calling, Others Say it's Just a Job*. University of Michigan News. https://news.umich.edu/some-see-work-as-a-calling-others-say-it-s-just-a-job/

3   Norton, K. (2022). *'I Work Just 4 Hours a Day': This 29-year-old's Side Hustle Brings in $2 million a Year—a Look at Her Typical Day*. CNBC. https://www.cnbc.com/2022/12/26/this-29-year-olds-side-hustle-brings-in-2-million-a-year-i-work-4-hours-a-week.html

Priorities

1   Thompson, D. (2019). Workism Is Making Americans Miserable. *The Atlantic*. https://www.theatlantic.com/ideas/archive/2019/02/religion-workism-making-americans-miserable/583441/

2   Mohajan, H. (2019). *The First Industrial Revolution: Creation of a New Global Human Era*. https://mpra.ub.uni-muenchen.de/96644/1/MPRA_paper_96644.pdf

3   Devaney, E. (2015). *Should You Strive for Work/Life Balance? The History of the Personal & Professional Divide*. blog.hubspot.com. https://blog.hubspot.com/marketing/work-life-balance

4   Chang, A., McDonald, P. and Burton, P. (2010). Methodological Choices in Work-life Balance Research 1987 to 2006: A Critical Review. *The International Journal of Human Resource Management*, 21(13), pp.2381–2413. https://doi.org/10.1080/09585192.2010.516592

5   Grant, A. (2023). *https://twitter.com/AdamMGrant*. X (formerly Twitter). https://twitter.com/AdamMGrant/status/1642180266234990594

6   Kroll, C. and Pokutta, S. (2013). Just a Perfect Day? Developing a Happiness Optimised Day Schedule. *Journal of Economic Psychology*, 34, pp.210–217. https://doi.org/10.1016/j.joep.2012.09.015

7   International Labour Organisation (2022). *Working Time and Work-Life Balance Around the World.* https://www.ilo.org/ wcmsp5/groups/public/---ed_protect/---protrav/---travail/ documents/publication/wcms_864222.pdf

8   Sverko, B. and Vizek-Vidovic, V. (1995). Studies of the Meaning of Work: Approaches, Models, and Some of the Findings. *Life Roles, Values, and Careers: International Findings of the Work Importance Study,* pp.3-21.

9   Parkinson, C.N. (1955). Parkinson's Law. *The Economist.* https://www.economist.com/news/1955/11/19/parkinsons-law

10   Wright, S. (2022). Worried Work: Australians' Long and Short Hours Hitting Life Quality. *The Sydney Morning Herald.* https://www.smh.com.au/politics/federal/worried- work-australians-long-and-short-hours-hitting-life-quality- 20220909-p5bgsq.html

11   Merle, A. (2023). *This Is How Many Hours You Should Really Be Working.* Atlassian Work Life. www.atlassian.com/blog/ productivity/this-is-how-many-hours-you-should-really-be- working

12   Vaillant, G.E. (2015). *Triumphs of Experience: The Men of the Harvard Grant Study.* Cambridge, MA: The Belknap Press of Harvard University Press. https://www.adultdevelopmentstudy .org/

13   Waldinger, R. (2023). *Author Talks: Robert Waldinger on 'The Good Life'.* https://www.mckinsey.com/featured-insights/ mckinsey-on-books/author-talks-the-worlds-longest-study-of- adult-development-finds-the-key-to-happy-living

14   Boncy, A. (2023). *A Matter of Time.* [online] Columbia College Today. https://www.college.columbia.edu/cct/issue/ winterspring-2023/article/matter-time

15   Fried, C. (2022). *Too Much Free Time? Blame Solitude or Lack of Productive Activity.* UCLA Anderson Review. https:// anderson-review.ucla.edu/too-much-free-time-blame-solitude- or-lack-of-productive-activity/

16   Finan, A. and Bloom, N. (2023). *How Working from Home Boosted Golf.* https://nbloom.people.stanford.edu/sites/g/files/ sbiybj24291/files/media/file/golfingfromhome.pdf

Happy go lucky

1 World Happiness Report (2023). *World Happiness Report.* https://worldhappiness.report/.

2 Ville Palonen (2021). *Sauna in Finland – the Ultimate Guide to Finnish Sauna Culture.* Featuring Finland. https://featuringfinland.com/finland-sauna-culture-guide

3 Eskelinen, S. (2023). *Happiness – it's Not About the Money for Finns.* University of Eastern Finland. https://www.uef.fi/en/article/happiness-its-not-about-the-money-for-finns.

4 Colston, P. (2023). The Finnish Secret to Happiness? Knowing When You Have Enough. *The New York Times.* 1 Apr. https://www.nytimes.com/2023/04/01/world/europe/finland-happiness-optimism.html

Work-and-spend cycle

1 Diderot, D. (1769). *Regrets for my Old Dressing Gown by Denis Diderot 1769.* https://www.marxists.org/reference/archive/diderot/1769/regrets.htm.

Handy man

1 Sutton, B. (2014). *Kurt Vonnegut, Joe Heller, and a Great Thanksgiving Message.* Bob Sutton. https://bobsutton.typepad.com/my_weblog/2012/11/kurt_vonnegut_a.html

2 Naish, J. (2008). *Enough: Breaking Free From the World of Excess.* Hodder.

3 Hari, J. (2022). *Stolen Focus: Why You Can't Pay Attention.* New York Crown.

4 Handy, C.B. (1990). *The Age of Unreason.* Boston, MA: Harvard Business School Press.

5 Quoidbach, J., Dunn, E.W., Petrides, K.V. and Mikolajczak, M. (2010). Money Giveth, Money Taketh Away. *Psychological Science*, 21(6), pp.759–763. https://doi.org/10.1177/0956797610371963.

Money and happiness

1 Kahneman, D. and Deaton, A. (2010). High Income Improves Evaluation of Life but Not Emotional Well-Being. *Proceedings*

of the National Academy of Sciences, 107(38). https://doi.org/
10.1073/pnas.1011492107.

2   Trapulionis, A. (2020). *'Money Buys Happiness Up to $75k' Is a
Bad Joke.* The Post-Grad Survival Guide. https://medium.com/
the-post-grad-survival-guide/money-buys-happiness-up-to-
75k-is-a-bad-joke-f19947ad3ea0

3   Dunn, E.W., Gilbert, D.T. and Wilson, T.D. (2011). If Money
Doesn't Make You Happy, then You Probably Aren't Spending
it Right. *Journal of Consumer Psychology,* 21(2), pp.115–125.
https://doi.org/10.1016/j.jcps.2011.02.002.

Ceiling cracks

1   Aguilar-Moreno, M. and Cabrera, E. (2011). *Diego Rivera:
A Biography.* ABC-CLIO.

2   Herrera, H. (2020). *Jose Clemente Orozco and Diego Rivera
- The Murals.* MexConnect. https://www.mexconnect.com/
articles/1085-jose-clemente-orozco-and-diego-rivera-the-
murals/

3   Nixey, C. (2020). Death of the Office. *The Economist.* https://
www.economist.com/1843/2020/04/29/death-of-the-office

4   Chen, H., Seo, Y. and Raine, A. (2023). *This Country Wanted a
69-hour Workweek. Millennials and Generation Z Had Other
Ideas.* CNN. https://edition.cnn.com/2023/03/18/asia/south-
korea-longer-work-week-debate-intl-hnk/index.html

5   Codrea-Rado, A. (2021). *Inside the Online Movement to End
Work.* Vice. https://www.vice.com/en/article/y3vwjw/inside-
the-online-movement-to-end-work-antiwork-sub-reddit

6   Moskin, J. (2023). Noma, Rated the World's Best Restaurant, Is
Closing Its Doors. *The New York Times.* 9 Jan. https://www
.nytimes.com/2023/01/09/dining/noma-closing-rene-redzepi
.html

7   Salzman, M. (2023). *Five Trends for 2023: Rethinking
Everything.* Marian Salzman. https://mariansalzman.com/
trends-report/

8   Niazi, A. (2022). *Losing My Ambition.* The Cut. https://www.
thecut.com/2022/03/post-pandemic-loss-of-ambition.html

9 World Health Organisation (2019). *Burn-out an 'Occupational Phenomenon': International Classification of Diseases.* https://www.who.int/news/item/28-05-2019-burn-out-an-occupational-phenomenon-international-classification-of-diseases

10 Baker, C. and Kirk-Wade, E. (2023). *Mental Health Statistics: Prevalence, Services and Funding in England.* House of Commons Library. https://commonslibrary.parliament.uk/research-briefings/sn06988/

11 Ledbetter, S. (2015). *America's Top Fears 2015.* The Voice of Wilkinson. https://blogs.chapman.edu/wilkinson/2015/10/13/americas-top-fears-2015/

12 Hoffman, R. (2023). LinkedIn. https://www.linkedin.com/posts/reidhoffman_ai-like-most-transformative-technologies-activity-7037481313934741504-wJjU/

13 Davidson, P. (2017). Automation Could Kill 73 Million U.S. Jobs by 2030. *USA TODAY.* https://www.usatoday.com/story/money/2017/11/29/automation-could-kill-73-million-u-s-jobs-2030/899878001/

14 Segrave, K. (2019). *Women and Bicycles in America, 1868-1900.* McFarland.

15 Satariano, A. and Alba, D. (2020). Burning Cell Towers, Out of Baseless Fear They Spread the Virus. *The New York Times.* 10 Apr. https://www.nytimes.com/2020/04/10/technology/coronavirus-5g-uk.html

16 Eloundou, T., Manning, S., Mishkin P. and Rock, D. (2023). *GPTs Are GPTs: An Early Look at the Labor Market Impact Potential of Large Language Models.* OpenAI. https://openai.com/research/gpts-are-gpts

17 Ledbetter, S. (2015). *America's Top Fears 2015.* The Voice of Wilkinson. https://blogs.chapman.edu/wilkinson/2015/10/13/americas-top-fears-2015/

18 Sabeti, A. (2023). *https://twitter.com/arram/.* X (formerly Twitter). https://twitter.com/arram/status/1642614341622181889

Myths and realities

1   Crowley, T. (2022). *https://twitter.com/tomiscrowley*. X (formerly Twitter). https://twitter.com/tomiscrowley/status/1504240943687692288?s=21

2   Chartr (2022). *Pandemic Trends: Remote Jobs Are In, Online yoga Is Out.* www.chartr.co. https://www.chartr.co/stories/2022-12-05-3-remote-work-stood-test-of-time

3   Bhattarai, A. (2022). The Great Mismatch: Remote Jobs Are in Demand, but Positions Are Drying Up. *Washington Post.* 27 Nov. https://www.washingtonpost.com/business/2022/11/27/remote-jobs-economy/

4   Aksoy, C.G., Barrero, J.M., Bloom, N., Davis, S.J., Dolls, M. and Zarate, P. (2023). *Time Savings When Working from Home.* Becker Friedman Institute. https://bfi.uchicago.edu/insight/research-summary/time-savings-when-working-from-home/

5   University of Queensland (2023). *How Many Career Changes in a Lifetime?* https://study.uq.edu.au/stories/how-many-career-changes-lifetime

The upside-down swan

1   Alburty, S. (1999). 'The Ad Agency to End All Ad Agencies'. *Fast Company.* https://www.fastcompany.com/27725/ad-agency-end-all-ad-agencies.

2   Coutu, D. (2000). 'Creating the Most Frightening Company on Earth'. *Harvard Business Review.* https://hbr.org/2000/09/creating-the-most-frightening-company-on-earth

3   Edge, C. (2013). St Lukes Documentary. Channel 4. https://vimeo.com/79397584

4   Beale, C. (2015). 'Why St Luke's Reminds Us of What's Really Possible'. *Campaign Live.* https://www.campaignlive.co.uk/article/why-st-lukes-reminds-us-whats-really-possible/1368442

5   Law, A. (1999). *Open Minds: 21st Century Business Lessons and Innovations from St.* Lukes. TEXERE Publishing.

Tool: Remote working

1   Abril, D. (2022). Yelp Shuts Some Offices Doubling Down on Remote; CEO calls Hybrid 'Hell'. *Washington Post.* 22 Jun.

https://www.washingtonpost.com/technology/2022/06/22/yelp-shutters-offices/.

2   Airbnb (2022). *Airbnb's Design for Employees to Live and Work Anywhere*. Airbnb Newsroom. https://news.airbnb.com/airbnbs-design-to-live-and-work-anywhere/.

3   Ren, H. (2022). In 10 Years, 'Remote Work' Will Simply Be 'Work'. *The Sydney Morning Herald*. https://www.smh.com.au/business/workplace/in-10-years-remote-work-will-simply-be-work-20220216-p59wsr.html

4   Smith, N. (2022). *Think Bigger About Remote Work*. Noahpinion. https://noahpinion.substack.com/p/think-bigger-about-remote-work

5   Choudhury, R., Foroughi, C. and Larson, B. (2021). Work-From-Anywhere: The Productivity Effects of Geographic Flexibility. *Strategic Management Journal* https://www.hbs.edu/ris/Publication%20Files/Work%20from%20Anywhere_forthcoming%20SMJ_ee8cc7c5-c90e-4ad9-a1f4-47309d693a5c.pdf.

Tool: Hybrid working

1   BBC Archive. (2022). *https://twitter.com/BBCArchive/*. X (formerly Twitter). https://twitter.com/BBCArchive/status/1566016654357565440

2   Flynn, J. (2022). *Remote Work Statistics [2022]: Facts, Trends, and Projections*. Zippia. https://www.zippia.com/advice/remote-work-statistics/

3   Saad, L. and Wigert, B. (2021). *Remote Work Persisting and Trending Permanent*. Gallup. https://news.gallup.com/poll/355907/remote-work-persisting-trending-permanent.aspx

4   Vice Media Group (2021). *Insights from the Future of Work Culture*. https://www.vicemediagroup.com/wp-content/uploads/2021/06/COVID-Future-of-Workplace-Culture-Global_030421.pdf

5   Bloom, N. (2023). The Five-Day Office Week Is Dead. *The New York Times*. 16 Oct. https://www.nytimes.com/2023/10/16/opinion/office-work-home-remote.html

6 Kessler, S. (2023). Getting Rid of Remote Work Will Take More Than a Downturn. *The New York Times*. 7 Jan. https://www.nytimes.com/2023/01/07/business/dealbook/remote-work-downturn.html

7 Choudhury, P. (2020). Our Work-from-Anywhere Future. *Harvard Business Review*. https://hbr.org/2020/11/our-work-from-anywhere-future

8 Tu, J. (2021). *'Team Anywhere': Atlassian's New flexible Work Model*. SmartCompany. https://www.smartcompany.com.au/people-human-resources/atlassian-team-anywhere-working-from-home/

9 Colvin, G. (2022). *Goldman Sachs Demands Return to Office Five Days a Week*. Fortune. https://fortune-com.cdn.ampproject.org/c/s/fortune.com/2022/03/10/goldman-sachs-office-hybrid-remote-work-david-solomon/amp/

10 Nippert-Eng, C. (1996). Calendars and Keys: The Classification of 'Home' and 'Work'. *Sociological Forum*, 11(3), pp.563–582. https://doi.org/10.1007/bf02408393

Tool: Flexible working

1 Boddy, N. (2022). 'Deal Breaker': How Flexibility Became Non-negotiable. *Australian Financial Review*. https://www.afr.com/work-and-careers/workplace/deal-breaker-how-flexibility-became-non-negotiable-20220503-p5ai0w

2 London Business School (2021). *Leadership Playbook – Are We Working Too Hard?* https://soundcloud.com/londonbusinessschool/working-too-hard

Tool: Four-day work week

1 Commonwealth of Australia (2023). *Select Committee on Work and Care: Final Report*. https://www.aph.gov.au/Parliamentary_Business/Committees/Senate/Work_and_Care/workandcare/Report

2 Timsit, A. (2023). A Four-day Week Pilot Was so Successful, Most Won't Go Back. *Australian Financial Review*. https://www.afr.com/work-and-careers/workplace/a-four-day-week-

pilot-was-so-successful-most-won-t-go-back-20230222-
p5cmkn

3   Stewart, H. (2023). Four-day Week: 'Major Breakthrough' as Most UK Firms in Trial Extend Changes. *The Guardian.* 21 Feb. https://www.theguardian.com/money/2023/feb/21/four-day-week-uk-trial-success-pattern

4   Smedley, T. (2019). *How Shorter Workweeks Could Save Earth.* BBC. https://www.bbc.com/worklife/article/20190802-how-shorter-workweeks-could-save-earth

5   Zaleznik, A. (2019). *The 'Hawthorne Effect' – The Human Relations Movement.* https://www.library.hbs.edu/hc/hawthorne/09.html

6   Brown, B. (2018). *Clear Is Kind. Unclear Is Unkind.* Brené Brown. https://brenebrown.com/articles/2018/10/15/clear-is-kind-unclear-is-unkind/

7   Kelley, L. (2023). Trial Run of 4-Day Workweek Wins Converts. *The New York Times.* 22 Feb. https://www.nytimes.com/2023/02/22/business/four-day-workweek-study.html

Tool: Career breaks

1   Lo, D. (2022). *The Great Resignation Has Morphed into the Great Sabbatical.* Fast Company. https://www.fastcompany.com/90715900/great-resignation-sabbatical-gap-year.

2   Schabram, K., Bloom, M. and DiDonna, D.J. (2023). Research: The Transformative Power of Sabbaticals. *Harvard Business Review.* https://hbr.org/2023/02/research-the-transformative-power-of-sabbaticals.

3   Hutchinson, A. (2022). LinkedIn Launches Expanded 'Career Break' Listing Option to All Users. *Social Media Today.* https://www.socialmediatoday.com/news/linkedin-launches-expanded-career-break-listing-option-to-all-users/619898/

Tool: Sabbath time

1   Klein, E. (2023). Sabbath and the Art of Rest. *The New York Times.* 3 Jan. https://www.nytimes.com/2023/01/03/opinion/ezra-klein-podcast-judith-shulevitz.html

Tool: Artificial intelligence

1   Gates, B. (2023). *The Age of AI Has Begun*. Gates Notes. https://
    www.gatesnotes.com/The-Age-of-AI-Has-Begun.
2   Frey, C.B. and Osborne, M.A. (2013). The Future of Employment:
    How Susceptible Are Jobs to Computerisation? *Technological
    Forecasting and Social Change*, 114(1), pp.254–280. https://www
    .sciencedirect.com/science/article/abs/pii/S0040162516302244.
3   Advertising Week (2023). *New Study Shows U.S. Companies
    Slow to Implement AI in the Workplace, Despite Over Half
    of Employees Expressing Desire for an AI Policy*. https://
    advertisingweek.com/new-study-shows-u-s-companies-
    slow-to-implement-ai-in-the-workplace-despite-over-half-of-
    employees-expressing-desire-for-an-ai-policy/

Tool: Better meetings

1   Microsoft (2021). *Research Proves Your Brain Needs Breaks*.
    https://www.microsoft.com/en-us/worklab/work-trend-index/
    brain-research
2   Thompson, D. (2022). This Is What Happens When There Are
    Too Many Meetings. *The Atlantic*. https://www.theatlantic
    .com/newsletters/archive/2022/04/triple-peak-day-work-from-
    home/629457/
3   Korn, J. (2023). This tech company is clearing out recurring
    meetings from employee calendar. *CNN Business*. https://
    edition.cnn.com/2023/01/03/tech/shopify-meetings/index.html
4   Elliott, B., Subramanian, S. and Kupp, H. (2022). Declare
    'Calendar Bankruptcy' to Move Beyond Meeting-Driven
    Culture. *MIT Sloan Management Review*. https://sloanreview
    .mit.edu/article/declare-calendar-bankruptcy-to-move-beyond-
    meeting-driven-culture/
5   Allen, J., Rogelberg, S. and Scott, J. (2008). Mind Your
    Meetings: Improve Your Organization's Effectiveness One
    Meeting at a Time. *Quality Progress*, 41, pp.48–53. https://
    digitalcommons.unomaha.edu/psychfacpub/93/?utm_source=
    digitalcommons.unomaha.edu%2Fpsychfacpub%2F93&utm_
    medium=PDF&utm_campaign=PDFCoverPages

Acknowledgements

The thick bundle of pages you're holding in your hands right now didn't start out like this. It underwent several major rewrites and drafting versions to get it into the succinct, snappy shape that you've just read, and I have an entire army of people to thank for that.

The first is my family, including my chosen family of my husband Ben and dog Winnie, and my original family of Anna, Andrew, Rachael and Chris, and all of their broods. This was the first big project I've completed without the ever-present encouragement of my dad, Phil, and although my mum's love now shines as brightly as two people, I could still hear his encouraging words powering me through late nights and early mornings. I just know he would have loved this book.

Thanks to everyone at my Australian and New Zealand publisher Pantera Press for bringing this project to life. Lex Hirst and Tom Langshaw were always able to see the end-goal clearer than I could to guide me to write my way there. Vanessa Lanaway and Cristina Briones prodded and poked the manuscript with expert eyes to make it better. Alison Green and Katy McEwen worked hard to help it find the right audiences. Kirsty van der Veer and Kate Cuthbert kept everything on track, and Kajal Narayan and Lauren Draper ensured the right people knew about it.

A big thanks to my international publisher Wiley who have done a wonderful job helping these important messages reach an even wider audience, especially Annie Knight, Alice Hadaway, Richard Samson, Elaine Bingham and the rest of the team. For that I'm forever grateful.

There are so many people who are experts in this field who were generous enough to share their learnings with me in person and on Zoom as I fought my way through this knotty topic. I loved getting inside the lives of everyday workers who are rethinking work around the world, and appreciate you trusting your stories with me. Thanks also to Patagonia for inspiring the 'Work Sucks' backwards poem that opens the book.

Some of the first people to read this book provided valuable words of encouragement, especially Seth Godin, Hugh van Cuylenburg, Benjamin Law and Kristina Karlsson, thank you.

Finally, the most important part of this entire process: you. The reader. Thank you for trusting me enough to let me inside your brain so we can figure out our way to a better future together. Without your support, this ambitious book wouldn't exist at all.

About the Author

Cybele Malinowski

Tim Duggan is an optimist who loves thinking about big ideas. He has co-founded several digital media ventures, most notably Junkee Media, one of the leading publishers for Australian youth.

His first book, *Cult Status: How to Build a Business People Adore*, was awarded the Best Entrepreneurship and Small Business Book at the 2021 Australian Business Book Awards, and his second book on creativity, *Killer Thinking: How to Turn Good Ideas Into Brilliant Ones*, was named one of the Best Books of 2022 by Apple Books.

Tim is the Chair of the Digital Publishers Alliance, an industry body that represents over 150 titles from leading independent digital publishers. He began his career as a music journalist for *Rolling Stone*, and currently lives with his husband in Mallorca.

Index

How to build a business
people **adore**

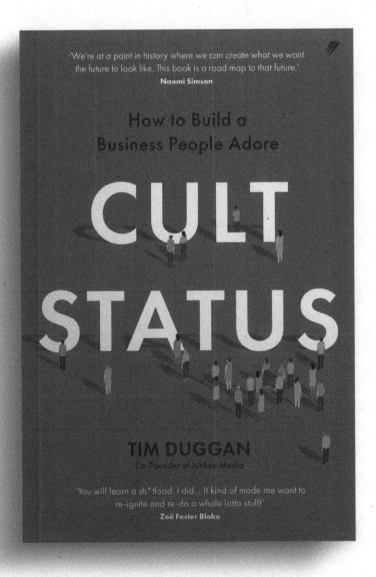

'We're at a point in history where we can create what we want
the future to look like. This book is a road map to that future.'
Naomi Simson

How to Build a
Business People Adore

CULT
STATUS

TIM DUGGAN
Co-Founder of Junkee Media

'You will learn a sh*tload. I did... It kind of made me want to
re-ignite and re-do a whole lotta stuff!'
Zoë Foster Blake

PANTERA
PRESS

SPARKING
IMAGINATION,
CONVERSATION
& CHANGE

How to turn good ideas
into **brilliant ones**

PANTERA
PRESS

SPARKING
IMAGINATION,
CONVERSATION
& CHANGE